New Headway Plus

Special Edition

Elementary
Teacher's Book

Liz and John Soars
Amanda Maris

OXFORD
UNIVERSITY PRESS

OXFORD
UNIVERSITY PRESS

Great Clarendon Street, Oxford, OX2 6DP, United Kingdom

Oxford University Press is a department of the University of Oxford.
It furthers the University's objective of excellence in research, scholarship,
and education by publishing worldwide. Oxford is a registered trade
mark of Oxford University Press in the UK and in certain other countries

© Oxford University Press 2011

The moral rights of the author have been asserted

First published in 2011

2015 2014 2013
10 9 8 7 6 5 4 3

All rights reserved. No part of this publication may be reproduced, stored
in a retrieval system, or transmitted, in any form or by any means, without
the prior permission in writing of Oxford University Press, or as expressly
permitted by law, by licence or under terms agreed with the appropriate
reprographics rights organization. Enquiries concerning reproduction outside
the scope of the above should be sent to the ELT Rights Department, Oxford
University Press, at the address above

You must not circulate this work in any other form and you must impose
this same condition on any acquirer

Links to third party websites are provided by Oxford in good faith and for
information only. Oxford disclaims any responsibility for the materials
contained in any third party website referenced in this work

Photocopying

The Publisher grants permission for the photocopying of those pages marked
'photocopiable' according to the following conditions. Individual purchasers
may make copies for their own use or for use by classes that they teach.
School purchasers may make copies for use by staff and students, but this
permission does not extend to additional schools or branches

Under no circumstances may any part of this book be photocopied for resale

ISBN: 978 0 19 471772 4   Teacher's Book
ISBN: 978 0 19 477003 3   Teacher's Book Pack

Printed in Dubai

This book is printed on paper from certified and well-managed sources

ACKNOWLEDGEMENTS

Illustrations by: Roger Fereday p.124; Oxford Illustrators pp.148, 151;
Gavin Reece p.130.

Contents

New Headway Plus Special Edition Elementary

Introduction

Unit 1	*am/is/are* – *my/your/his/her* – Everyday objects – Numbers – Hello and goodbye	6
Unit 2	*am/is/are*: questions and negatives – Possessive *'s* – Family – Opposites – In a café	11
Unit 3	Present Simple 1: *he/she/it* – Questions and negatives – Jobs – What time is it?	18
Unit 4	Present Simple 2: *I/you/we/they* – Leisure activities – Social expressions 1	26
Stop and check 1	138	
Unit 5	*There is/are* – Prepositions – *some/any* – *this/that* – Furniture – Directions 1	34
Progress test 1	146	
Unit 6	*can/can't/could/couldn't* – *was/were* – Words that sound the same – On the phone	42
Unit 7	Past Simple 1: regular verbs – Irregular verbs – Words that go together – Social expressions 2	51
Unit 8	Past Simple 2: negatives/*ago* – Forming nouns and adjectives – What's the date?	60
Stop and check 2	140	
Unit 9	Count and uncount nouns – *I like/I'd like* – *much/many* – Food – Polite requests	69
Unit 10	Comparatives and superlatives – *have got* – City and country – Directions 2	77
Progress test 2	149	
Unit 11	Present Continuous – *Whose?* – Clothes – Words that rhyme – In a clothes shop	87
Unit 12	*going to* future – Infinitive of purpose – The weather – Making suggestions	96
Stop and check 3	142	
Unit 13	Question forms – Adverbs and adjectives – Describing feelings – Catching a train	105
Unit 14	Present Perfect + *ever, never, yet,* and *just* – At the airport	113
Stop and check 4	144	
Progress test 3	152	

PHOTOCOPIABLE MATERIAL

Photocopiable material and extra ideas

Units 1–4	122
Units 5–8	124
Units 9–12	128
Units 13–14	131

Stop and checks	138
Progress tests	146
Answer keys	155
Workbook Answer key	161

Introduction

New Headway Plus Special Edition Elementary

Why *New Headway Plus Special Edition*?

New Headway Plus Special Edition Elementary is an adaptation of the world-renowned *New Headway Elementary*. Texts and topics, together with all photos and illustrations, have been carefully selected to suit students and teachers throughout the Middle East and North Africa. This edition can also be used successfully wherever the material is considered more appropriate.

Headway key ingredients

Methodology
- The basic *Headway* methodology is use of proven traditional approaches alongside those which have been developed and researched more recently.

Grammar
- The grammatical syllabus is the same as in other editions of *Headway Elementary* because the requirements of lower level students are usually more predictable than at later levels.

Practice
- There is a great variety of practice activities covering all the skills.

Vocabulary
- Vocabulary is not only integrated throughout, but also developed in its own section.

Skills work
- Skills work is integrated and balanced. All the texts for listening and reading come from authentic sources and are simplified and adapted to suit the level.

Everyday English
- There is an *Everyday English* section which focuses primarily on aspects of spoken English.

Starter
- Each unit begins with a *Starter* section, which is designed to be a warmer to the lesson. It is a short activity and always has direct relevance to the language to be introduced in the unit.

Grammar Spot
- Each grammar presentation contains a *Grammer Spot*. This is a mix of explanation, questions, and self-check tests to reinforce the grammar being taught. Each *Grammar Spot* has a link to the fuller *Grammar Reference* section at the back of the book.

What's in the Teacher's Book?

- **Full teaching notes**, answers, and possible problems.
- ***Don't forget!* section** which refers to relevant exercises in the Workbook and to the Word list.
- **Tapescripts** in the main body of the teaching notes.
- **Extra ideas section** with notes on how to use them for use after Units 1–4, 5–8, 9–12, and 13–14.
- **Stop and check tests**
  There are four Stop and check revision tests which cover Units 1–4, 5–8, 9–12, and 13–14. These can either be set in class, or given for homework (preferably over a weekend) and then discussed in the next lesson. Students can work in small groups to try to agree on the correct answer, then you can go over it with the whole class, reminding students of the language items covered. It is important that, in the translation sentences which come at the end of each Stop and check test, students translate the ideas and concepts, and not word by word.
- **Progress tests**
  There are three Progress tests which cover Units 1–5, 6–10, and 11–14.

What's in the Workbook?

The Workbook is an important component of the course. It revises the grammatical input of the Student's Book and contains the writing syllabus. Many of the exercises are on the Student's Workbook recording, for use in class or at home.

Finally!

In all our *New Headway* material we try to guide students to an understanding of new language, rather then just have examples of it on the page. We attach great importance to practice activities, both controlled and free, personalized and impersonal. The skills work comes from a wide range of material – newspapers, magazines, biographies, short stories, radio programmes – and features both British and American English. We hope you and your students enjoy using the books, audio, and DVD-ROM, and have success with them whether using *Headway* for the first time or having learned to trust its approach from previous use.

1

am/is/are • *my/your/his/her*
Everyday objects • Numbers
Hello and goodbye

Hello everybody!

Introduction to the unit

As you begin *New Headway Plus Special Edition Elementary*, you are probably starting a new course with a new group of students. The title of Unit 1 is 'Hello everybody!', and one important aim is that students get to know each other and you, and you get to know them. Obviously students will have relatively little English to use at this stage, but nevertheless a convivial classroom atmosphere can be established through quite basic interchanges.

Language aims

Grammar – *am/is/are* The verb *to be* is introduced in all persons, singular and plural. The focus is on the positive and questions with question words (*where*, *what*, and *how*). The negative and *Yes/No* questions are dealt with in Unit 2.

Possessive adjectives *My*, *your*, *his*, and *her* are introduced in the unit. The other possessive adjectives are given in Grammar Reference 1.2 on p124.

Vocabulary Names of countries are introduced as part of the work on introductions. In the *Vocabulary and pronunciation* section, the alphabet is introduced and practised. Students look at the organization of a bilingual dictionary entry, and everyday objects such as *ticket* and *key*. If possible, bring enough bilingual dictionaries for students to share at least one between two. Students are asked to work out the rules for using *a/an* and the formation of regular plurals with *-s*.

Everyday English Numbers 1–20 are revised and practised. The situational focus includes practice on exchanging telephone numbers and work on saying hello and goodbye.

Workbook Nationality adjectives (*German*, *French*); the numbers 1–20 are practised. The writing syllabus begins in Unit 3.

Notes on the unit

STARTER (SB p6)

1   Say your own name – *I'm (Ali)* – and point to yourself to make the meaning clear. Then invite students to say their names – *I'm Ghada, I'm Samir*, etc. Encourage students to listen to each other's names and to memorize as many as they can. If appropriate, play a memory game by pointing to individual students and yourself and getting the group to say just the name, e.g. *Ali! Ghada!* Encourage students in a multilingual group to pronounce each other's names (and your name!) as accurately as possible.

2   Check students understand 'alphabetical order' by putting letters *a–g* on the board in random order and asking students to re-order them alphabetically. (Don't worry too much if students pronounce the letters wrongly as the alphabet is covered later in the unit.) Check by asking students to put the names in *Starter 1* in order.

Ask students to stand up in alphabetical order and say their name. If appropriate, repeat this getting progressively faster each time.

If there are not too many students in the class, put their names on the board so everyone can begin to learn them.

INTRODUCTIONS (SB p6)

am/is/are, my/your

1. **T 1.1** [CD 1: Track 2] Ask students to read and listen. Play the recording two or three times, repeat as a class first, then practise it in both open (i.e. students ask and answer the question across the room with the rest of the class listening) and closed pairs (i.e. the whole class working in pairs). Make sure students can accurately produce the contracted form *I'm*.

GRAMMAR SPOT

Focus attention on the contractions. Ask students to circle the contracted forms in exercise 1.

2. Ask students to complete the conversation. Remind them to use contracted forms.

   T 1.2 [CD 1: Track 3] Play the recording and let students check their answers. If you feel students need more practice, ask them to say the dialogue in open and closed pairs.

   Answers and tapescript
   A Hello. My **name's** Richard. **What's your** name?
   B Kurt.
   A **Where** are you from, Kurt?
   B **I'm** from Berlin. Where **are** you from?
   A **I'm from** London.

3. This is a mingle activity. If you want to you can demonstrate the dialogue first in open pairs, and then get students to move around the class and talk to as many people as possible. Don't let this activity go on too long. If you have a large class, it will be impossible for all the students to talk to everyone.

ADDITIONAL MATERIAL

Workbook Unit 1
Exercises 1–3 These practise *What's your name?, Where are you from? I'm from ...* , and *I'm (a) ...* .

Countries, his/her

If you have access to a world map or a globe, it would be useful for presenting the names of the countries.

4. Focus attention on the table with the names of the countries. Explain stress and the system of stress marks used in *Headway* with an example on the board, e.g. ● •
   England. You could use L1 to explain, and you could perhaps take some examples of words with more than one syllable in L1 (if L1 is stress-timed itself, not syllable-timed) to show how there are stressed and unstressed syllables.

   T 1.3 [CD 1: Track 4] Ask students to read the list of countries as you play the recording. Then they can listen and repeat the second time. Practise the countries as a class, then in closed pairs.

5. Ask students to look at the photographs and read about the people.

GRAMMAR SPOT

Focus attention on the contractions. Ask students to circle the contracted forms in the sentences in exercise 5.

6. Ask students in pairs or groups to write where the people are from. Students are *not* expected to know how to say *Hello!* in all the different languages! This is merely a fun way to introduce countries and the third person singular and plural. Some students will know a few, others will know more.

   Answers
   1 This is Richard.
      He's from England.
   2 This is Tomoko.
      She's from Japan.
   3 This is José and Miguel.
      They're from Brazil.
   4 This is Marco.
      He's from Italy.
   5 This is Irina.
      She's from Russia.
   6 This is László and Ilona.
      They're from Hungary.
   7 This is Yalda.
      She's from Syria.
   8 This is Kurt.
      He's from Germany.
   9 This is Pierre.
      He's from France.

7. Introduce the questions *What's his/her name?* and *Where's he/she from?* Point to some of the pictures in exercise 6, ask the questions yourself, and let the students reply. Then drill the questions and correct any mistakes in the use of *he/she* and *his/her* carefully. Practise the questions and answers in open pairs.

   Ask the students to continue the activity in closed pairs. Monitor and check for correct use of *he/she* and *his/her*, and if necessary, drill the language again using the pictures in the book. At the end of the activity, consolidate the positive form by asking students to say *His/Her name's ...* , *He's/She's from ...* or *They're from ...* .

Unit 1 • Hello everybody! 7

GRAMMAR SPOT

Ask students to complete the table with *am*, *is*, and *are*. Check the answers.

Answers

I	am	
He / She / It	is	from England.
We / You / They	are	

Briefly check comprehension of the subject pronouns which are not covered in exercise 6 (*we*, *it*, and *you* plural) by using the photographs and the students themselves. *It* can be checked using international food and drinks, e.g. *pasta – It's from Italy*.

Read Grammar Reference 1.1 on p124 together in class, and/or ask students to read it at home. Encourage them to ask you questions about it.

PRACTICE (SB p9)

Talking about you

1 If you want to you can demonstrate the activity by getting students to ask and answer the same questions in open and/or closed pairs about the other people in the class. Obviously this will work better in a multilingual class. In a monolingual class where everyone knows each other, you could make role cards giving students a new country of origin, or the identity of a famous person whose country of origin the class would know. This practises the vocabulary of the exercise, too.

2 Ask the students to introduce their partner to the rest of the class. Check for the correct use of *he/she* and for the correct stress on the names of countries.

Listening and pronunciation

3 **T 1.4** [CD 1: Track 5] Play the recording. Ask students to tick the sentence they hear. This is an exercise that tests discrimination, but you can make it productive afterwards by asking students in pairs to practise the pairs of sentences. Pay particular attention to the sounds /ɪ/ and /iː/.

Answers and tapescript
1 He's from Spain.
2 What's her name?
3 They're from Brazil.
4 Where's she from?
5 He's a teacher in Italy.

Check it

4 Ask students to work in pairs to put *am*, *is*, *are*, *his*, *her*, or *your* into the gaps. Afterwards, you can ask them to make the contractions in numbers 1, 3, and 7.

Answers
2 Where **are** you from?
3 I **am** from Japan.
4 'What's **your** name?' 'My name's Tomoko.'
5 Max and Lisa **are** from Chicago.
6 This **is** my teacher. **His** name's Richard.
7 Where **is** he from?
8 This is my sister. **Her** name's Emma.

Reading and writing

NOTE
The aim of this section is to allow students to see how much English they already know. In exercise 7, students write about themselves. Encourage them to follow the models in exercises 5 and 6, but also give better students the opportunity to show off!
The verbs *have*, *live*, and *want* appear in their Present Simple form, but you don't need to review this tense at this stage.

5 **T 1.5** [CD 1: Track 6] Ask students to read and listen to the text about Rafael. Make sure students understand *married* and *children*. You could ask one or two students to read the text aloud, or in closed pairs, and the students can help each other with pronunciation.

6 Ask students to complete the text about Jana. Make sure students understand *flat*, *international*, and *language*.

T 1.6 [CD 1: Track 7] Play the recording to check. Again, you could practise the text around the class and/or in closed pairs.

Tapescript and answers
My name's Jana and I'm a student. **I'm** 19. I'm not married. I have one **sister** and two brothers. I **live** in a flat in Amman, Jordan. I **want** to learn English because it's an international **language**.

7 Ask students to write about themselves. After quite a lot of oral class work, some silent, individual work provides variety and balance. Ask them to read what they have written to the class. Don't worry if there are a lot of pronunciation mistakes. The aim is for students to show what they can do, and to say a little about themselves and their families. You can't do everything at once!

If you have a large class, not all the students will be able to read out what they have written. Collect it in.

If you have a smaller class, it can be interesting to record the students. Play the recording back and correct mistakes that are common to the whole class.

ADDITIONAL MATERIAL

Workbook Unit 1
Exercises 4 and 5 Third person *is* and *are*, and short and long forms.
Exercises 6 and 7 Possessive adjectives.
Exercises 8 and 9 Countries and nationalities with stress practice.

VOCABULARY AND PRONUNCIATION (SB p10)

> **SUGGESTION**
> Some students may be quite familiar with the letters of the alphabet, while others may not remember many of them. Whatever your students' knowledge at this stage of the course, remember that they will all need regular practice in the alphabet and spelling. This can easily be integrated into any lesson when teaching new vocabulary (*How do you think you spell ... from the sound?*), or when reviewing vocabulary (*How do you spell ... ?*), and by the use of spelling games.
>
> If your group cannot remember much of the alphabet, you may want to write it on the board and drill the letters in groups of five before moving on to the chant.

1 **T 1.7** [CD 1: Track 8] Tell the students that they are going to listen to the alphabet in the form of a chant. Ask them to join in where they can. Play the recording and note down the letters students get wrong or don't know, paying particular attention to *a, j, e, g, i, y, u, w, r*, which cause problems for many students. Drill the letters which students found difficult.

Practise the letters as a class and in closed pairs. Listen to the chant again and let the students join in if they want to. It certainly helps them to remember the pronunciation of the alphabet!

> **T 1.7 The alphabet chant**
> A B C D E F G
> H I J K L M
> N O P Q R S T U
> V W X Y Z

Pre-teach the question *How do you spell ... ?* and the use of *double* for spelling (e.g. *apple* = a, double p, l, e). Get students to practise asking the question and spelling in pairs, using their own names or the names of famous people. Do not focus on the use of *do* to form questions in the Present Simple as in *How do you spell ... ?* This will be covered in full in Units 3 and 4.

2 In the previous lesson, check who has a bilingual dictionary. If there are not likely to be enough, bring some yourself. Ask students to find *apple* in the dictionary. You could have a conversation in L1 to compare the dictionary entries, but don't let this go on too long.

3 Students match the words and pictures. Encourage them to work in pairs and match the words that they recognize first. Then they can use a dictionary to complete the activity. Monitor and check for pronunciation.

> **Answers and tapescript**
> a a dictionary   g an apple
> b an orange   h a letter
> c a newspaper   i a magazine
> d a stamp   j a ticket
> e a bag   k a key
> f a camera   l a postcard

T 1.8 [CD 1: Track 9] Play the recording and get students to repeat the words as a class and individually. If students have problems with incorrect stress, refer them to the table to help them self-correct. If necessary, drill the words, stopping the recording after each example.

4 If you want to you can demonstrate the activity by saying the letter of some of the photographs and asking a student to tell you what the object is and how you spell it. Students continue in closed pairs.

5 Ask students to look at the words and to work out the rule if they don't already know it.

> **Answers**
> The letters *a, e, i, o,* and *u* are vowels.
> *a* goes before a word with a consonant, *an* goes before a vowel.

Point out the following sound rules:
• when we pronounce *u* /juː/, we use *a*, e.g. *a university*
• when *h* is silent, we use *an*, e.g. *an hour*.

6 Ask students to look at the plurals and work out the rules for the formation of plurals. Refer students to Grammar Reference 1.4 and 1.5 on p124.

> **Answers**
> Most nouns add -*s*. Nouns ending in a consonant + *y*, take away the -*y* and add -*ies*.
> Get students to say the plurals of the other words in exercise 2.

ADDITIONAL MATERIAL

Workbook Unit 1
Exercises 10 and 11 *a/an*
Exercise 12 Check it

EVERYDAY ENGLISH (SB p11)

Hello and goodbye

1 Get students to say numbers 1–20 around the class. If necessary, drill the numbers and check for correct stress on numbers 13–19, e.g. *thirteen*.

2 **T 1.9** [CD 1: Track 10] Ask students to read and listen to the telephone numbers. Focus attention on the use of *double* for repeated numbers and the use of 'oh' for 0, rather than *zero*. Make sure students realize that each number is read individually in English, unlike some languages where 94 would be read as *ninety-four*.

3 **T 1.10** [CD 1: Track 11] Tell students they are going to hear six sentences, each of which contains a number. Ask students to write down the numbers they hear. If necessary, pause the recording after each sentence, or play the recording a second time. Check the answers.

> **Answers and tapescript**
> 1 Hello. **01913 786 499**.
> 2 My brother has **four** children.
> 3 I have **10** stamps in my bag.
> 4 Hello, extension **4177**.
> 5 I live at number **19**.
> 6 Goodbye. See you at **five**.

Get students to practise the numbers in the sentences.

4 Drill the question and answer. Then get students to ask other people what their phone number is and to write a list. If you have a big group, check a few of the numbers across the class. If you have a small group, you could check the numbers by writing up the list on the board.

5 Ask students to write the conversations in the correct order. **T 1.11** [CD 1: Track 12] Play the recording to check.

> **Answers and tapescript**
> 1 A Hello, extension 3442.
>   B Hello, John. This is Mark. How are you?
>   A I'm fine, thank you. And you?
>   B I'm OK, thanks.
> 2 A Goodbye, Marcus.
>   B Goodbye, Filipe. Have a nice day.
>   A Thanks, Marcus. See you this evening!
>   B Yes, at seven in the restaurant.
> 3 A Hello, 270899.
>   B Hi, Peter! It's me, Leo. How are you?
>   A Not bad, thanks. And you?
>   B Very well. How are the children?
>   A They're fine.

6 Students practise the dialogues in open and then closed pairs. Then ask students to practise again, using their own names and telephone numbers.

Don't forget!

Workbook Unit 1
Exercises 13–14 These are exercises on numbers 1–20.

Word list
Look at the Word list on p135 of the Student's Book as a class. Tell students that the most important words from the unit are here. They could translate the words, or look at them at home, or transfer some of the words to their vocabulary notebook.

2

am/is/are – questions and negatives
Possessive *'s* • Family
Opposites • In a café

Meeting people

Introduction to the unit

The title of Unit 2 is 'Meeting people', and various characters are introduced to practise the grammar. The first real fluency activity of *New Headway Plus Special Edition Elementary* is the reading and listening exercise – Fahad's email to Nabil. It is important for elementary-level students to be exposed to language in a natural context.

Language aims

Grammar – questions and negatives The verb *to be* is given further practice, with an emphasis on questions, negatives, and short answers. The question words *what*, *where*, *who*, *how old*, and *how much* are revised or introduced.

Note that in the negative, we use the contracted forms of *not*, not the contracted forms of the verb *to be*: i.e. *she isn't, they aren't, you aren't, we aren't*, and not *she's not, they're not, you're not, we're not*. Try to keep to these forms as you speak to the class. The contraction **I amn't* isn't possible, and this is pointed out in the *Grammar Spot* in the *Negative and short answers* section.

Having been introduced to contracted forms, students are tempted to use them in short answers, for example, *Are you married? *Yes, I'm*, but this is not possible. Where other languages will answer an inverted question with simply *yes* or *no*, English prefers to add a short answer. Without the short answer, the speaker can sound rather abrupt.

Possessive *'s* It can come as quite a surprise to students to learn that not only does *s* signify a plural noun, but *'s* is both the contracted form of the verb *to be* and an indicator of possession. This needs to be pointed out very carefully and regular practice given in distinguishing the different forms.

Vocabulary Members of the family (*father*, *aunt*, etc.); common adjectives and their opposites.

Everyday English This section practises the language required in a café. *Can I have … ?* is taught idiomatically. Vocabulary to do with food and drink is introduced, and prices are practised. You might feel your students would benefit from doing exercises 13 and 14 in the Workbook before doing the *Everyday English* section.

Workbook The spelling of plural nouns is practised.

Notes on the unit

STARTER (SB p12)

> **POSSIBLE PROBLEMS**
> The *Starter* section revises and practises numbers. Numbers 1–20 and phone numbers were introduced in Unit 1, but you might feel that your students need more classroom work on these areas.
> Learners of English often experience difficulty in recognizing and producing the difference between the 'teen' numbers (13–19) and the corresponding 'ten' numbers (30, 40, 50, etc.). Point out the different word stress.
>
> ● •   • ●
> thirty   thirteen

Unit 2 • Meeting people   11

1 Get students to count from 1–20 around the class. Repeat so that everyone has a chance to practise or if students make mistakes.

2 Now ask students to count in tens from 10–100 around the class. Check for correct stress, and repeat until students can say the numbers quickly and accurately.

3 If you want to, tell students your own age and then briefly revise numbers that reflect the age of your students. Drill the question *How old are you?* Ask students to work in groups of three or four and ask and answer about ages. Ask for a few examples of ages to practise *He's …* , *She's …* , *They're …* , and *We're …* . (Unless your students query the use of *be* as different from how they express age in their own language, do not spend time on this.)

WHO IS SHE? (SB p12)

Questions and negatives

1 Ask students to read about Keesha Anderson. Check comprehension of the key vocabulary: *surname*, *first name*, *address*, and *journalist*.

2 If you think that your students will be familiar with most of the question words in this exercise, you can ask them to do this exercise in pairs. Otherwise, do it as a class.

T 2.1 [CD 1: Track 13] Play the recording so students can check their answers. Point out that *isn't* is the negative, and that *n't* is the short form of *not*.

Tapescript and answers
1 What's **her** surname? Anderson.
2 What's her first name? Keesha.
3 Where's she from? London, England.
4 What's **her** job? She's a journalist.
5 What's **her** address? 42, Muswell Hill Road, London N10 3JD.
6 What's **her** phone number? 020 8863 5741.
7 How old **is she**? Twenty-eight.
8 Is she **married**? No, she isn't.

Before you ask students to practise the questions and answers in pairs, let them practise in open pairs, focusing on accurate intonation. English has a very wide voice range, and this is apparent in questions. Questions with a question word start high and fall.

What's her surname?

Listen to the models on the recording and ask students to imitate them. Point out that the question in number 8 is different as you can answer *Yes/No* and it has a different intonation pattern. Inverted questions usually rise at the end. (Students will practise this more fully in the *Negatives and short answers* section that follows.)

Is she married?

Practise the questions as much as possible without boring the class! Have a mixture of open and closed pairs.

3 Students write questions about Keesha's brother, basing their questions on exercise 2.

Answers
Where's he from?   What's his phone number?
What's his job?   How old is he?
What's his address? Is he married?

Encourage students to ask you questions about Keesha's brother. Insist on accurate intonation. You can give any information you want, but here is a sample profile.

Keesha's brother
Surname   Anderson
First name   Rudi
Country   England
Job   Policeman
Address   70, London Road, Oxford OX3 5AL
Phone number   01865 753 4991
Age   21
Married?   No

Negatives and short answers

4 Tell students they are going to continue asking questions, first about Keesha and then about her brother.

Asking about Keesha

T 2.2 [CD 1: Track 14] Ask students to read and listen to the *Yes/No* questions and short answers. Play the recording. Play the recording again and ask students to repeat, emphasizing the rising intonation on the question and the pronunciation of the contracted form *isn't*.

Allow students to practise the questions and answers which appear in full in the Student's Book in open and closed pairs. Insist on accurate intonation. Then ask students to ask questions 1 and 2, following the same pattern.

Answers
1 Is she a doctor?   No, she isn't.
   Is she a teacher?   No, she isn't.
   Is she a journalist?   Yes, she is.
2 Is she eighteen?   No, she isn't.
   Is she twenty-one?   No, she isn't.
   Is she twenty-eight?   Yes, she is.

5 **Asking about Keesha's brother**
Students continue asking about Keesha's brother, following the same pattern and working in closed pairs.

Answers
1. Is his first name Peter? — No, it isn't.
   Is his first name Daniel? — No, it isn't.
   Is his first name Rudi? — Yes, it is.
2. Is he a journalist? — No, he isn't.
   Is he a student? — No, he isn't.
   Is he a policeman? — Yes, he is.
3. Is he sixteen? — No, he isn't.
   Is he thirty? — No, he isn't.
   Is he twenty-one? — Yes, he is.

GRAMMAR SPOT

SUGGESTION
This is the first time that students have seen all the short answers and negative forms of the verb *to be*, so deal with the information in the *Grammar Spot* very carefully. You might want to practise the short answers in open pairs and drill the negative sentences.

1. Students complete the short answers, using the contracted form where possible (*No, it **isn't***). Check the answers.

   Answers
   Is Keesha English? — Yes, she **is**.
   Is her surname Smith? — No, it **isn't**.
   Are you a journalist? — No, I'm **not**.

   Make sure students understand that positive short answers can't be contracted to **Yes, she's*.

2. Focus attention on the negative forms and point out especially that we cannot say **I amn't*.

   Read Grammar Reference 2.1 on p125 together in class, and/or ask students to read it at home. Encourage them to ask you questions about it.

PRACTICE (SB p13)

Who is he?

1. Photocopy the identity cards on p122.

POSSIBLE PROBLEMS
This is the first information gap activity in *New Headway Plus Special Edition Elementary*, and it might even be the first time your students have ever done such an activity. Students may find it strange that Student A has different information from Student B, so explain this activity very carefully, in L1 if you can. Stress that they mustn't show each other the information! Read the instructions as a class. Allocate the pairs, and give the photocopied card to Student A. You could do the first two questions yourself as an example. Give students enough time to complete the information exchange.

Answers
SURNAME	**Binchey**
FIRST NAME	Patrick
COUNTRY	**Ireland**
JOB	Accountant
ADDRESS	**82, Hill Road, Dublin**
PHONE NUMBER	1232 4837
AGE	**47**
MARRIED?	Yes

2. Students ask and answer questions about Patrick.

POSSIBLE PROBLEMS
Students first saw the short answers *Yes, he/she is*, *No, he/she isn't*, and *No, I'm not* in *Negatives and short answers*. This speaking exercise and the exercises in *Talking about you* extend and consolidate this focus. It is inadvisable to embark on an explanation of what short answers are and how they operate, as you run the risk of overloading students with too much information. It is better to let students see them in context and use them in controlled exercises. Demonstrate the activity by asking this first question about Patrick's surname and getting students to answer. Students continue to ask and answer in closed pairs. Monitor and check for correct formation of questions and short answers.

Answers
1. Is his surname Smith? — No, it isn't.
   Is his surname Jones? — No, it isn't.
   Is his surname Binchey? — Yes, it is.
2. Is he from Italy? — No, he isn't.
   Is he from England? — No, he isn't.
   Is he from Ireland? — Yes, he is.
3. Is he a policeman? — No, he isn't.
   Is he a teacher? — No, he isn't.
   Is he an accountant? — Yes, he is.

Talking about you

3. Photocopy the forms on p122. This is a mingle activity. Read the instructions as a class and get two or three pairs of students to model the examples. Students stand up and ask and answer questions. The students should complete the information exchange with at least two other students, but stop the activity before they get tired. Ask four or five students to tell the rest of the class about one of the others. They could well have problems with the shift from first and second persons to third person, i.e. *your* to *her*, *are* to *is*, etc., but allow students to feed back without correcting every mistake.

ADDITIONAL MATERIAL

Workbook Unit 2
Exercises 1–7 Verb *to be*, questions, negatives, short answers, short forms, and long forms.

Patrick's family
Possessive *'s*

1 Focus attention on the vocabulary table and on the example. Make sure students understand that the words are in male–female pairs. Students complete the table working with a partner and using a dictionary if necessary. Monitor and check for correct pronunciation, especially of *daughter* /ˈdɔːtə/ and of *grandmother/grandfather* /ˈɡrænmʌðə/, /ˈɡrænfɑːðə/. Check the answers. Drill some of the words to practise the pronunciation.

> **Answers**
> | | | | |
> |---|---|---|---|
> | **husband** | **father** | son | **brother** |
> | **wife** | mother | **daughter** | sister |
> | uncle | **nephew** | grandfather | |
> | **aunt** | niece | **grandmother** | |

2 **T 2.3** [CD 1: Track 15] Focus attention on the photograph. Ask students to read and listen and put the names next to the right person. Check the answers by pointing to each person and asking students for the correct name.

> **GRAMMAR SPOT**
>
> 1 Focus attention on the use of *'s* as the contraction of *is* and as an indicator of possession.
>
> 2 Refer students back to the text about Patrick Binchey. Get them to work in pairs and underline the use of possessive *'s* and circle the use of *'s* as the contraction of *is*.
>
> **Answers**
> | Possession | *is* |
> |---|---|
> | wife's name | She's a teacher. |
> | daughter's name | She's twenty-one |
> | son's name | she's a nurse |
> | | He's nineteen and he's a student. |
>
> Refer students to Grammar Reference 2.2 on p125.

3 Students ask and answer questions about Patrick's family.

> **Answers**
> Who's Brenda? She's Lara and Benny's mother.
> Who's Lara? She's Patrick's/Brenda's daughter.
> She's Benny's sister.
> Who's Benny? He's Patrick's/Brenda's son.
> He's Lara's brother.

> **SUGGESTION**
> You could revise the possessive *'s* and family relationships by referring to famous people and their relations.

PRACTICE (SB p15)

You and your family

1 Students write down the names of some of their relatives on a piece of paper. Then they exchange pieces of paper with a partner and ask and answer questions about each other's families.

> **SUGGESTION**
> You could revise the possessive *'s* at the beginning of the next lesson by asking ten or so students for a personal belonging of theirs. Put them all in the middle of the room. Students then have to point at an object and say *That's Hassan's book*, etc.

2 This exercise consolidates the verb *to be* in a range of persons, and allows students to make some sentences about themselves. Check comprehension of *at home*, *at work*, and *coffee bar*.

> **Answers**
> There can be no set answers for this exercise, but check that students haven't made mistakes in the forms of *to be*.

Check it

3 Students work in pairs or small groups to identify the correct sentence.

> **Answers**
> 1 I'm a doctor.
> 2 I am twenty-nine years old.
> 3 I'm not married.
> 4 My sister's name is Lara.
> 5 She's married.
> 6 I'm an uncle.
> 7 I have two brothers.
> 8 Ahmad's my sister's son.

ADDITIONAL MATERIAL

Workbook Unit 2
Exercises 8 and 9 Possessive *'s*

VOCABULARY (SB p16)

Opposites

1 Students use their dictionaries to match the opposite adjectives.

Answers			
big	small	hot	cold
new	old	expensive	cheap
lovely	horrible	fast	slow
easy	difficult		

Drill the words to practise pronunciation. Ask students to mark the stress on words with two syllables or more.

Answers		
●••	•●•	●•
difficult	expensive	lovely
horrible		easy

2 This exercise practises the vocabulary and revises the verb *to be*. Students write sentences for each picture.

T 2.4 [CD 1: Track 16] Play the recording so students can check their answers. Students practise saying the sentences in pairs.

Answers and tapescript
1 He's old. She's young.
2 It's easy. It's difficult.
3 It's new. It's old.
4 It's fast. It's slow.
5 It's lovely. It's horrible.
6 They're hot. They're cold.
7 They're cheap. They're expensive.
8 It's small. It's big.

READING AND LISTENING (SB p16)

An email from America

> **POSSIBLE PROBLEMS**
> This is the first piece of extensive skills work in *New Headway Plus Special Edition Elementary*. Students read and listen to the email at the same time even though this might be deemed an unnatural activity. Learners of English find reading easier than listening because they can recognize cognates without the interference of different pronunciation. However, if they read the email silently at their own speed, they could become distracted by unknown and not terribly important vocabulary.
> The aim of this activity is to show students a lot of the language that they have already been exposed to in a relatively natural context. If you feel your students would not be able to cope with the activity as it stands, you could pre-teach the following items of vocabulary, or set them as a homework task prior to the lesson.
>
> | | | |
> |---|---|---|
> | *nice* | *subway* | *happy* |
> | *apartment* | *use* (*v.*) | *soon* |
> | *girl* | *park* (*n.*) | |
> | *friendly* | *snow* (*n.*) | |
>
> However, if you feel your students don't need so much support, simply encourage them not to worry about other unknown words.

1 Read the introduction as a class.

T 2.5 [CD 1: Track 17] Students read and listen to the email.

2 If you feel your students would be happy to correct the false sentences in pairs or small groups, ask them to do this. Otherwise, answer the questions as a class.

Answers
3 ✓
4 ✗ No, he isn't. He's at a language school.
5 ✗ No, it isn't. It's a small class – nine students.
6 ✗ No, they aren't. They're all from different countries.
7 ✗ No, they aren't. Bobby is a policeman.
8 ✓

Unit 2 · Meeting people 15

3 Students often have problems with the formation of questions, so it is worth taking the opportunity to provide some practice.

If you feel students would be happy to work in pairs or small groups to answer these questions, let them do so.

Answers
2 Where are the (other) students from?
3 What's his/the teacher's name?
4 Who are Bobby and Matt?
5 How old are Bobby and Matt?
6 Is New York busy/exciting/expensive?

You could drill the questions for pronunciation practice. Careful with intonation!

4 **T 2.6** [CD 1: Track 18] Students listen to three conversations. After each conversation ask and answer the two questions with the students. Then ask them to look at the tapescript on p114 of the Student's Book and play the recording again.

Answers
F = Fahad   O = Orlando
1 F Hello. My name's Fahad.
  O Hello, Fahad. I'm Orlando.
  F Where are you from, Orlando?
  O I'm from Italy, from Rome. And you? Where are you from?
  F I'm from Lebanon.
  O From Beirut?
  F Yes, that's right.

M = Martin   C = class   F = Fahad
2 M Good morning everybody.
  C Good morning, Martin.
  M How are you all?
  C Good.
    OK.
  M How are you, Fahad?
  F I'm fine, thank you. And you?
  M Very well. Now listen, everybody ...

M = Matt   F = Fahad   B = Bobby
3 M Bye, Fahad. Have a nice day.
  F Pardon?
  B Have a good day at the school of English.
  F Oh, yes. Thank you. Same to you.
  M What's your teacher called?
  F My teacher called?
  B Your teacher's name – what is it?
  F Ah, yes. His name's Martin.
  M And is he good?
  F My teacher good?
  B Yeah. Martin, your teacher, is he a good teacher?
  F Oh yes, yes. Very good, very nice.

Answers
1 He's with the students in his school.
2 He's in school with the teacher.
3 He's at home with Bobby and Matt.

5 This is a free writing activity. Set it for homework, and mark it sympathetically.

EVERYDAY ENGLISH (SB p18)

In a café

SUGGESTION
The activities in the *Starter* section allow students to focus just on prices before being exposed to them in a fuller context. If you feel your students need to do more work on prices prior to the lesson, see the Workbook Unit 2, Exercises 13 and 14.

1 1 **T 2.7** [CD 1: Track 19] Students read and listen to the prices to familiarize themselves with the system and pronunciation.

Play the recording again and get students to repeat the prices. Make sure students realize we only use 'p' for prices under a pound.

2 **T 2.8** [CD 1: Track 20] Tell students they are going to hear six prices, each in a context. Get them to write down the prices they hear. (In number 6, they have to write the *correct* price.) Check the answers.

Answers and tapescript
1 That's **five pounds fifty**, please.
2 Look, it's only **twelve pounds**.
3 Here you are. **Twenty p** change.
4 Pizza is **three pounds seventy-five**.
5 **One hundred pounds** for that is very expensive.
6 **Nine pounds fifteen**, not nine pounds fifty.

2 Students read the menu and match the food with the pictures. Drill the pronunciation of the food and drink. Pay particular attention to *burger and chips* /'bɜːgərən 'tʃɪps/, *chocolate cake* /'tʃɒklət ˌkeɪk/, and *orange juice* /'ɒrɪndʒ ˌdʒuːs/.

Students practise the menu items in pairs by pointing to the pictures and saying the names.

3 **T 2.9** [CD 1: Track 21] Students listen and repeat. Do this chorally, stopping the recording, and individually. Check comprehension of the question *How much ... ?* Make sure students practise the intonation of the *How much ... ?* questions, and draw attention to word-joining, e.g. *an orange juice*.

Students ask and answer questions about the prices. Do this first in open pairs, then in closed pairs. Correct pronunciation carefully.

4 **T 2.10** [CD 1: Track 22] Students listen to the conversations and fill in the gaps.

> **Answers and tapescript**
> A Good morning.
> B Good **morning**. Can I have **a coffee**, please?
> A Here you are. Anything else?
> B No, thanks.
> A **One pound fifty p**, please.
> B Thanks.
> A Thank you.
>
> A Hi. Can I help?
> B Yes. Can I have a **tuna and egg** salad, please?
> A Anything to drink?
> B Yeah. A **mineral water**, please.
> A OK. Here you are.
> B **How much** is that?
> A **Six** pounds **thirty-five**, please.
> B Thanks.

5 Students practise the conversations in pairs. Then make the activity a little freer by roleplaying. Take the role of the person working in the café yourself first and choose one of the students to be the customer. You can increase the vocabulary according to the level of your students, asking for example *Do you want mayonnaise in your sandwich?* etc.

Then ask students to take both roles and practise the conversations in the Student's Book and their own conversations. You could record some conversations for later examination and correction.

Don't forget!

Workbook Unit 2
Exercise 10 Practice of family vocabulary and possessive *'s*.
Exercise 11 This exercise looks at adjectives and nouns that go together.
Exercise 12 Spelling of plural nouns.

Word list
Remind your students of the Word list for this unit on p135. They could write in the translations, learn them at home, and/or write some of the words in their vocabulary notebook.

3

Present Simple 1 – *he/she/it*
Questions and negatives
Jobs • What time is it?

The world of work

Introduction to the unit

Work and jobs are the themes of this unit as they lend themselves to the practice of the grammatical aim, which is the introduction of the third person singular of the Present Simple. The skills work includes a reading text about a man who lives on a remote Scottish island and has twelve jobs! This was chosen to complement both the themes and grammar of the unit. The text also acts as a preview of other forms of the Present Simple in context.

Language aims

Grammar – Present Simple 1 The Present Simple is the most used tense in the English language. It is therefore important to introduce it early in an elementary course. In *New Headway Plus Special Edition Elementary* the introduction is staged over two units. In this unit only the third person singular with its questions and negatives is presented and practised. All the other persons are introduced in Unit 4.

POSSIBLE PROBLEMS
- The English language does not have many inflections. Unfortunately this seems to mean that the few that exist cause a disproportionate amount of difficulty for foreign learners. The *s* on the third person singular of the Present Simple is a classic example of this. Therefore we introduce it first in the hope that it will be more memorable and students will be less likely to omit it.
- The *s* can be pronounced in three ways:
  comes   /kʌmz/
  works   /wɜːks/
  teaches /ˈtiːtʃɪz/
  So you need to spend some time highlighting the /s/, /z/, /ɪz/ endings and practising them.
- The use of *does/doesn't* in the question and negative often seems strange to students, because of the absence of the auxiliary in the positive.

NOTE
For the first nine units of *New Headway Plus Special Edition Elementary*, the verb *have* is introduced and practised as a full verb with its *do/does* forms. *Have got* is introduced in Unit 10. This is for several reasons:
- By introducing the *do/does* forms, the verb *have* operates like any other verb in the Present Simple (with the exception of *has* in the third person singular).
- When students have just learned the Present Simple and have been introduced to the auxiliary verbs *do/does*, it is very difficult and confusing for them when they come across the verb form *have got*, which operates differently.
- Although *have got* is common, especially in the spoken language, the full verb *have* with its *do/does* forms covers all the uses in a way that *have got* doesn't. *Have got* expresses possession, but it cannot express a habitual action. So students can learn *How many children have you got?*, but then it is very confusing when they are introduced to *What time do you have lunch?* We cannot say **What time have you got lunch?*
- Finally, *have* with its *do/does* forms is becoming more common in spoken British English. It is the standard form in American English.

Vocabulary and pronunciation A variety of jobs with related activities are introduced. Dictionary work is encouraged and there is a certain amount of work on the phonetic spelling of some of the words.

Everyday English Students focus on how to tell the time in English. This is practised in short dialogues.

Workbook The spelling of the third person singular is practised (*watches, goes*).

Question words such as *Where?* and *How much?* are practised.

Verbs of daily routine (*get up, get dressed*) are introduced, and some verbs and nouns that go together (*have a shower, wear a uniform*).

The writing syllabus of *New Headway Plus Special Edition Elementary* begins in this unit.

Object pronouns (*me, him, them*) are introduced and practised.

Notes on the unit

STARTER (SB p20)

The *Starter* activity recycles the family vocabulary from Unit 2 and allows students to use some of the jobs vocabulary they already know. Give some examples of jobs then get students to give examples of jobs in pairs. If students ask for the names of individual jobs, give some examples that are common to the whole class, but do not let the *Starter* activity go on too long or reduce the usefulness of the *Vocabulary and pronunciation* section.

THREE JOBS (SB p20)

Present Simple *he/she/it*

> **SUGGESTION**
> We suggest that *before* you start this unit you set the following vocabulary homework in preparation for the presentation texts on Alison and Bob. This will save a lot of classroom time where you would have to check vocabulary either by mime, dictionary work, or translation (in a monolingual class), and it will give you more time to focus on the grammar.
>
> **Homework prior to lesson**
> Ask students to write the translation of the following words and *learn* them for the lesson. They can use a bilingual dictionary to look up words they don't know.
> **Verbs** come fly go help like love speak work
> **Nouns** day hour summer town walk week winter
> **Adjectives** free (time) ordinary
> Pre-teach *scientist* and *flying doctor*.

1 Ask students to look at the photographs. Ask them *What's her job?* (scientist), *What's his job?* (flying doctor). Then ask them to look quickly at the texts and ask *Where's she from?* (Cambridge, England), *Where's he from?* (England).

T 3.1 [CD 1: Track 23] Now play the recording and ask your students to read and listen to the texts at the same time. If you think your class will experience some difficulty, you could deal with the texts one at a time, doing the *Grammar Spot* exercises with them for the first text and then asking them to repeat the process on their own for the second.

> **GRAMMAR SPOT**
> 1 Ask students to work on their own to underline the verbs and then check their answers with a partner before you conduct a full class feedback. You could ask them to call out the verbs for you to write on the board in columns according to their pronunciation.
>
> **Answers and pronunciation guide**
> /z/ comes flies lives loves is has
> /s/ works likes speaks
>
> Refer students to Grammar Reference 2.2 on p125.
>
> 2 Ask the whole class what the last letter is and point out that this is the ending for the third person singular – *he, she, it* – of the Present Simple tense.
>
> 3 Before you ask your students to practise the verbs in pairs, ask them to chorus them with you from the board and draw their attention to the different pronunciations of the endings.
>
> You may also want to point out that *is* and *has* are irregular.
>
> Now ask them to practise in pairs and read one of the texts to each other. Go round and monitor. You could round off the activity by asking one or two students to read a text aloud to the whole class.

2 Ask your students to write in the answers on their own and then check with a partner. Make it clear that each gap represents a word and that number 8 requires a positive verb in the second sentence because of the negative expressed by *never*.

T 3.2 [CD 1: Track 24] Students listen and check their answers.

> **Answers and tapescript**
> 1 She's a scientist. He's a doctor.
> 2 Alison comes from England. Bob **comes from** England, too.
> 3 She lives in a big city, but he **lives** in a **small** town.
> 4 She **works** three days **a** week. He **works** 16 hours a day **non-stop**.

5   He **speaks** to sick people on his radio. She **speaks** three languages.
6   She loves her job and he **loves his job**, too.
7   She **has a** daughter. He **isn't** married.
8   She **likes** skiing and going **for** walks in her free time.* He never **has** free time.
*   Note that *like* + *-ing* is dealt with in Unit 4.

PRACTICE (SB p21)

Talking about people

1   The aim of this activity is to give students the chance not just to produce single sentences, but to speak at some length to describe Philippe. It is both useful and satisfying for low-level students to use language for 'display' purposes in this way and not always engage in the more 'natural' question and answer activities.
    Ask the whole class to look at the picture of Philippe and the information about him. Start to build a profile of him orally with contributions from different students.

2   Then ask one or two individuals to speak at length about Philippe.

Sample answer
Philippe is a waiter. He comes from France and he lives in Paris. He works in the centre of Paris. He speaks French and a little English. He's married, and he has two sons. In his free time he likes reading and playing football.

3   Now ask your students to write some notes about a friend or relative. Students work in pairs and talk about their friend/relative to their partner. Go round the class to check and help them. Bring the whole class together again, and ask one or two students to tell the others about their friend/relative.

ADDITIONAL MATERIAL

Workbook Unit 3
Exercises 1 and 2 These provide further practice of the third person positive of the Present Simple. Exercise 2 focuses on the spelling.
Exercise 3 This is a vocabulary activity in preparation for Exercise 4. It should be done with a dictionary. (It is *not* an opportunity to practise other persons of the Present Simple, only to see the verbs in their infinitive forms!) It would be a good idea to set this exercise for homework and then follow it in class with Exercise 4 – the pictures of Rupert's daily routine are particularly suitable for a classroom activity, where the story is built orally *before* students are asked to write it.

WHAT DOES SHE DO? (SB p22)

Questions and negatives

NOTE
Be prepared for some students to make mistakes in the use of *does/doesn't* to form the question and negative. In the Present and Past Simple tenses, where there is no auxiliary in the positive, the use of the auxiliary verbs can seem very strange. Many students feel that it would be much more logical to say:
*Lives he in Paris?
*Where lives she?
*She lives not in London.
The short answers *Yes, he does./No, he doesn't.* also cause problems and need highlighting for students.

1   You need to signal that you are going to introduce the question form. You can do this by drawing a large question mark on the board and/or repeating the sentences yourself with exaggerated intonation.

    T 3.3 [CD 1: Track 25] Play the recording and ask your students to read and listen to the questions and complete the answers.

Answers and tapescript
Where does Alison come from?	Cambridge, **in** England.
What does she do?	She's **a** scientist.
Does she speak French?	**Yes**, she does.
Does she speak Spanish?	**No**, she doesn't.

Play the recording again and get students to repeat both chorally and individually. Then get them to ask and answer the questions in open pairs across the class.

NOTE
Encourage good pronunciation at all times. Highlight the pronunciation of *does* and *doesn't*, getting students to repeat the weak and strong forms in isolation and as part of the question and short answers:
the weak /dəz/ in all the questions *What does she do? Does she speak French?*
and the strong form /dʌz/ and /dʌznt/ in the short answers *Yes, she does./ No, she doesn't.*
Also take care with the intonation, falling at the end in the *wh-* questions and rising in the inverted questions.

Where does she come from? /weə dəz ʃɪ kʌm frɒm/

Does she speak French? /dəz ʃɪ spiːk frentʃ/

> **GRAMMAR SPOT**
>
> 1 Make sure students understand that *What does she/he do?* means the same as *What's her/his job?* but that *What does she/he do?* is the more normal question.
>
> 2 Ask students to complete the sentences using the verb *come*.
>
> > **Answers**
> > **Positive**: She **comes** from England.
> > **Negative**: She **doesn't come** from America.
> > **Question**: Where **does** she **come** from?
>
> 3 Read Grammar Reference 3.1 on p126 together in class, and/or ask students to read it at home. Encourage them to ask you questions about it.

2 **T 3.4** [CD 1: Track 26] Ask your students to complete the sentences on their own and then check their answers with a partner. Play the recording and get them to listen and check. Finally, ask individuals to read aloud their answers to the class and check the pronunciation.

> **Answers and tapescript**
> 1 Where **does** Bob **come** from? England.
> 2 What **does** he **do**? He's a doctor.
> 3 **Does** he fly to help people? Yes, he **does**.
> 4 **Does** he **speak** French and German? No, he **doesn't**.

3 Students write similar questions about Philippe and then ask and answer in pairs.

> **Sample questions and answers**
> 1 Where does Philippe come from? Paris.
> 2 What does he do? He's a waiter.
> 3 Does he work in the centre of Paris? Yes, he does.
> 4 Does he speak German? No, he doesn't.

PRACTICE (SB p22)

Asking about people

1 Get students to read about Mona or Mark. Check comprehension and drill the pronunciation of *interpreter* /ɪnˈtɜːprɪtə/, *journalist* /ˈdʒɜːnəlɪst/, *United Nations* /juːˈnaɪtɪd ˈneɪʃnz/, and *Moscow* /ˈmɒskəʊ/.

2 Get students to say a sentence about each person as an example. Students choose Mona or Mark and describe her/him to a partner. Go round the class to check and help them. Round off the activity by bringing the whole class together again, and asking one or two students to tell the others about Mona and Mark.

3 Ask each student in a pair to choose either Mona or Mark. Students work on their own and write the questions about their character.

> **Answers**
> 1 Where does Mona/Mark come from?
> 2 Where does Mona/Mark live?
> 3 What does Mona/Mark do?
> 4 Where does Mona/Mark work?
> 5 Does Mona/Mark speak French/German?
> 6 What does Mona/Mark do in her/his free time?
> 7 Does Mona/Mark go skiing?
> 8 How many children does Mona/Mark have?

Check their questions quickly round the class, getting students to read them aloud.

4 Ask your students to close their books. Write the names Mona and Mark on the board, then ask students to work in pairs and take it in turns to ask and answer questions about them. Don't make the activity too laborious by insisting they ask *every* question about *both* characters, as this would probably take too long. Let your students choose their questions and character they use.

Round off the activity by asking for a few questions and answers in open pairs across the class.

5 This is a personalized activity. Tell students they can answer questions about any relative or a friend. Feed in any necessary vocabulary, e.g. *cousin, (brother)-in-law* if students request this. Go round and check as they do the activity, focusing on the formation of questions. Ask one or two students to tell the whole class about their or their partner's relative.

> **SUGGESTION**
> Students can play a guessing game in which one student describes another (without saying his/her name!) and the rest of the class guess who it is. This can also be used to practise *Yes/No* questions, where the student who has thought of the person replies *Yes* or *No* to the rest of the class and does not give any additional information. This can be set up as a whole-class activity and then continued in groups/pairs.

Listening and pronunciation

6 Do this exercise as briskly as possible with the whole class. Demonstrate the activity by going through the sample sentences with them and practising the responses *Yes, that's right, No, he/she doesn't, No, he isn't.*

T 3.5 [CD 1: Track 27] Play the recording or read the sentences yourself and nominate individuals in the class to respond.

Encourage other members of the class to correct if a wrong answer is given. It should be quick and fun to do, so *don't* insist on the full correct answer if it slows down the activity. *No, he/she doesn't* is enough.

> **Answers and tapescript**
> 1 Philippe comes from Paris.
>   **Yes, that's right.**
> 2 Philippe lives in London.
>   **No, he doesn't.** (He lives in Paris.)
> 3 He works in the centre of Paris.
>   **Yes, that's right.**
> 4 He speaks English very well.
>   **No, he doesn't.** (He speaks a little English.)
> 5 He's married.
>   **Yes, that's right.**
> 6 Mona lives and works in New York.
>   **Yes, that's right.**
> 7 She speaks French and German.
>   **No, she doesn't.** (She speaks Arabic, English, and French.)
> 8 She plays tennis in her free time.
>   **No, she doesn't.** (She likes reading.)
> 9 She isn't married.
>   **Yes, she is.**
> 10 Mark works in an office in Moscow.
>   **Yes, that's right.**
> 11 He has three sons.
>   **No, he doesn't.** (He has three daughters.)
> 12 He likes playing football in his free time.
>   **No, he doesn't.** (He likes to go skiing.)

7 **T 3.6** [CD 1: Track 28] This should follow on immediately from the previous exercise. Play the recording. Ask students to tick the sentence they hear. This exercise tests receptive comprehension, but you can make it productive afterwards by asking students to say the pairs of sentences in pairs.

> **Answers and tapescript**
> 1 She likes her job.
> 2 She loves walking.
> 3 He isn't married.
> 4 Does he have three children?
> 5 What does he do?

Check it

8 Ask students to work in pairs or small groups and tick the correct sentence. Ask them to work quite quickly, then conduct a full class feedback. Try to get students to correct each other and explain any mistakes they hear.

> **Answers**
> 1 She comes from Japan.
> 2 What does he do in his free time?
> 3 Where does she live?
> 4 He isn't married.
> 5 Does she have two sons?
> 6 He doesn't play football.
> 7 She doesn't like pizza.
> 8 What's his address?

ADDITIONAL MATERIAL

Workbook Unit 3
Exercises 4–8 Questions and negatives in Present Simple third person singular.
Exercise 12 Using pronouns.
Exercise 13 Rewriting a short text about Mona.

READING AND LISTENING (SB p24)

Seumas McSporran – the man with twelve jobs!

> **NOTE**
> This is an important activity because it brings together in a text much of the grammar your students have been studying so far. It should give them great satisfaction to feel that they can already master a piece of continuous prose of this length.
> It also acts as a preview of the work on daily routine in Unit 4.
> Seumas McSporran is a real person (and a real name), and the text is based on a newspaper article. However, it has been carefully simplified and graded for students of this level.

You could begin the lesson by asking students:
How many jobs do you/most people have?
What time do you/most people start and finish work?

1 Ask students to look quickly at the photographs on the page and tell you a little about what and who they can see. Do not insist on accuracy at this stage – use this as an opportunity for students to get into the topic and predict what they might read in the text.
Briefly revise the times that go with each photograph.

2 Ask students to work in pairs and match the sentences with the photographs. Tell them not to worry about new vocabulary but to use the words that they recognize and the information in the photographs to help them with the matching.
Check the answers.

> **Answers**
> 1 g 2 a 3 e 4 c 5 b 6 d 7 h 8 f

Check the key vocabulary by giving short definitions accompanied by mime and getting students to tell you the word, e.g. *You eat this in the morning – breakfast; the people who stay in a hotel – guests; you need this in your car to drive it – petrol*, etc.

3 Pre-teach/check some of the key vocabulary before the students start to read, so that they do not stop at every word they do not recognize to ask for an explanation. You can teach/check the following through mime or short definitions: jobs – *policeman, fireman, taxi-driver, school-bus driver, boatman* (a man you pay to take you out in a boat or for the use of a boat), *ambulance man, petrol attendant, undertaker*; verbs – *get up, make breakfast, watch TV, make supper, go to bed.*

Ask students to work in pairs or small groups to find the answers. Tell them not to worry about words they do not recognize and just to focus on the key information. They can consult the text whenever necessary.

Check the answers. Decide according to the speed and ability of your students whether you want quick, short answers or fuller answers (see brackets).

Answers
1 On the Island of Gigha (pronounced /giːə/). (He lives on the Island of Gigha in the north of Scotland.)
2 60. (He's 60 years old.)
3 Twelve. (He has twelve jobs.)
4 Margaret. (His wife's name is Margaret.)
5 She works in the shop.
6 120. (120 people live on Gigha.)
7 150. (150 tourists visit Gigha in summer.)
8 He makes breakfast, drives the children to school, collects the post from the boat, and delivers the post to the houses.
9 Margaret makes supper, and Seumas does the accounts. They have a mug of tea and then go to bed.

If appropriate, ask students for their reaction to the text. Ask if they know anyone who has a lot of jobs and what they do.

4 Ask students to look back at the photographs on p24. Demonstrate the activity by getting two students to ask and answer using the example in the Student's Book. Students continue to ask and answer questions about the times in Seumas's day. Go round the class to check. Feed back on any common errors.

5 **T 3.7** [CD 1: Track 29] Ask students to mask the conversations in exercise 6. Focus attention on the three questions and demonstrate the activity by playing conversation 1 and checking the answers (see below).
Play the remaining three conversations, stopping after each one to allow students to complete their answers. Check the answers with the whole class.

Answers
Conversation 1
1 Afternoon
2 Seumas and a customer in Seumas's shop
3 Shopkeeper
Conversation 2
1 Morning
2 Seumas and a woman who lives on the island
3 Postman
Conversation 3
1 Evening
2 Seumas and Margaret
3 No job – Seumas isn't working
Conversation 4
1 Morning
2 Seumas and schoolchildren
3 School-bus driver

6 Students complete the conversations as far as they can, using what they can remember from the first listening and from the reading text, and the information from exercise 4. Students can then exchange information with a partner.

Play the conversations again to allow students to complete their answers. Then check the answers with the whole class.

Answers and tapescript
1 A Good **afternoon**. Can I **have** two ice-creams, please?
  B Chocolate or vanilla?
  A One chocolate, one vanilla please.
  B That's **£1.80**. Anything **else**?
  A No, thank you.
2 A Only **two** letters for you this **morning**, Mrs Craig.
  B Thank you very much, Mr McSporran. And **how**'s Mrs McSporran this **morning**?
  A Oh, she's very well, thank you. She's **busy** in the shop.
3 A A mug of **tea** before bed, my dear?
  B Oh, yes please.
  A **Here** you are.
  B Thank you, my dear. I'm very **tired** this **evening**.
4 A Hello, Mr McSporran!
  B Good **morning**, boys and girls. Hurry up, we're late.
  A Can I sit here, Mr McSporran?
  C No, no, **I want** to sit there.
  B Be quiet **all** of you, and SIT DOWN!

Put students into pairs to practise the conversations. An additional idea is to ask them to choose *one* of the conversations and learn it by heart to act out to the rest of the class. You could also encourage more confident students to improvise some further dialogues. (Asking students to act really seems to help their pronunciation, particularly stress and intonation.)

VOCABULARY AND PRONUNCIATION (SB p26)

Jobs

1 Ask students to look at the pictures and tell you any of the jobs they know already. Then get them to work in pairs and match a picture with a job in column A, checking any words that are still unknown in their dictionaries. You could ask them to mark the stress.

Conduct a full class feedback on the correct answers and drill the words both chorally and individually as you go, taking care with the stress (see below). Keep revising as you go by asking *Tell me again! What's '1'? What's '4'?* etc.

Answers
1 d   A chef
2 f   A journalist
3 a   A pilot
4 b   An interpreter
5 c   A nurse
6 i   A shop assistant
7 e   An accountant
8 h   An architect
9 g   A postman

2 Ask students to work in pairs or small groups and match a job in column A with a line in column B. They will probably need to continue to use their dictionaries *or* if you have a monolingual class and you think dictionary work will take too much time, you could give quick translations of any words they ask about. Afterwards you could either conduct a full class feedback (try not to make this too laborious with too much correction), or ask different students to come to the board and write the answers for the others to comment on and read aloud.

Answers
a   A pilot flies planes.
b   An interpreter translates things.
c   A nurse looks after people in hospital.
d   A chef cooks in a restaurant.
e   An accountant looks after money.
f   A journalist writes for a newspaper.
g   A postman delivers letters.
h   An architect designs buildings.
i   A shop assistant sells things.

3
> **NOTE**
> The idea of this activity is to give a very short introduction to and practice of the phonetic script. It is also an opportunity to start getting your students familiar with the phonetic symbols chart on p143 of their book.
> You need to make clear what exactly phonetic script is, i.e. that it is only the sounds of the words that are transcribed and that it is important to know this in English because the spellings and the sounds often do not relate exactly.

Ask the whole class to look at all the phonetic transcriptions and say if they can recognize any of the words. Ask them to turn to p143, *not* to study it, but so that they get the idea of what phonetic script is.

Now ask them to write the spellings of the words and then check them with a partner and practise saying them together. Let them use the phonetic chart to help them.

Answers
1 nurse   4 shop assistant
2 postman   5 architect
3 accountant   6 pilot

If you have time, you could put a few additional words in phonetic script on the board for students to do after you have asked for feedback on the words in the exercise. For example:

/ˈhɒspɪtəl/   (hospital)
/ˈpiːpl/   (people)
/wɜːks/   (works)
/lʊks/   (looks)
/selz/   (sells)
/pleɪnz/   (planes)
/ˈhaʊzɪz/   (houses)

4 Make this exercise fun, like a game, and do it as quickly as possible. Ask students to learn the sentences by heart, then to close their books. Call out the name of a job and tell your students to call out to complete the sentence.

Teacher   **Student(s)**
A journalist …   *writes for a newspaper!*
A pilot …   *flies planes!* etc.

Finally, ask students to work in pairs for a few minutes with their books still shut, and ask and answer questions about the jobs. Demonstrate the first example yourself to remind them of the question, e.g.

What does an interpreter do? He/She translates things.

ADDITIONAL MATERIAL

Workbook Unit 3
Further vocabulary exercises:
Exercise 9 This practises more verbs and nouns that go together, e.g. *have a shower*.
Exercise 10 This revises a selection of vocabulary from all the units so far. It requires students to sort words into related groups.

EVERYDAY ENGLISH (SB p27)

What time is it?

Introduce the subject of telling the time by asking *What time is it now?* and *What time does the lesson end?* Accept answers in the hour + minutes form, e.g. *five thirty*, but explain that the system used in *New Headway Plus Special Edition Elementary* uses *past* and *to*.

> **NOTE**
> The first eight clocks on this page are positioned in such a way that those with gaps underneath are next to clocks with *similar* times which students can use to help them write in the correct answers.
> The next eight practise the time in five-minute intervals around the clock. You probably will *not* need to point this out to students. It should be obvious what to do from the pictures.

1 Ask students to work in pairs, look carefully at the clocks, and write in the times.

 T 3.8 [CD 1: Track 30] Now play the recording for students to check their answers.

> **Answers and tapescript**
> It's five o'clock.   It's eight o'clock.
> It's half past five.   It's half past eleven.
> It's quarter past five.   It's quarter past two.
> It's quarter to six.   It's quarter to nine.
> It's five past five.   It's ten past five.
> **It's twenty past five.**   It's twenty-five past five.
> **It's twenty-five to six.**   It's twenty to six.
> It's ten to six.   **It's five to six.**

Get students to practise saying the times either from the recording or repeating them after you. If possible, bring a toy clock with moveable hands to the lesson as an easy way of getting further practice. First, *you* can change the times on the clock and then your students can also have turns, coming to the front of the class, moving the hands, and asking *What time is it?*

2 This exercise introduces *about* as a useful expression for times just before or after an exact division of the clock. Read through the examples with the class and practise with the toy clock (if you have one!) or by drawing further examples on the board.

3 **T 3.9** [CD 1: Track 31] Play the recording and ask your students to repeat the sentences giving very special attention to the stress and intonation. Tell them that they must try to sound *very* polite. Really encourage good imitation from the recording, or by giving the sentences yourself. Practise the dialogue across the class with your own examples first, then ask everyone to draw about three clocks on a piece of paper and practise the conversation again in pairs. Round off the lesson by asking one or two pairs to act out the conversations in front of the class. Tell them to imagine that they are stopping someone in the street to ask the time and that they must be very, very polite.

The *more* you insist on good stress and intonation in such activities, the more fun it will be!

ADDITIONAL MATERIAL

Workbook Unit 3
Exercise 11 This gives more practice of telling the time.

Don't forget!

Workbook Unit 3
Exercises 12 and 13 You might want to do the writing activities now, if you haven't done them earlier.

Word list
Remind your students of the Word list for this unit on p136. They could write in the translations, learn them at home, and/or write some of the words in their vocabulary notebook.

4

Present Simple 2 – *I/you/we/they*
Leisure activities
Social expressions 1

Take it easy!

Introduction to the unit

The theme of this unit is free time and leisure activities. This lends itself to much practice, personalized and otherwise, of the main grammatical aim, which is the introduction of all other persons (those without the *s*!) of the Present Simple tense. The skills work includes reading and listening tasks where people from three different countries talk about seasons and what they do. This provides the opportunity to bring together and revise all persons of the Present Simple.

Language aims

Grammar – Present Simple 2 This unit follows on from the introduction of the third person in Unit 3 and introduces all other persons of the Present Simple, *I, you, we, they*, and the question and negative. The verb forms with these are all the same, without the inflection *s*, and tend to cause less difficulty as a result. The third person is constantly revised alongside the other persons so that students can perceive the differences in form.

Vocabulary A variety of leisure activities (sports and hobbies) are introduced and these are practised in a personalized activity with the verb *to like*.

Everyday English Some common and useful social expressions are introduced and practised in short dialogues.

Workbook Adverbs of frequency, e.g. *always, sometimes, never* are practised.

In the vocabulary section, 'opposite' verbs, e.g. *love/hate, open/close, leave/arrive* are revised.

The writing syllabus continues with an introduction to informal letter writing via a letter to a penfriend.

Notes on the unit

> **SUGGESTION**
> Setting some vocabulary for homework before you start this unit will give you more time to focus on the grammar. It is also worthwhile to get your students used to the idea of taking some responsibility for the learning of vocabulary. Encourage them to enter the new words in their vocabulary notebooks.

Homework prior to the lesson

1 Ask students to learn the days of the week in English. You could give them a handout with phonetic script such as this:

Saturday /ˈsætədi/   Tuesday /ˈtʃuːzdi/   Friday /ˈfraɪdi/
Sunday /ˈsʌndi/   Wednesday /ˈwenzdi/
Monday /ˈmʌndi/   Thursday /ˈθɜːzdi/

2 Give students these new verbs to look up in a bilingual dictionary. Ask them to learn them and write down the translations.

interview _____   go out _____
chat _____   relax _____
cook _____   stay _____
get up _____   visit _____

26 Unit 4 · Take it easy!

STARTER (SB p28)

1 Use a calendar that shows the year, months, and days as a visual aid. (Alternatively, write the day, month, and year on the board in abbreviated form, e.g. Tu., Sept., 2006). Focus attention on the year and elicit how we say this in English. Do the same for the month. (Do not spend too long on this, as students will focus on months more fully before the *Reading and listening* section.)

> **POSSIBLE PROBLEMS**
> Students often try to say years in English in the same way as in their own language, e.g. 1999 is read as **one thousand nine hundred and ninety-nine* instead of *nineteen ninety-nine*. If necessary, highlight on the board how we divide dates beginning 18-, 19-, into two pairs of numbers and give practise of similar dates.
>
> You may also need to remind students of the use of *and* in dates like 2001 = *two thousand and one*.

2 Use the calendar and get students to go through the days of the week. Say the days yourself and ask them to repeat each one both chorally and individually. This will take less time if you have set the above for homework.

> **POSSIBLE PROBLEMS**
> **Days**
> Take particular care with the pronunciation of *Tuesday* /ˈtʃuːzdi/ and *Thursday* /ˈθɜːzdi/ which students can easily confuse because they sound quite similar. Also the pronunciation of *Wednesday* /ˈwenzdi/ can be a problem because of the spelling, and the consonant cluster /nzd/ that results from it being pronounced as *two* syllables not three.

- Ask *What day is it today?* Chorus through the days of the week with the whole class and then make the individual practice fun by getting one student after another to give consecutive days *very* quickly round the class until they are firmly fixed. (If time, you could then ask one or two students to go through the whole week and perhaps also ask them to spell some of the days, to revise the alphabet.)
- Ask *Which days are the weekend?* This will check that students understand the word *weekend* which is needed in the exercises.
- Ask students to ask and answer the *Starter* questions in pairs. Go round and check students' pronunciation and feed back on any common errors.

> **EXTRA SUGGESTIONS**
> If you feel your students needs more practice on days, months, and years, try the following activities:
> - rearranging the jumbled spelling of days and months
> - matching phonetic script to days and months
> - conducting a favourite day or birthday survey
> - a word association activity for different days/months
> - doing an 'important year' quiz with simple headline-style sentences (to avoid the use of the past simple), e.g. *the first man on the moon*, and students supply the correct year, e.g. *1969*.

WEEKDAYS AND WEEKENDS (SB p28)

Present Simple 2 *I/you/we/they*

1 This text reminds students of the third person of the Present Simple before they are introduced to the other persons. Focus attention on the photographs and on the headline. Elicit basic information about Gary. You may need to point out that in New Zealand, the weekend is Saturday and Sunday.

> **Answers**
> Gary **is** 45 years old and **lives** in Queenstown, New Zealand. He **works** hard as a lawyer in Queenstown from Monday to Friday, but he **doesn't relax** at weekends. He **races** stock cars for the McKay Racing Team. On Saturdays he **trains** with the team and works on his car, and on Sundays he **races** in the National Stock Car League. He **doesn't have** much free time, but he **loves** his busy life.

Ask a few questions to revise the third person.
Examples

Teacher	Student(s)
Where does Gary live?	*In New Zealand.*
How old is he?	*Forty-five.*
What does he do?	*He's a lawyer.*
What does he do at weekends?	*He races stock cars.*

2 **T 4.1** [CD 1: Track 32] Tell students that Gary Seaman is now talking about his weekdays and weekends. Ask students to first read and listen to the text and not to write anything. Explain that they will complete the text at the next stage. Check or pre-teach the following vocabulary from the text: *garage, repair, race track, gym*. Play the recording.

3 Ask students to work in pairs and check the verbs in the box. This can be done quite quickly if they have done the preparatory homework. If they haven't, encourage students to look up new words in their dictionary and work together to complete the text with the verbs from the box. You will need to make clear that some of the verbs will need an *s* because they are third person singular. The others can be copied exactly from the box.

T 4.1 Play the recording again so that students can check their answers.

> **Answers and tapescript**
> **Gary Seaman's Week**
> I **like** my job as a lawyer because it's very interesting. And I **like** stock car racing too, because it's so exciting – they're very different things! My life is very busy, because it's non-stop, but I enjoy it! On Tuesday and Wednesday evenings I **go** to the garage and work on my car – there's always a lot of repair work to do. And on Thursday evenings I **train** with my team at the race track. I like to keep fit, so three days a week I **get up** at 5.30 and **go** to the gym before work. On Friday evenings I just **relax** at home because I'm very tired. I usually **cook** a nice dinner for my wife, Sarah. We both **love** cooking. After dinner we often **watch** TV. On Saturdays I sometimes **visit** my parents for lunch. They **live** in the centre of Queenstown, too. I never **go out** on Saturday evenings, because I always **race** on Sundays and I get up very early. I **want** our team to win the National Stock Car League this year!

Ask one or two students to read parts of the text aloud to the rest of the class and, if time, to each other in pairs.

4 **T 4.2** [CD 1: Track 33] Ask students to complete Gary's answers and play the recording for them to check their answers.

> **Answers**
> **In** Queenstown.   No, I **don't**.
> Yes, I **do**.   **Because** I race stock cars.

Play the recording again or model the questions and answers yourself. Practise the questions and answers in open pairs across the class so that you can correct any mistakes. Take particular care with the pronunciation:

Sounds
The weak vowel sound /dʊ/ in the question, and the strong vowel sound /duː/ in the short answer.
Do you like your work?   *Yes, I do.*
/dʒʊ laɪk jɔː wɜːk/   /jes aɪ duː/

Stress and intonation
The intonation rises at the end of inverted questions and falls at the end of short answers and *wh-* questions.

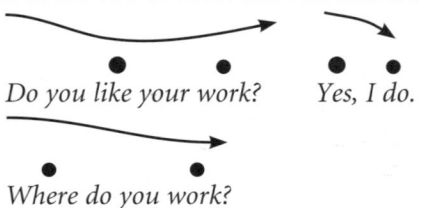

Do you like your work?   *Yes, I do.*

Where do you work?

Roleplay

5 Tell students to read the texts on p28–9 again first, but then to cover them and try to remember the information about Gary's life. Ask students to work in pairs and take it in turns to be Gary Seaman. Demonstrate the activity by getting two students to ask and answer the first two questions across the class. Ask students to continue the activity in pairs. Go round and check for the correct use of the auxiliary *do/does* and for the correct use of strong and weak forms in the pronunciation of *do*.

GRAMMAR SPOT

1 Ask students to complete the table with the positive and negative forms. Check the answers.

> **Answers**
>
> | | Positive | Negative |
> |--------|----------|--------------|
> | I | work | don't work |
> | You | work | don't work |
> | He/She | works | doesn't work |
> | It | works | doesn't work |
> | We | work | don't work |
> | They | work | don't work |

Ask students to focus on the positive forms in the table. Ask them which have a different form (*he/she/it*) and how they are different (they end in *-s*).

Ask students to focus on the negative forms in the table. Ask them how the *I/you/we/they* forms are different from the positive forms (they use the auxiliary *don't*). Ask students to focus on the *he/she/it* forms and ask them how they are different from the other negative forms (they use the auxiliary *doesn't*).

2 Ask students to complete the questions and answers. Check the answers.

> **Answers**
> Where **do** you work?
> Where **does** he work?
> **Do** you work in Queenstown? Yes, I **do**.
> **Does** he work in Auckland? No, he **doesn't**.

Ask students which auxiliary verb is used in questions with *I/you/we/they* (*do*) and which with *he/she/it* (*does*). Remind students that questions can begin with a question word, or have no question word and the answer *Yes/No*. Ask students to give you examples of each type of question from the table.

Read Grammar Reference 4.1 and 4.2 on p127 together in class, and/or ask students to read it at home. Encourage them to ask you questions about it.

3 Students find the adverbs of frequency in the text about Gary Seaman.

SUGGESTION
Do Exercises 6 and 7 in the Workbook to introduce adverbs of frequency before this activity.

> **Answers**
> I **usually** cook a nice dinner . . .
> . . . we **often** watch TV.
> . . . I **sometimes** visit my parents for lunch.
> I **never** go out on Saturday evenings . . .
> I **always** race on Sundays . . .

SUGGESTION
- Student A describes their weekday routine as if they do a certain job and the rest of the class has to guess what the job is. They can ask *Yes/No* questions.
- Student A describes their weekday routine as if they were a famous person and the rest of the class has to guess who they are pretending to be. They can ask *Yes/No* questions to help them if necessary. (You might provide role cards of people who are often in the news, so that students don't choose characters who are too obscure.)

PRACTICE (SB p30)

Talking about you

1 Ask students to work on their own to do this activity. Students who finish early can then check their answers with a partner.

> **Answers and tapescript**
> 1d What time do you go to bed? At 11 o'clock.
> 2b Where do you go on holiday? To Spain or Portugal.
> 3e What do you do at weekends? I always relax.
> 4c When do you do your homework? After dinner.
> 5a Who do you live with? My mother and sisters.
> 6f Why do you like your job? Because it's interesting.
> 7g How do you travel to school? By bus.
> 8h Do you go out in the evenings? Yes, I do sometimes.

T 4.3 [CD 1: Track 34] Play the recording and let students check their answers. As preparation for the next activity, ask students to listen and repeat the questions and answers chorally and individually. Take particular care with intonation.

2 This activity gives practice of the first and second persons only. Ask students to work in pairs to ask and answer the questions in *Practice* 1. Demonstrate the activity by getting a pair of students to ask and answer the first question across the class. Remind students to have the whole question ready before they speak. Go round and check as students do the activity, listening for correct intonation. Students who finish early can be encouraged to ask similar questions but with different question words, e.g. *When do you go on holiday? Where do you do your homework?*

3 This activity practises the third person singular alongside the other persons. It also pulls the class together after the pairwork. Ask a few individuals to tell the rest of the class about themselves and their partner. If necessary, remind students they need to use the third person *-s* when talking about their partner. (Unless you have a small class, it would take too long to give everyone a turn.)

Listening and pronunciation

4 **T 4.4** [CD 1: Track 35] Play the recording. Ask students to listen carefully and tick the sentence they hear. Play the recording again. Stop after each one and ask students to discuss the answer with a partner before you establish the correct one. You can make this exercise productive by asking students to read aloud the pairs of sentences.

> **Answers and tapescript**
> 1 What does she do on Fridays?
> 2 Do you stay home on Thursday evenings?
> 3 He lives here.
> 4 What do you do on Thursday evenings?
> 5 I read a lot.
> 6 Why don't you like your job?

A questionnaire

5 Focus attention on the verbs in the questionnaire. Students answer the questions and complete the *Me* column about themselves.

6 Get students to practise the questions and answers from the questionnaire, encouraging good pronunciation with rising intonation for inverted questions.

Ask all the class to stand up and 'mingle' to do the next part of the activity (if there is enough space to do so!). Tell them to take it in turns with two other students to ask and answer the questions.

7 This part of the activity is designed to revise the third person singular again alongside the other persons. (It could be set for homework or done orally.)

Ask students to use the information they have collected and write and compare themselves with another student. Then ask one or two students to read their answers aloud for the others to comment on.

> **Sample answer**
> I cook, but she doesn't. She drinks a lot of tea. We both like shopping, and we both sometimes have a big breakfast. She plays tennis, but I don't. We both get up early on weekdays. She also watches TV a lot, but I don't.

Positives and negatives

8 This exercise revises the verb *to be* alongside other verbs in the Present Simple. The exercise could be set for homework, but it can be quite fun if done orally and at a brisk pace with the whole class. Students could then write their answers afterwards.

> **Answers**
> 3 She speaks Arabic.
> 4 They don't want to learn English.
> 5 We aren't tired and we don't want to go home.
> 6 Roberto doesn't like watching football on TV, but he likes playing it.
> 7 I don't work at home because I don't have a good Internet connection.
> 8 Amelia is happy because she has a new mobile phone.
> 9 I don't drink coffee, I don't watch TV a lot, and I go to bed early.
> 10 He drinks coffee, he watches TV a lot, and he doesn't go to bed early.

> **SUGGESTIONS**
> - You can 'test' how much students can remember about each other's lives by using the ideas in the 'How do you live?' questionnaire and getting the others to guess who is being referred to.
> - Students imagine they have a very extravagant and luxurious lifestyle and interview each other, practising *Wh-* and *Yes/No* questions.
>   Where do you work?   I don't work.
>   What time do you get up?   About 11 o'clock.
>   Where do you live?   In a very big house in Paris.
>   Do you have children?   Yes, but they don't live with me.
>   Do you like cooking?   No, I never cook. I have a chef at home.
>   Do you have a busy life?   Of course! I go shopping every day and I go to a restaurant every night!

ADDITIONAL MATERIAL

Workbook Unit 4
Exercise 1 This practises all persons of the Present Simple. Part 3 focuses on question formation.
Exercise 2 This practises *do* and *does*, and the verb *to be*.
Exercises 3–5 Questions and negatives in the Present Simple.
Exercises 6 and 7 More adverbs of frequency.

READING AND LISTENING (SB p32)

My favourite season

> **SUGGESTION**
> It would save time in the lesson if you could ask your students to learn the names of seasons and months in English for homework before the lesson. You could give them this list to learn by heart and test them in class.
>
> **Seasons**
> *spring* /sprɪŋ/   *autumn* /ˈɔːtəm/
> *summer* /ˈsʌmə/   *winter* /ˈwɪntə/
>
> **Months**
> *January* /ˈdʒænjəri/   *July* /dʒuːˈlaɪ/
> *February* /ˈfebruəri/   *August* /ˈɔːɡəst/
> *March* /mɑːtʃ/   *September* /sepˈtembə/
> *April* /ˈeɪprɪl/   *October* /ɒkˈtəʊbə/
> *May* /meɪ/   *November* /nəʊˈvembə/
> *June* /dʒuːn/   *December* /dɪˈsembə/

1 Ask students to work in pairs and answer the questions in exercise 1. They will obviously find this easier if you set it for homework. Monitor, noting any problems with pronunciation and confusion with the months of the year.

> **POSSIBLE PROBLEMS**
> **Months and seasons**
> Students often confuse the months *March* and *May*, and *June* and *July*. They may also need particular help with the pronunciation of *February* /ˈfebruəri/ and *autumn* /ˈɔːtəm/.
>
> If your students had difficulties with the questions in exercise 1, now is a good time to present the key language again. Use a calendar as a visual aid, and go through the seasons and months. Say them first yourself and ask students to repeat each one in order both chorally and individually. Repeat the months and seasons a few times, making it fast and fun if you can. If necessary, check further by asking:
>   *What's before/after September?* etc.
>   *Which month were you born in?*
>
> Then ask students the questions in exercise 1 again, checking for accurate pronunciation.

If your students had few difficulties with the questions in exercise 1, briefly go through the answers as class feedback, highlighting any specific problems you noted earlier. If necessary, do further spot checks by asking similar questions to those above.

2 Ask students to look at the photographs and see if they can identify the seasons. Ask students which colours they can see.

3 **T 4.5** [CD 1: Track 36] Ask students to read the text and listen to the recording at the same time. Ask them which seasons are mentioned.

It may be wise to pause after *each* text to ask for feedback. You can also ask for the *nationality* of the speaker. (Careful with stress in the nationalities.)

Answers
Al Wheeler is Canadian. He mentions summer, winter and autumn.
Manuela da Silva is Portuguese. She mentions summer and winter.
Hamad Saleh is Bahrainian. He mentions spring.

4 Ask students to do this in groups of three if possible. Ask each one in the group to read about a different person. Then they can share the information to answer the questions, which will generate more speaking. Ask someone in each group to write down their answers. Give them 5–10 minutes and then bring the whole class together to conduct the feedback. Encourage them to give short answers where applicable but then to expand on these if possible (see suggestions in brackets in the answer key).

Answers
1 Yes, they do. (Hamad goes diving. Al plays baseball and ice hockey and goes ice-skating and sailing. Manuela goes swimming.)
2 Al goes ice-skating and plays ice hockey. Manuela meets friends in restaurants and coffee shops and they chat.
3 Yes, they do. (They both go to coffee shops with friends.)
4 Near a lake.
5 Fish.
6 They drive to the beach and go swimming.
7 No, we don't. We only know Hamad's job. (He works for Gulf Pearls.)
8 Because he likes the colours of the trees.
9 Because it's too noisy.
10 Red, gold, orange, yellow, brown, grey.
(Ask students to point to things of these colours in the room to check their understanding.)

5 Ask students to remain in their groups to find the six mistakes in the summary and get one or two students to read aloud the corrected version to the rest of the class.

Answers
Al comes from Canada. In winter he plays ice hockey and goes (1) **ice-skating**. He has a holiday home near (2) **a lake**.
Manuela comes from (3) **Portugal**. She likes going to the beach and (4) **swimming** in summer.
Hamad comes from Bahrain. He (5) **doesn't have** a lot of free time. He likes taking underwater photographs, but he (6) **doesn't like** motor racing.

6 **T 4.6** [CD 1: Track 37] Ask students to listen and decide which one is Al, Manuel, and Hamad. Play the recording and stop it after each conversation. Ask *Who is it? Where are they? How do you know?* and let students discuss their answers in pairs before checking with the whole class.

Answers and tapescript
Conversation 1: Manuela. (She is with some Portuguese friends and an English friend called Jane.) They are in a Brazilian café. We know this because they talk about the food.
Conversation 2: Hamad. (He is with a British colleague, Ann Jones from London.) They are in Bahrain in an office (the headquarters of Gulf Pearls). We know this because Hamad says Welcome to Bahrain.
Conversation 3: Al. (He is with a Scottish friend called Mick.) They are at Al's holiday home, near the lake. We know this because they talk about going sailing and fishing.

T 4.6 Who's who?
1 **M = Manuela J = Jane F = Manuela's friends**
M Hello, everybody! This is my friend Jane from England.
F Hi!
    Hello!
    Hello, Jane!
J Hello. Pleased to meet you.
M Sit down here, Jane.
J Thanks.
M Do you like Brazilian food, Jane?
J Yes, I do.
M Great! Would you like to see the menu?

2 **H = Hamad J = Ann Jones**
H Mrs Jones! How do you do?
J How do you do?
H Please come in. You're from our office in London, aren't you?
J Yes, that's right.
H Welcome to Bahrain! Do you like our headquarters here?
J Yes. It's very big. How many people work here?
H About eight hundred people. Do you want to see our offices?

3 **A = Al M = Mick**
A What do you want to do today, Mick?
M Ooh, I don't know. What do you . . .
A Ah! Do you like sailing?

Unit 4 · Take it easy! 31

> **M** Yes, very much. I sometimes go sailing in Scotland but not very often.
> **A** OK – so today it's sailing and fishing on the lake.
> **M** Fantastic. I love fishing too – we go fishing a lot in Scotland.

You could round off the activity by playing the recording again and suggesting that students read the tapescripts on p116 at the same time.

What do you think?

This is an attempt to generate some personalized discussion and give further freer practice of the Present Simple. Don't worry if at this level it turns out to be quite a short activity. Just a little free speaking is still worthwhile.

It can be helpful to ask students to discuss the topic together in small groups first before you conduct feedback with the whole class.

It would also be a nice idea to encourage them to ask *you* questions about *your* favourite season.

> **SUGGESTIONS**
> - You could do a favourite month/season survey where students interview each other in groups and then transfer the information into chart form. (This would work well in a class of students from different countries.) Students write notes to accompany the chart and highlight the key information. You will need to feed in expressions like: *Most of the class prefer … because … , Nobody prefers … .*
> - Students interview each other to find out when the best month/season is for a certain activity in their country: *When's the best month for* (*skiing, walking, playing tennis, shopping, visiting your city,* etc.)?
> - Students write a description of how their home area changes from season to season. Get them to include information on the weather, the colours they can see, the activities people do, and the number of visitors/tourists.

VOCABULARY AND SPEAKING (SB p34)

Leisure activities

1 In pairs or small groups, students look at the pictures and match as many as they can with the names of the activities. Ask them to check the others in their bilingual dictionary. Encourage them to enter any new words in their vocabulary notebooks. Then ask students to tick the activities they like doing.

> **Answers**
> 1 playing football   3 sailing
> 5 ice-skating   10 listening to the radio
> 8 going on picnics   11 swimming
> 16 watching TV   4 reading
> 13 going to the gym   15 eating in restaurants
> 9 taking photographs   14 going to the museum
> 6 cooking   7 jogging
> 12 playing computer games   2 going shopping

2 Highlight the form *like + -ing*. Choose a student and give examples of what you think he/she likes doing. Then ask students what *they* think *you* like doing. Ask them to continue in groups, choosing five activities from the Student's Book.

Encourage students to ask you questions to find out if they were correct about what you like, following the examples in the Student's Book. (Students are often interested to find out about their teacher, but keep this fairly short to allow time for the personalized stage.)

3 First build a dialogue with two students, using the example in the book and highlighting the possible follow-up questions. Then tell the students some true things about yourself, encouraging them to respond to your likes and dislikes as in the example.

Now ask students to continue in pairs and go round the class to check and help them. Make sure they use the *-ing* form.

4 Ask students to think about other activities which are not in the Student's Book. They can look them up in their bilingual dictionary, or ask you or their partner for help. Encourage students to mime or describe the activities rather than ask in L1. Finally, ask a few students in the class to report back on themselves and their partners (thereby practising different persons of the Present Simple).

EVERYDAY ENGLISH (SB p35)

Social expressions (1)

These dialogues introduce and practise little expressions that 'lubricate' day-to-day conversational exchanges.

1 **T 4.7** [CD 1: Track 38] Ask students to work in pairs and complete the dialogues with the expressions given. Then play the recording for them to listen and check their answers.

32 Unit 4 · Take it easy!

Answers and tapescript
1. A **I'm sorry I'm late.** The traffic is bad today.
   B **Don't worry.** Come and sit down. We're on page 25.
2. A **Excuse me.**
   B Yes?
   A Do you have a dictionary?
   B **I'm sorry**, I don't. It's at home.
   A **That's OK**.
3. A It's very hot in here. **Can I open the window?**
   B **Really?** I'm quite cold.
   A OK. **It doesn't matter.**
4. A **Excuse me!** Can I have a coffee with milk, please?
   B Do you want a macchiato?
   A **Pardon?** Can you say that again?
   B A macchiato. Do you want a macchiato?
   A Sorry. **What does macchiato mean?**
   B It's a strong white coffee.
   A **Ah, I see!** Fine. I'll try one. Thank you.

> **EXTRA IDEAS UNITS 1–4**
> On p123 of the Teacher's Book there is an additional reading activity. If you have time and feel that your students would benefit from this, you can photocopy it and use it in class. The reading exercise revises Units 1–4 and could also be done for homework.
>
> An activity to exploit the reading is provided and the answers are on p155.

2 Ask students where each conversation takes place and who the speakers are. Play the recording again so that they can copy the stress and intonation. Ask each pair to learn one of the dialogues by heart and then act it out for the rest of the class. Acting out can improve their pronunciation considerably.

Don't forget!

Workbook Unit 4
Exercise 8 Prepositions of time.
Exercise 9 This vocabulary exercise practises verbs with opposite meaning, e.g. *love/hate*.
Exercise 10 Writing an informal letter to a friend.
Word list
Remind your students of the Word list for this unit on p136. They could write in the translations, learn them at home, and/or write some of the words in their vocabulary notebook.

5

There is/are • Prepositions
some/any • *this/that*
Furniture • Directions 1

Where do you live?

Introduction to the unit

The theme of this unit is places. Students describe a living room, a kitchen, their classroom, and where they live themselves. There is a reading text about a man who has an unusual home – a bubble! This text consolidates the language of the unit and hopefully students will be interested in the man and his less-than-average living space. There are also four very short listenings about homes around the world, as far apart as Toronto and Samoa.

Language aims

Grammar – *There is/are*

> **POSSIBLE PROBLEMS**
>
> Students often confuse *It's a …* with *There's a …* . The difference is that *It's a …* defines something and gives it a name. *There's a …* expresses what exists. This is quite a subtle area, and we don't suggest that you explore it with students, unless absolutely necessary, and preferably in L1, using translation as a support.
>
> Learners confuse *there* and *their*. For such a short structural item, there are a lot of pronunciation problems. Many nationalities have difficulty with the sound /ð/. In *There's*, the *r* is often silent. In *There are* and the question when the following word begins with a vowel, the *r* is pronounced as a linking sound. Again, students need to be encouraged to start questions 'high' and fall, ending with a rise in inverted questions. It is worth working on these pronunciation areas, but not to the point of exhaustion!

Prepositions Simple prepositions of place, such as *on*, *under*, and *next to*, are introduced and practised.

some/any In this unit, *some* and *any* are presented only with countable nouns. In Unit 9, they are presented with both countable and uncountable nouns.

> **POSSIBLE PROBLEMS**
>
> *Some* also presents problems of pronunciation with its weak form /səm/.
>
> *Some* as a concept has a tangible meaning, i.e. a certain, unspecified number of (something). The same cannot be said of *any*. It is a determiner used often (though by no means exclusively) in questions and negatives. We suggest you do not go into the deeper areas of *any* expressing fundamentally negative ideas, or *any* expressing *It doesn't matter what*, as in *Take any book you want*. This is unnecessary, and difficult for elementary-level students.

Vocabulary There is quite a high vocabulary load in this unit, including furniture and electrical appliances, classroom and business items, and local amenities. The vocabulary is taught and recycled alongside the main target structures and, for this reason, there is no self-contained *Vocabulary* section.

It is worth checking from time to time how students are progressing with their vocabulary notebooks. Are they still adding to them? Have they started a new one? Do they try to revise regularly? Have they thought of new ways of organizing their notebooks? Probably not!

Everyday English This is the first activity on directions. This topic is picked up again in Unit 10, where prepositions of movement are introduced.

Workbook There is further practice on *there is/are, some/any*, prepositions, and *this/that/these/those*. There are also exercises to help students distinguish *There's a …/ It's a …* and *this/that/these/those*.

In the vocabulary section, rooms and objects/appliances are revised through a labelling activity. There is also an exercise on verb and noun collocations.

In the writing section, there is the first exercise on linking words, *and, so, but*, and *because*. Students are invited to write a description of their house or flat.

Notes on the unit

> **SUGGESTION**
> We suggest that you set some vocabulary for homework before you start this unit to maximize classroom time.

Homework prior to the lesson

Ask students to look up the following words in their dictionary, and put them in their vocabulary notebook.

sofa	shelf	fire	bedroom
armchair	cupboard	rug	bathroom
video	curtains	flowers	living room
stereo	lamp	mirror	kitchen

STARTER (SB p36)

1 Focus attention on the vocabulary and ask students to give two or three examples of correct words to go in *The living room* column. Students continue categorizing the vocabulary in pairs. Check the answers with the whole class. (Note that these are the most usual answers and that students may highlight different places for some items, e.g. a television in the kitchen.)

> **Answers**
> | The living room | The kitchen | both |
> |---|---|---|
> | an armchair | a fridge | a shelf |
> | a television | a cooker | a plant |
> | a coffee table | a washing machine | a cupboard |
> | a lamp | a cup | |
> | a telephone | | |
> | a stereo | | |
> | a sofa | | |

Drill the pronunciation of the words chorally and individually. Take care with the stress on the compound words *coffee table* and *washing machine*. Students may need help with pronunciation of *cupboard* /ˈkʌbəd/ and with distinguishing *cook* and *cooker*, thinking quite logically that *cooker* should be a person and not a thing.

2 If you want to you can demonstrate the activity by saying what's in your own living room. You can do this in a natural way starting the sentence *In my living room there's a/an …* but do not give too much extra detail like size, colour, etc. as the main focus here is the core lexis of furniture and appliances. Students continue the activity in pairs. More able students may be able to include *There is/are …*, but do not insist on this and keep the activity brief.

WHAT'S IN THE LIVING ROOM? (SB p36)

There is/are, prepositions

1 You could briefly revise/check the names of the main rooms in a house or flat, *living room, kitchen, bedroom, bathroom*, and *toilet*. Avoid overloading students with relatively low-frequency words like *study, balcony*, etc.

Students look at the photograph of Helen's living room. Call out the following words and get students to point to the objects in the photograph: *armchair, sofa, coffee table, plants, bookshelves, cupboard, television, stereo, telephone, lamps, rug, fire, mirror, magazines, pictures*. (If students have looked up the words for homework, this shouldn't take too long.)

Model the words yourself, and drill them around the class. Correct pronunciation carefully.

Read the example sentences as a class. In a monolingual class, you might want to ask for a translation of *There's* and *There are*. You could ask 'Why *is* and why *are*?' to establish singular and plural.

Again, model the sentences yourself and do some individual drilling. Insist on accurate linking between *There's‿a/an …* and *There‿are …* . Point out that with plural nouns students need to state the exact number. You do not want them to try to produce *some* at this stage.

Students then work in pairs to produce more sentences. Allow them enough time to give four or five examples each, but do not let the activity go on too long. Monitor and check for correct use of *there is/are*.

Round off the activity by bringing the whole class together again to check the answers. Correct mistakes carefully.

> **Answers**
> | | |
> |---|---|
> | There's a sofa. | There's a telephone. |
> | There's a coffee table. | There's a mirror. |
> | There's a cupboard. | There's a fire. |
> | There's a television. | There's an armchair. |
> | There's a stereo. | There are three plants. |
> | There's a table. | There are two lamps. |
> | There's a shelf. | There are two pictures. |
> | There's a rug. | There are three bookshelves. |

2 **T 5.1** [CD 1: Track 39] Students read and listen to the questions and complete the answers.

> **Answers and tapescript**
> A Is there a television? B Yes, there **is**.
> A Is there a radio? B No, there **isn't**.
> A Are there any books? B Yes, there **are**.
> A How many books are there? B There **are** a lot.
> A Are there any photographs? B No, there **aren't**.

Play the recording again and get students to repeat. Students then practise the questions and answers in open pairs and then closed pairs. Monitor and check for accurate pronunciation (sounds, intonation, stress).

GRAMMAR SPOT

Focus attention on the tables. Check students are clear about which words are singular and which words are plural. Get students to complete the tables, using contracted forms where they can.

Check the answers with the whole class.

> **Answers**
> **Positive**
> There's a television. There **are** some books.
> **Negative**
> There **isn't** a radio. There **aren't** any photos.
> **Question**
> **Is** there a television? **Are** there any books?

Briefly highlight the use of *some* in the positive plural sentence and *any* in the negative plural and question, but do not go into a long grammatical explanation at this stage. (*Some/any* is covered in the next presentation *What's in the kitchen?*)

Read Grammar Reference 5.1 on p127 together in class, and/or ask students to read it at home. Encourage them to ask you questions about it.

3 Focus attention on the sets of words and make sure students realize that the first set are singular, and the second set are plural and that they are going to ask and answer questions about Helen's living room.

Students work in pairs to ask and answer questions. Go round the class monitoring, helping as necessary. If most students are having problems, drill the question and answers and get students to try again.

Check the answers with the whole class, getting students to repeat their questions and answers in open pairs.

> **Answers**
> Is there a sofa? Yes, there is.
> Is there a fire? Yes, there is.
> Is there a rug? Yes, there is.
> Is there a cat? Yes, there is.
> Is there a mirror? Yes, there is.
> Is there a computer? No, there isn't.
> Is there a clock? No, there isn't.
> Are there any plants? Yes, there are.
> Are there any lamps? Yes, there are.
> Are there any flowers? No, there aren't.
> Are there any pictures? Yes, there are.
> Are there any newspapers? No, there aren't.
> Are there any bookshelves? Yes, there are.
> Are there any photos? No, there aren't.

4 This exercise practises/revises prepositions. If you think they will be new to your class, you will need to present them first. Do this very simply, perhaps using classroom objects, such as a book or chair (*The book is on the desk*), or the students themselves (*Khaled is next to Hassan*).

Refer students back to the photo of Helen's living room. Ask students to work in pairs to put a preposition into each gap. Check the answers.

> **Answers**
> 1 The television is **on** the cupboard.
> 2 The coffee table is **in front of** the sofa.
> 3 There are some magazines **under** the table.
> 4 The television is **next to** the stereo.
> 5 There are two pictures **on** the wall.
> 6 The cat is **on** the rug **in front of** the fire.

Point out that *in front of*, like *next to*, is two-dimensional. You can do this by using gestures.

You could practise the prepositions further by using your actual classroom, if you haven't already used this situation to present the items.

PRACTICE (SB p37)

What's in your picture?

1 You will need to photocopy the pictures on p124 of the Teacher's Book, enough copies for half of the class to see picture A and half picture B. Read the instructions as a class. Make sure students understand that each Student B has a complete picture and that each Student A has to draw in objects in the correct place to make a 'mirror' image. These objects are set above Student A's picture so that he/she knows what to ask about. (This is another information gap activity, so use L1 if you want to clarify what students have to do. Naturally, the most important thing is that they don't look at their partner's picture!)

36 Unit 5 • Where do you live?

Look at the example questions for Student A, pointing out the use of *Where exactly?* to get precise information about the position of the different objects.

Look at the example answers for Student B, pointing out the use of the prepositions for giving exact positions.

Point out that we say *on the sofa*, but *in the armchair*. Ask students to work in pairs, asking and answering so that Student A can complete their picture. Allow students enough time to complete the information exchange.

When students have finished, get them to compare their pictures and see how well they transferred and interpreted the key information.

Answers
The lamp is on the small table next to the sofa.
The magazines are on the coffee table, next to the radio.
The photographs are on the bookshelves.
The plants are on the floor. In front of the window.
The clock is on the television.
The rug is on the floor. Under the coffee table.

2 **T 5.2** [CD 1: Track 40] Ask students to look at the complete picture together. (It's probably wise to ask students to use the printed picture, rather than Student A's completed version just in case there are some objects wrongly located.) Read the instructions as a class. Students listen and shout 'Stop!' when they hear a mistake. You could do some work on contrastive stress as students correct the mistakes.
There aren't two people. There are three people.

Answers and tapescript
These are the mistakes:
1 There aren't two people. There are three people.
2 The girl isn't in the armchair. She's in front of the television.
3 There isn't a cat.
4 There are some photographs on the bookshelves.
5 There aren't any flowers on the table next to the sofa. They're in front of the mirror.

T 5.2
There are two people in the living room. A man on the sofa and a little girl in the armchair. There's a radio on the coffee table and a rug under it. There's a cat on the rug in front of the fire. There are a lot of books on the bookshelves but there aren't any photographs. There are two plants on the floor next to the television and some flowers on the small table next to the sofa.

ADDITIONAL MATERIAL

Workbook Unit 5
Exercises 1–4 *There is/are, some/any,* and prepositions.

WHAT'S IN THE KITCHEN? (SB p38)

some/any, this/that/these/those

1 Pre-teach/check the following vocabulary: *plate, cup, saucer, fork, spoon, knife*. Check the plural of these words, highlighting the irregular form *knives*. Ask students to look at the photographs and say what they can see. Take the opportunity for students to recycle *There is/ are …* , but do not expect or insist on the use of *some*. Correct mistakes in pronunciation.

Answers
(There's) a fridge, a cooker, a toaster
(There are some) cupboards, cups, knives, forks, flowers

2 **T 5.3** [CD 1: Track 41] Students listen to the conversation about the kitchen and fill in the gaps. Let them check in pairs, then play the track again. Ask for feedback. Notice that students are not expected to produce *some* until they have seen and heard it in context.

Answers and tapescript
H = Helen   L = Laura
H And this is the kitchen.
L Mmm, it's very nice.
H Well, it's not very big, but there **are a lot** of cupboards. And **there's** a new fridge, and a cooker. That's new, too.
L But what's in all these cupboards?
H Well, not a lot. There are some cups, but there aren't any saucers. And I have **some** knives and forks, but I don't have **any** spoons!
L Do you have **any** plates?
H Yes, I do. Here they are.
L Good. We can use those plates for this cake.

3 Students now need to practise using *There is/are* and *a/some/any* in context. Focus attention on the photo of Helen's kitchen. Model some sentences yourself in both affirmative and negative and with singular nouns with *a* and noun phrases with *some*. Make sure *some* is weak /səm/. Drill the sentences around the class, correcting mistakes carefully.

Examples
There's a cooker.   *There are some cupboards.*
There aren't any saucers. *There's a new fridge.*
There are some flowers.   *There aren't any spoons.*

Students continue talking about Helen's kitchen in pairs. You could ask your students to close their books and try to remember what is (and isn't!) in the kitchen. Move on to the personalization fairly quickly, so do not allow this pairwork stage to go on too long.

Get students to talk about their own kitchen in pairs. Go round checking and helping where necessary, but don't correct grammar mistakes unless incomprehensible. The emphasis here is on fluency.

Bring the class back together and ask for any interesting examples you heard, e.g. the washing machine being kept in the bathroom, or in a special room on its own, or on a balcony. You could ask follow-up questions like *Where's the fridge? How big is it? Where do you keep food?*, etc.

GRAMMAR SPOT

1 Look at *Grammar Spot* question 1 as a class. Allow students time to think before checking the answer.

2/3 Get students to work in pairs to answer question 2 and complete the sentences in 3.

Check the answers with the whole class.

Answers
1 *Two magazines* gives us the exact number. *Some magazines* doesn't give us the exact number.
2 We say *some* in positive sentences. We say *any* in negative sentences and questions.
3 1 I like **this** juice.
   2 **These** biscuits are lovely.
   3 **That** cooker is new.
   4 Give me **those** cups.

SUGGESTION
If students have difficulty with the use of *this/that/these/those*, use the classroom environment to briefly revise this language focus. Choose objects near to you to demonstrate *this/these*, e.g. *This is my desk. I like these posters* and objects that you have to point to demonstrate *that/those*, e.g. *That cupboard is new. We use those books.* Give students objects to hold or point to objects and get students to say sentences using *this/that/these/those*.

Refer students to Grammar Reference 5.3 and 5.4 on p127–8.

PRACTICE (SB p39)

In our classroom

1 Students work in pairs or small groups to fill the gaps.

Answers
1 In our classroom there are **some** books on the floor.
2 There aren't **any** plants.
3 Are there **any** new students in your class?
4 There aren't **any** Greek students.
5 We have **some** dictionaries in the cupboard.
6 There aren't **any** pens in my bag.

2 Get students to work in pairs and briefly describe their classroom. If necessary, give word cues to help get a variety of forms, e.g. *television, video, flowers, photos*, etc.

3 Briefly revise the use of *this/that/these/those* and relevant adjectives, e.g. *big, small, new, old*, etc. Get students to continue talking about things in the classroom in pairs.

What's in Pierre's briefcase?

4 **T 5.4** [CD 1: Track 42] Focus attention on the photo of Pierre and get students to say who they think he is, where he is, and what his job is. Read the instruction as a class to check.

Students listen to Pierre describing what is in his briefcase, and tick the things they hear.

Answers and tapescript
✔ a newspaper   ✘ a letter
✔ a dictionary   ✔ photos
✘ a sandwich   ✔ a mobile phone
✔ pens   ✘ stamps
✔ a notebook   ✘ an address book
✔ keys
✘ a bus ticket

T 5.4
What's in my briefcase? Well, there's a newspaper – a French newspaper – and there's a dictionary – my French/English dictionary. I have some pens, three I think. Also I have a notebook for vocabulary, I write words in that every day. And of course I have my keys, my car keys and my house keys. Oh yes, very important, there are some photos of my family, my wife and my daughter and there's my mobile phone. I ring my home in Paris every night. That's all I think. I don't have any stamps and my address book is in my hotel.

5 Get students to practise the questions in the Student's Book in open pairs. Students continue working in closed pairs. Ask one or two students to say what is in their or their partner's bag. This can be very interesting! However, try not to be over-curious, as some students may consider it too personal.

Check it

6 Students work in pairs and tick the correct sentence.

Answers
1 There aren't any sandwiches.
2 Do you have a good dictionary?
3 I have some photos of my daughter.
4 I have a lot of books.

5 How many students are there in this class?
6 Next to my house there's a park.
7 Look at that house over there!
8 Henry, this is my mother. Mum, this is Henry.

ADDITIONAL MATERIAL

Workbook Unit 5
Exercises 5–8 *this/that/these/those* and *it/they*

READING AND SPEAKING (SB p40)

Living in a bubble

You could lead in to the topic of the reading text by asking students: *What type of home do you/most people have? Do you know anyone who lives in an unusual home?* (e.g. on a houseboat, in a castle).

1 Get students to brainstorm rooms in a house and write a list on the board. Elicit possible actions for each room, e.g. *have a shower – bathroom*. Focus attention on exercise 1 and get students to match the sentence halves. Check the answers.

> **Answers**
> We cook in the kitchen.
> We watch TV in the living room.
> We sleep in the bedroom.
> We eat in the dining room.
> We work in the study.

If appropriate, elicit other true sentences for each of the rooms.

2 Focus attention on the photos and elicit the rooms shown.

> **Answers**
> living room, dining room, bedroom, kitchen, garden room

3 Tell students they are going to read a text about a man with an unusual home. Pre-teach/check *bubble* and *round* using the photos. Check comprehension of the questions. Ask students to work in pairs. Tell them not to worry about words they do not recognize and just to focus on finding the answers. (You may want to set a time limit for this to discourage students from reading too intensively.)

Check the answers. Decide according to the speed and ability of your students whether to settle for quick short answers or whether you want fuller answers (given in brackets).

> **Answers**
> 1 In the south of France. 40 years old. (It's in the south of France. It's 40 years old.)
> 2 Because it's (completely) round. (Because the house is (completely) round.)
> 3 He's a designer.
> 4 Coins, clocks, and round furniture. (He collects coins, clocks, and round furniture.)
> 5 Six. (The living and dining room is one room. There's also a kitchen, garden room, reading room, bedroom and bathroom.)
> 6 Yes, there is.

4 Give students time to read through the questions and check the vocabulary. Get them to answer the questions in pairs. Check the answers with the whole class. Encourage students to correct some of the false answers.

> **Answers**
> 1 False. The house is 40 years old.
> 2 False. There are more bubble houses like this in the south of France.
> 3 True.
> 4 False. The centre of the house is the living room and dining room.
> 5 False. He has a reading room.
> 6 True.
> 7 False. There are two rooms – a bedroom and bathroom.
> 8 False. Lovag is the architect of the bubble houses.

5 Practise the questions and answers in open and closed pairs. Check students can reproduce highlighted stress patterns in the bubbles, and drill the pronunciation of the list of things students have to ask about.

Students continue to ask and answer about the things in the list. Monitor and check for accurate use of *Is there a/an … ?* and *Are there any … ?* and feed back on any common errors. Check the answers with the whole class.

> **Answers**
> Is there a study? No, there isn't.
> Are there any pictures? No, there aren't.
> Are there any curtains? No, there aren't.
> Are there any clocks? Yes, there are.
> Is there a TV? Yes, there is.
> Are there any plants? Yes, there are.
> Are there a lot of kitchen cupboards? No, there aren't.

What do you think?

Ask students for a few examples of things they like and don't like about Cyril's home, and then allow them to continue exchanging opinions in pairs. Ask students for any interesting opinions they or their partner gave and find out what they both liked and disliked. Focus attention on the next question. Ask students for their ideas on the perfect home. Write the ideas on the board. If students show interest, give them time to discuss their ideas in pairs or smaller groups.

The aim is to generate some personalized discussion, so do not insist on complete accuracy.

LISTENING AND SPEAKING (SB p42)

Homes around the world

> **POSSIBLE PROBLEMS**
> The listening texts contain quite a lot of words that may be new, or that students might not remember. We intend this listening exercise to be for gist understanding only, so students should be encouraged, if possible, not to worry about unknown words.
>
> You *could* ask them to look at the tapescripts while they listen, or you could do this after they have heard the texts once or twice and then study the vocabulary. However, try if possible not to do this – but only you know your class!
>
> Even for gist comprehension, you will need to check the following words first:
> *near   river   light (n.)   alone   shops   basement room   swimming pool   sports centre   blinds*
>
> You could ask students to look at the tapescript for homework.

1 Focus attention on the photos of the four places and get students to match the correct names.

Answers
d Lisbon   a Toronto   b Malibu   c Samoa

Ask students to give any facts or personal experience of the places. Allow students to continue briefly in pairs. (Again, this is a personalization activity, so do not insist on accuracy.)

2 **T 5.5** [CD 1: Track 43] Students listen to the five people talking about where they live and fill in the chart, supplying any extra information (see below the chart) that they have understood.

Answers and tapescript

	Manola from LISBON	Ray and Elsie from TORONTO	Brad from MALIBU	Alise from SAMOA
House or flat?	flat	house	house	house
Old or modern?	old	old	we don't know	new house, but in old style
Where?	in the old town, near the sea	near the city centre	next to the sea	very near the sea
How many bedrooms?	one	three	five	one
Live(s) with?	her cat	each other – children not at home now	alone	her family

Extra information
Manola from Lisbon
- lives in old town called the Alfama
- has beautiful flat – one very big room with one very big window
- bed next to window so can see sea and lights of city when she goes to sleep
- has a cat and lives near shops
- lots of friends visit her
- loves flat

Ray and Elsie from Toronto
- house about 50 years old
- near the city centre
- have living room, quite a big kitchen, but favourite room is their family room
- family room has TV, stereo, large comfortable sofa, some big old armchairs. Love sitting there in winter with snow outside
- children aren't at home now – both have jobs in the USA. Most of the time just Ray and Elsie in house

Brad from Malibu
- house is fantastic
- neighbours very rich
- ten rooms in house. Everything white – carpets, curtains, sofa
- also has a swimming and sports centre
- not married at the moment. Ex-wife is French – lives in Paris with three sons

Alise from Samoa
- house doesn't have any walls because is very hot in Samoa
- have blinds to stop the rain and sun
- new house but in old style
- one room for living and sleeping. Have rugs – sit and sleep on the floor

T 5.5
1 Manola from Lisbon
I live in the old town near the sea. It is called the Alfama. I have a very beautiful flat. There's just one room in my flat, one very big room with one very big window. My bed's next to the window so I see the sea and all the lights of the city when I go to sleep. I live alone, but I have a cat and I'm near the shops and lots of friends come to visit me. I love my flat.

2 Ray and Elsie from Toronto
Elsie Our house is quite old, about fifty years old. It's quite near to the city centre. We have a living room, quite a big kitchen and three bedrooms, but the room we all love is our family room.

Ray Yes, there's a TV and a stereo and a large comfortable sofa in there, and some big, old armchairs. We love sitting there in winter with the snow outside.

Elsie Our children aren't at home now, they both have jobs in the USA, so most of the time it's just Ray and me.

3 Brad from Malibu
My house is fantastic. It's right next to the sea. My neighbours are very rich. Some of them are famous. In my house there are ten rooms, five are bedrooms, and everything is white, the floors, the walls, the sofas, everything. I also have a swimming pool and an exercise room. I live here alone. I'm not married at the moment. My ex-wife is French. She lives in Paris now with our three sons.

4 Alise from Samoa
I live with my family in a house near the sea. We have an open house,... er... that is... er... our house doesn't have any walls. Houses in Samoa don't have walls because it is very, very hot, but we have blinds to stop the rain and sun. Our house is in the old style. We have only one room for living and sleeping, so it is both a bedroom and a living room. We have rugs and we sit and sleep on the floor.

3 Get students to ask you questions about where you live. Then get students to continue in pairs or groups of three. Get students to share any interesting information with the whole class.

4 Students write about where they live for homework. Before you set this, do the writing exercises 10 and 11 in the Workbook, which will prepare them for the task.

EVERYDAY ENGLISH (SB p43)

Directions 1

1 Ask students to look at the street map. Make sure they understand the words on the map. As a class, ask where you can buy the items in the Student's Book.

> **POSSIBLE PROBLEMS**
> There might not be the direct equivalent of a newsagent's in your students' countries. A newsagent sells newspapers, magazines, sweets, and little items such as chewing gum and soft drinks.

Answers
buy aspirin: at the pharmacy
buy some bread: at the baker's
buy a book: at the bookshop
buy milk: at the supermarket
buy a DVD: at the newsagent's/supermarket
buy stamps: at the post office (sometimes at the supermarket/newsagent's)
send an email: at the Internet café
go for a walk: in the park
read a book: in the library
have a meal: at the Lebanese restaurant, the Italian restaurant or the Internet café
catch a bus: at the bus stop

2 **T 5.6** [CD 1: Track 44] Students listen to the conversations and complete them. You might want to play them all through first before students begin to write, or pause after each conversation to allow students time to write. Play the recording again to check answers.

Answers and tapescript
1 A Excuse me! Is **there** a pharmacy **near** here?
   B Yes. It's over **there**.
   A Thanks.
2 A **Excuse** me! Is there a **newsagent's** near here?
   B Yes. **It's in** Silver Street. Take the first **street on the** right. It's **next to** the flower shop.
   A Oh yes. Thanks.
3 A Is there a post office near here?
   B Go straight ahead, and it's **on the** left, **next to** the museum.
   A Thanks a lot.
4 A Excuse me! Is there a **restaurant** near here?
   B There's one in Park Lane **next to** the bank, and there's an Italian restaurant in Silver Street next to the **travel agent's**.
   A Is that one **far**?
   B No. Just two minutes, that's all.

Check that the class understand *Excuse me!*, *over there*, *first/second*, and *near/far*. If necessary, highlight the difference between *next to* and *near* (*next to* is two-dimensional, whereas *near* is three-dimensional.) Students work in pairs to practise the conversations.

3 Students then make more conversations about the places listed. Drill the pronunciation of the places in the list and practise one or two conversations in open pairs across the class. Students continue to work in closed pairs. You could ask some of the pairs to act out their dialogues for the rest of the class.

4 Students talk about their own situation. You could do this as a group activity or as a class.

Don't forget!

Workbook Unit 5
Exercise 9 Vocabulary of rooms and objects found in them, and verbs and nouns that go together.
Exercises 10 and 11 The writing section focuses on basic linking words.
Word list
Remind your students of the Word list for this unit on p137. They could write in the translations, learn them at home, and/or write some of the words in their vocabulary notebook.

6

can/can't/could/couldn't • was/were
Words that sound the same
On the phone

Can you speak English?

Introduction to the unit

Skills and ability are the themes of this unit. These are particularly suitable topics to introduce and practise *can/can't* (ability). However, the unit has two main aims in that we also introduce some past tenses for the first time: the past of *can* (ability) – *could*, and the Past Simple of the verb *to be* – *was/were*. The skills work includes a jigsaw reading about two young entrepreneurs and provides a further context for and practice of the grammar.

Language aims

Grammar – *can/can't* Students have already met the form *can* in the *Everyday English* section of Unit 2, but it is used only as a polite request *Can I have … ?* In Unit 2 it is introduced idiomatically because it is a useful expression, and the grammar is not explored.

Here, in Unit 6, the use is extended to ability, and all aspects of the form (statements, questions, negatives) are fully explored and practised.

> **POSSIBLE PROBLEMS**
> 1. Sometimes after all the practising of the Present Simple, students want to use *do/don't* and *does/doesn't* to form the question and negative.
>   **Do you can swim?*
>   **I don't can swim.*
> 2. A major problem with *can* and *can't* is the pronunciation. Often students find the different realizations of the vowel sounds (/ə/ or /æ/ in *can* and /ɑː/ in *can't*) confusing and, because the final *t* in *can't* tends to get lost, they can't recognize whether the sentence is positive or negative and they have difficulty producing the correct sounds themselves.
>   *I can swim.*   /aɪ kən swɪm/
>   *Can you swim?*   /kən ju swɪm/
>   *Yes, I can.*   /jes aɪ kæn/
>   *I can't come.*   /aɪ kɑːŋ kʌm/
>   For these reasons we highlight the pronunciation in the unit and include exercises both for recognition and production.

was/were* and *could/couldn't These forms are the first introduction to a past tense. We have chosen to present them in a simple and straightforward manner by having students complete a table about the present and past.

> **POSSIBLE PROBLEMS**
> Again pronunciation is a problem. The vowel sounds in *was* and *were* have both weak and strong realizations: *was* /ə/ and /ɒ/; and *were* /ə/ and /ɜː/.
> *He was at home.*   /hɪ wəz ət həʊm/
> *Was he at home?*   /wəz hɪ ət həʊm/
> *Yes, he was./No, he wasn't.*   /jes hɪ wɒz/ /nəʊ hɪ wɒznt/
> *Were they at home?*   /wə ðeɪ ət həʊm/
> *Yes, they were./No, they weren't.*   /jes ðeɪ wɜː/ /nəʊ ðeɪ wɜːnt/

The pronunciation is highlighted and practised in the unit.

Vocabulary and pronunciation We focus on words that sound the same but have a different spelling and meaning, i.e. homophones, for example *see* and *sea*. This provides the opportunity to give more practice of phonetic script.

There are many homophones in English (because of the non-phonetic spelling), and students confuse the two meanings, especially when hearing them (as opposed to seeing them when reading).

Everyday English Language useful for making phone calls is introduced and practised.

Workbook There is further practice on *can/can't*, *was/were*, and *could/couldn't*. The question *How much … ?* is practised with *is* and *was*.

In the vocabulary section, more words that commonly go together are practised (*ask a question*, *get up early*).

There is an exercise to revise and extend coverage of prepositions.

The writing syllabus continues with work on simple formal letters.

Notes on the unit

STARTER (SB p44)

1 Briefly check the pronunciation of the languages. Students work in pairs and say a sentence about where each language is spoken.

Check the answers. If necessary, drill the pronunciation of the countries and languages in pairs, especially where there is a change in stress, e.g. *Japan*, *Japanese*

> **Answers**
> They also speak French in Switzerland, Belgium, and some parts of Africa.
> They speak Spanish in Spain, Mexico, parts of South and Central America, Cuba, and the USA.
> They speak Farsi in Iran.
> They speak Italian in Italy and Switzerland.
> They speak Portuguese in Portugal, Brazil, Angola, and Mozambique.
> They speak Japanese in Japan.
> They speak English in Great Britain, the USA, Canada, Australia, New Zealand, Singapore, The West Indies, and India (and in many other countries as the language of tourism, business, and technology).
> They speak Arabic in Algeria, Bahrain, Egypt, Iraq, Jordan, Kuwait, Lebanon, Libya, Morocco, Oman, Qatar, Saudi Arabia, Sudan, Syria, Tunisia, United Arab Emirates and Yemen. (Note: these are amongst the countries where Arabic has official status. There are many more countries where Arabic is spoken.)

2 Tell the class which languages you can speak. Students continue to work in pairs or small groups. If you have a small group, allow each student to tell the rest of the class about their language skills. If you have a big group, select just a few students to feed back, but make sure you choose different students at the next feedback stage, so that everyone gets a chance.

WHAT CAN YOU DO? (SB p44)

can/can't

1 This is quite a simple presentation. The aim of the pictures is to illustrate the meaning of *can* and *can't*. The sentences are recorded to provide models of the different realizations of the vowel sounds and to raise students' awareness of these from the start.

First, ask students to look at the pictures and read the sentences. (Most of the vocabulary should be familiar or obvious from the picture, but check that there are no isolated difficulties.) Students then match the sentences to the pictures and write the appropriate sentence number in the boxes provided in the pictures.

T 6.1 [CD 1: Track 45] Students can discuss their answers with a partner before listening to the recording and checking. Then check the answers with the whole class. Ask students to repeat the sentences after listening to each one.

> **Answers**
> 1d 2a 3c 4f 5e 6b

GRAMMAR SPOT

1 Focus attention on the *Grammar Spot* questions. Students work in pairs and say all the persons of *can/can't*. Ask them what they notice about the verb form for each person. Check students are clear about the answer.

> **Answer**
> *Can/can't* are the same for all persons, so there is no *-s* added in the *he/she/it* forms.
> We do not use the auxiliary *don't/doesn't* to form the negative.

2 **T 6.2** [CD 1: Track 46] This activity highlights the pronunciation of *can/can't* in the positive, question, and short answers. Play the recording and get your students to read and listen very carefully to the pronunciation of *can* and *can't*. First, ask generally *Can you hear differences?* If necessary, repeat the sentences yourself, exaggerating the vowel sounds in *can* and *can't* and isolating them /ə/, /æ/, /ɑː/, so that your students can fully appreciate the differences. Play the recording again and get students to repeat chorally and individually.

3 Focus attention on the sentence stress in the positive and negative sentences. Drill the sentences and then get students to practise in pairs. Read Grammar Reference 6.1 on p128 together in class, and/or ask students to read it at home. Encourage them to ask you questions about it.

> **SUGGESTION**
> If your students need more practice with the pronunciation of *can/can't*, play the sentences from exercise 1 again and get students to repeat. (The sentences are produced below in phonetic script.)
> 1 /hi: kən ski: veri wel/
> 2 /ʃi: kən pleɪ tʃes/
> 3 /kən elɪfənts swɪm/   /jes ðeɪ kæn/
> 4 /kən ju: spi:k dʒæpəni:z/   /nəʊ aɪ kɑ:nt/
> 5 /aɪ kən drɔ: bət aɪ kɑ:nt raɪt/
> 6 /wi: kɑ:nt ʌndəstænd ðə kwestʃən/

2 **T 6.3** [CD 1: Track 47] This is a dictation to check that your students can recognize what they hear. Pre-teach/check *cook*, and *drive*. Ask students to listen and write in the answers. Pause the recording after each sentence. Then ask them to check their answers with a partner. Play the recording again as you conduct a full class feedback. (They could read the tapescript on p116 of their books as you do this.)

> **Answers and tapescript**
> 1 I **can speak French**, but I **can't speak German**.
> 2 He **can't fly**, but he **can drive**.
> 3 '**Can** you **cook**?' 'Yes, I **can**.'
> 4 They **can ski**, but they **can't swim**.
> 5 We **can read** and we **can write**.
> 6 '**Can** she **drive**?' 'No, she **can't**.'

Although this is a recognition exercise, you can make it productive by asking your students to read some of the sentences aloud to each other.

PRACTICE (SB p45)

Tina can't cook. Can you?

1 This again is a recognition exercise that moves into a production stage. This time the recording is much more natural-sounding, not being a series of sentences for dictation, but a girl talking about her abilities.

T 6.4 [CD 1: Track 48] Ask your students to listen to Tina and put a ✔ next to things she can do or a ✘ next to the things she can't do in the first column in the chart. Play the recording.

Put students into pairs to compare their answers. Then conduct a full class feedback to establish the correct answers. Let students listen again if necessary.

> **Answers and tapescript**
>
> | Can ... ? | Tina |
> |---|---|
> | drive a car | ✘ |
> | speak French | ✘ |
> | speak Italian | ✔ |
> | cook | ✘ |
> | play tennis | ✔ |
> | ski | ✔ |
> | swim | ✔ |
> | play chess | ✘ |
> | use a computer | ✔ |
>
> **T 6.4**
> Well, there are a lot of things I can't do. I can't drive a car, but I want to have lessons soon. I can't speak French but I can speak Italian. My mother's Italian, and we often go to Italy. My mother's a really good cook, she can cook really well, not just Italian food, all kinds of food, but I can't cook at all. I just love eating! What about sports? Er . . . I think I'm good at quite a lot of sports. I can play tennis, and ski, sometimes we go skiing in the Italian Alps, and of course I can swim. And . . . I can't play chess, but I really want to learn. Of course I can use a computer – all my friends can.

2 The exercise now becomes personalized. Students complete column 2 of the chart about themselves.

3 This is the productive phase of the activity. Practise the questions in the Student's Book in open and closed pairs.

> **SUGGESTION**
> 1 Make sure students use appropriate rising intonation with the inverted questions, and falling intonation with the short answers.
>
> *Can you ski? Yes, I can.*
>
> 2 Make sure that they pronounce the *t* on the end of the negatives. The two consonants *nt* together are difficult for many nationalities.
> Students work in pairs and ask and answer questions about each of the activities in the chart. Go round and monitor and help as they do this. Then round off the activity by asking a few members of the class to tell the others about their and their partner's abilities. Highlight the use of contrastive stress, e.g. *Laila can ski, but I can't.*

What can computers do?

4
> **NOTE**
> This can be quite a contentious activity because students tend to disagree about what exactly computers can do, and/or the degree to which they can do it. There is a growing belief that the initial very high expectations of computer ability in terms of real human-like behaviour have not been met.

Check comprehension of the key vocabulary: *poetry*, *laugh*, *play chess*, *hear*, *feel*. Put your students into pairs to do this activity. (We are hoping that discussion and disagreement will generate some freer speaking in English, in which case the activity can last some while. However, be grateful at any efforts at expressing their opinions and don't worry if the activity is quite short.)

In the sample answers we have included an extra section (*They can … but …*), which is for your information only. You can choose how/if you deal with the extra information.

> **Sample answers**
> **They can …**
> play chess   check spellings   give directions
> **They can … but …**
> translate (but word for word, not overall meaning)
> speak English (only in limited fashion with unnatural intonation)
> hear (they can recognize some speech, but limited)
> have conversations (but limited with many misunderstandings of context)
> **They can't …**
> write poetry   laugh   feel   think (because they work completely in numbers)

Conduct a feedback session with the whole class. This could be quite lively.

5 Ask students what people can do that computers can't do, *or* you could list some things that you think computers can't do and encourage the class to react: *drink*, *eat*, *sleep*, etc.

ADDITIONAL MATERIAL

Workbook Unit 6
Exercises 1 and 2 These practise *can* and *can't*.

WHERE WERE YOU YESTERDAY? (SB p46)

was/were, can/could

This is a very direct presentation of the past of the verbs *to be* and *can*. It revises the present of the verbs and then moves straight to the past tense equivalents.

Pre-teach/check *yesterday*, by doing the first example with the class. Let the students work in pairs to write in the answers. When they have finished, go through the exercise with them, modelling the questions and answers for them to repeat, and highlighting the weak vowel sounds of *was* and *were* (/wəz/ and /wə/) in statements and questions, and the strong vowel sounds (/wɒz/, /wɒznt/, /wɜː/, /wɜːnt/) in short answers and negatives.

> **POSSIBLE PROBLEM**
> **The negatives**
> The groups of consonants in the negatives *wasn't*/wɒznt/, *weren't* /wɜːnt/ and *couldn't* /kʊdnt/ may be difficult for some students and may need extra choral and individual repetition.
> Also, as you go through, keep backtracking by asking individual students to answer the earlier questions again.
> Finally, get your students to ask and answer the questions in open pairs across the class. Use the opportunity to check and correct them carefully. You can move on to practise in closed pairs, unless you think this may prove too laborious.

GRAMMAR SPOT

1 Put your students into pairs to complete the table with the past of *to be*. Quickly check through the answers with the whole class.

Answers	Positive	Negative
I	was	wasn't
You	were	weren't
He/She/It	was	wasn't
We	were	weren't
They	were	weren't

2 **T 6.5** [CD 1: Track 49] This is a repetition exercise with some more questions and answers to help consolidate the pronunciation. There are pauses on the recording for students to repeat. Insist on accurate pronunciation of the strong and weak forms.

3 Students complete the positive and negative forms of *can*.

> **Answer**
> **Positive could** (all persons)
> **Negative couldn't** (all persons)

Read Grammar Reference 6.1 and 6.2 on p128 together in class, and/or ask students to read it at home. Encourage them to ask you questions about it.

PRACTICE (SB p46)

Talking about you

1 Drill the first question and answer in open pairs. Students continue asking and answering the questions in closed pairs. Go round the class to help them. Encourage them to ask about times other than those listed in the

book. Round the activity off by asking one or two students to tell the others about their partner.

2 **T 6.6** [CD 1: Track 50] Set the scene of the conversation by asking your students to look at the picture and telling them that two friends are talking about what they did last Saturday. Check that they realize that they can only use *was*, *were*, *wasn't*, *weren't*, and *couldn't* to fill the gaps.

Ask students to work in pairs to do the exercise. Play the recording for them to listen and check their answers. Play it again and ask students to focus on the pronunciation, not only of *was* and *were*, but of the stress and intonation of the questions and answers.

Ask one or two pairs of students to take the parts of Bob and Peter and read aloud the conversation across the class. Encourage lively and natural pronunciation.

> **Answers and tapescript**
> B = Bob   P = Peter
> B **Were** you at Barnaby's wedding last Saturday?
> P Yes, I **was**.
> B **Was** it good?
> P Well, it **was** OK.
> B **Were** there many people?
> P Yes, there **were**.
> B **Was** Henry there?
> P No, he **wasn't**. And where **were** you? Why **weren't** you there?
> B Oh . . . I **couldn't** go because I **was** at a conference. It **was** boring!

Now ask the class to practise the conversation again in closed pairs. Go round and help and check them as they do this. (Don't let this go on too long otherwise it will become boring!)

You could move on to some other situations, e.g. *John's picnic last Sunday, the meeting last Friday evening, the football match last week*. Put some skeletal dialogue prompts on the blackboard and ask pairs of students to come to the front of the class and act out another situation, e.g.

… the picnic last Sunday?
… good?
… many people?
… (Tom) there?
… brilliant!

> **SUGGESTION**
> Try to personalize the language as much as possible by getting students to use real events they have been to recently as the basis for similar conversations.

Four child prodigies!

This section brings together *could*, *couldn't*, and *was* and it also introduces *to be born* and *until*. It continues the theme of skills and talents, but this time focuses on some famous characters. Students are also given the opportunity to personalize the language.

3 First ask students to look at the pictures and see if they know the people. Teach the word 'child prodigy', meaning a child who can do things that normally only very clever adults can do. Do the exercise as a class as a contrast to the pairwork in the previous activity, and so it can be done quite quickly.

> **Answers**
> 1 Al-Mutanabbi was a poet.
> 2 Einstein was a physicist, famous for his theory of relativity.
> 3 Michelle Wie is a golfer.
> 4 Fabiano Caruana is a chess player.

> **POSSIBLE PROBLEM**
> *(I) was born* is taught here as an expression, *not* as an example of the passive. Don't be tempted to go into the grammar. Some students translate from their own language and want to say **I am born*.

4 Focus attention on the example. Check comprehension of *was born* and drill the pronunciation. Ask students to give you a complete sentence about Al-Mutanabbi, matching lines in columns A, B, and C, and adding a comparison about themselves.

Check the rest of the answers with the whole class. (It really is true that Einstein couldn't speak until he was eight!)

> **Answers (Sample personalized sentences in brackets)**
> 1 Al-Mutanabbi was born in Iraq in 915. He could write poems when he was nine. (I couldn't write poems until I was twelve.)
> 2 Einstein was born in Germany in 1879. He couldn't speak until he was eight! (I could speak when I was one.)
> 3 Michelle Wie was born in Hawaii in 1989. She could play golf when she was four. (I couldn't play golf until I was sixteen.)
> 4 Fabiano Caruana was born in Miami in 1992. He could play chess when he was five. (I couldn't play chess until I was fourteen.)

5 Drill the questions in the Student's Book, highlighting the falling intonation in the *wh-* questions. Students continue working in pairs, asking and answering about the child prodigies.

6 This is the personalization stage. Drill the questions in the *you* form, getting students to repeat them in chorus and individually. Make sure the students can hear the difference between *where* and *were*, and again insist on accurate intonation.

Students work in small groups and ask and answer the questions. At the end of the activity, ask a few students to tell you what information they can remember, e.g. *Sara was born in Damascus in 1980. She could read when she was five.*

> **SUGGESTION**
> Students could think of some famous talented people that they know and make similar sentences about where/when they were born and what skills they had at different ages.

Check it

This exercise practises the grammar of the unit.

7 Ask students to work in pairs or small groups to choose the correct sentence. Ask them to work quite quickly, then conduct a full class feedback on which are the correct answers. Try to get students to correct each other and explain any mistakes they hear.

> **Answers**
> 1 I can't use a computer.
> 2 Were they at the wedding?
> 3 I'm sorry. I can't go to the meeting.
> 4 She wasn't at home.
> 5 He could play chess when he was five.
> 6 I can speak English very well.

ADDITIONAL MATERIAL

Workbook Unit 6
Exercises 3–5 These practise *was* and *were*. Exercise 4 is also very suitable for oral work and could well be used in class either to supplement or replace one of the activities in the Student's Book. Exercise 5 brings together past and present tense forms covered so far.
Exercise 6 This practises *could* and *couldn't* with *was*, *were*, and *can*.

READING AND SPEAKING (SB p48)

Young entrepreneurs

This activity is a jigsaw reading. This means that it should result in not only reading practice, but also some freer speaking.

The class divides into two groups and each group reads a different but similar text about a young entrepreneur and answers the questions. After this, students from the different groups get together to exchange information about the person in their text. This means that they should get some speaking practice whilst their main attention is on the completion of the reading task.

Yahya Stapic is the winner of the 2009/10 *Big Start* competition. *The Big Start* is open to all final year students in the United Arab Emirates who are planning to start a business, and offers full funding and support from Al Tamimi Investments. Yahya's *United Designers* opened in Dubai in 2011 to provide a platform for up-and-coming fashion talent in the UAE. Visit *www.bigstart.ae* and *www.uniteddesigners.ae* for more information.

Louis Barnett is a licensed chocolatier who started his own company at the age of 14. He now supplies major retail outlets throughout the UK and hopes to expand his business overseas. One of his most recent products is the environmentally friendly *Biting Back* bar, which is free from palm oil and artificial colours, flavours and additives.

You need to be very clear when giving instructions for any jigsaw activity. If necessary and possible, give them in L1.

1 Focus attention on the title of the section *Young entrepreneurs*. Ask students what they think the section is about. Ask students to look at the photographs of Louis and Yahya and offer guesses about their special talent. Ask the questions.

2 Divide the class into two groups. Tell Group A to read about 'The Chocolate Maker' and Group B to read about 'The Student CEO'. Ask each group to read through their text as quickly as possible to get a general understanding of it and to check if their guesses about the children were correct.

3 Get students to read the text again more slowly and find the information in their text to answer the questions about Louis or Yahya. Most of the vocabulary in the texts should be known, but allow students to use dictionaries to check if they can't guess from the context.

When they have read the texts, they could either go through the questions on their own and then check with others from the same group, or work with a partner from the same group to answer the questions. Each group has the same questions to answer.

Check the answers with Group A students and Group B students separately. The main idea of these questions is to check understanding, therefore short answers are perfectly acceptable. However, when you have a full class feedback you might want to encourage further language production such as you can see in the brackets in the answers below.

Unit 6 • Can you speak English? 47

Answers

Group A – Louis Barnett
1 He's eighteen.
2 He set up his own business selling chocolates.
3 (He was born) in Staffordshire, England.
4 (He lives) with his parents.
5 No, it was very difficult.
6 'Chokolit.' Because he couldn't spell 'chocolate' when he was young.
7 He makes the boxes with chocolate.
8 His parents. (His mother works in the chocolate factory and his father does the accounts.)
9 'Nobody makes mistakes, we only learn lessons.'

Group B – Yahya Stapic
1 He's twenty-one.
2 He's the CEO of a company.
3 (He was born) in Sharjah, in the United Arab Emirates.
4 (He lives) with his father and seven brothers and sisters.
5 Yes, it was.
6 'United Designers.' Because it brings fashion students together.
7 Students can show their work to the public and the public can buy their designs.
8 The competition organiser, Al Tamimi Investments.
9 'Be who you were born to be!'

4 Tell each student to find a partner from the other group and go through the questions and answers together, telling each other about the entrepreneur in their article. Try not to offer help at this stage – let students exchange the information themselves as far as possible.

Roleplay

5 Assign roles of the journalist and Louis or Yahya, or allow students to choose the role they want. Get students to prepare the interview using the questions in exercise 3 to help them. Allow sufficient time for students to make notes, but discourage them from writing out the interview word for word. Get students to practise the interview in pairs and then act it out in class.

VOCABULARY AND PRONUNCIATION (SB p50)

Words that sound the same

This activity introduces your students to words that have different spellings and meanings but *sound* the same, i.e. homophones. Of course, it is not important that your students learn the linguistic term *homophone*, but it is important that they are aware of such words, as there are so many in English and they can be particularly confusing when listening. The use of phonetic script in the activity serves not only to continue the process of getting to know it, but also to highlight the fact that there is often no relation between sounds and spellings in English.

1 This is to illustrate what is meant by *words that sound the same*. Ask your students to read aloud the sentences to themselves and then ask for suggestions about the words highlighted in **bold**. They should easily notice that the words sound the same but are spelt differently and have different meanings.
/siː/ = *see* and *sea*
/nəʊ/ = *no* and *know*

2 Ask students to work in pairs to do this. Most of the words are taken from previous units and should be familiar, but allow them to check new words either with you or in their dictionaries. Whilst they are doing the exercise, write the words in box A on the board in a column.

Bring the class together to go through the exercise and invite students, in turn, up to the board to write the words that sound the same next to each other.

Answers

A		B
hear	/hɪə/	here
write	/raɪt/	right
there	/ðeə/	their
wear	/weə/	where
see	/siː/	sea
eye	/aɪ/	I
for	/fɔː/	four
hour	/aʊə/	our
by	/baɪ/	buy
too	/tuː/	two
know	/nəʊ/	no
son	/sʌn/	sun

3   This exercise puts some of the words which have the same sound but different spelling in context and should be good fun to do. Again, ask students to work in pairs to do it. Then check through with the whole class, asking individuals to read the sentences aloud and spell the correct word.

> **Answers**
> 1 I can **hear** you, but I can't **see** you.
> 2 **There** are three bedrooms in **our** house.
> 3 I don't **know where** Jill lives.
> 4 My **son** lives near the **sea**.
> 5 Don't **wear** that hat, **buy** a new one!
> 6 **No, I** can't come to the meeting.
> 7 You were **right**. Sally and Peter can't come **for** dinner.
> 8 **Their** daughter could **write** when she was three.
> 9 I **know** my answers are **right**.

4   You could begin this by asking the class to chant through the phonetic transcriptions all together to check their progress in reading them.

Ask students to work on their own to do the exercise and then check their answers with a partner before you go through it.

> **Answers**
> 1 /nəʊ/   know   no
> 2 /sʌn/   son   sun
> 3 /tuː/   too   two
> 4 /raɪt/ write right
> 5 /hɪə/   hear   here
> 6 /weə/   wear   where

ADDITIONAL MATERIAL

Workbook Unit 6
Exercise 7 This is a vocabulary exercise that practises words that go together, e.g. *get up early*.

EVERYDAY ENGLISH (SB p50)

On the phone

1   Read the introduction as a class.

T 6.7 [CD 1: Track 51] Focus attention on the first name and address (Nancy Wilson). Students listen and answer the operator's questions and get Nancy's telephone number. Do this as a class activity, getting students to call out the answers.

> **Answers and tapescript**
> **Operator** International Directory Enquiries. Which country, please?
> **You**   Australia, please.
> **Operator** And which city?
> **You**   Perth.
> **Operator** Can I have the last name, please?
> **You**   Wilson.
> **Operator** And the initial?
> **You**   N.
> **Operator** What's the address?
> **You**   302 Erindale Road.
> **Recorded message** The number you require is **006198 4681133**.

Check students have written Nancy's phone number down correctly.

2   Students work in pairs to roleplay the operator and someone wanting Khaled's and Mauricio's number. Write the numbers on bits of paper to give to the operators:

Khaled Abdullah's phone/fax number is 00971 4294 1734.

Mauricio Ferreira's phone number is 005511 253 1162, and his fax number is 005511 253 5879.

Briefly check students have exchanged the information correctly.

3   > **SUGGESTION**
> This activity includes some of the typical expressions used over the phone in English. Make sure students understand that each language uses different expressions over the phone and if they translate from their own language, they may cause confusion or surprise! Point out in particular that in English you cannot say **I'm (Joe)* when saying who is speaking.
>
> Check comprehension of: *get someone* (as in *fetch*), *message, Great!, Never mind, ring back*. Focus on line 1 as an example with the whole class. If students are unsure what would come before this line, tell them they need to make a question with *can* (*Can I speak to Joe, please?*). Ask students to work in pairs and

continue the activity. Tell them not to worry about getting exactly the right answers, as you will focus on these at a later stage. Ask them to take the opportunity to exchange their ideas.

Focus attention on the use of *will* to make offers or promises. (Do not focus on other uses of *will*, e.g. simple future at this stage, as this may confuse students.)

Sample answers
1 **Can I speak to Joe, please?**
   This is Joe.
   Hello, it's X here.
2 **I'm afraid X isn't here**.
   Can I take a message?
   Yes, please. Ask him/her to call X.
3 **Sunday is OK for me**.
   Great! See you on Sunday at ten, then. Bye!
   Yes, OK. Bye!
4 **I'm afraid I can't come to your picnic**.
   Oh, never mind. Perhaps next time. Bye!
   Yes, OK. Bye!
5 **Is that X?**
   No, it isn't. I'll just get him.
   Hello, X speaking.
6 **X isn't here at the moment**.
   I'll ring back later.
   OK. Bye!
7 **Hi, X**.
   There's an interesting lecture at the university on Saturday. Can you come?
   Yes. That's great, thanks.
8 **Hello, (company name)**.
   Can I speak to the manager, please?
   Yes, can I ask who's calling, please?

4 Students work in pairs to complete the three telephone conversations, using the lines from exercise 3.

T 6.8 [CD 1: Track 52] Students listen and check. If necessary, get students to listen and repeat the conversations before continuing to practise in pairs.

Answers and tapescript
1 A Hello.
  B Hello. Can I speak to Joe, please?
  A **This is Joe**.
  B Oh! Hi, Joe. This is Pat. Is Sunday still OK for tennis?
  A Yes. That's fine.
  B **Great! See you on Sunday at ten, then. Bye!**
  A Bye!

2 A Hello.
  B Hello. Is that James?
  A **No it isn't. I'll just get him**.
  (pause)
  C Hello, James here.
  B Hi, James. It's Tom. Listen! **There's an interesting lecture at the university on Saturday. Can you come?**
  C Oh sorry, Tom. I can't. It's my sister's wedding.
  B **Oh, never mind. Perhaps next time. Bye!**
  C Bye!
3 A Good morning. Allied Bank. How can I help you?
  B Good morning. **Can I speak to the manager, please?**
  A I'm afraid Mr Smith isn't in his office at the moment. **Can I take a message?**
  B Don't worry. **I'll ring back later**.
  A All right. Goodbye.
  B Goodbye.

Then ask students to invent more telephone conversations, based on the ones in the Student's Book. They can change the names, times, arrangements, etc. but can keep the basic format of each conversation the same.

Don't forget!

Workbook Unit 6
Exercise 8 Prepositions
Exercise 9 The writing activity is a simple formal letter applying for a job.

Word list
Remind your students of the Word list for this unit on p137. They could write in the translations, learn them at home, and/or write some of the words in their vocabulary notebook.

7

Past Simple 1 – regular verbs
Irregular verbs
Words that go together • Special occasions

Then and now

Introduction to the unit

The past (the early part of the 20th century) and more recent past (the 1990s) are the themes of this unit. Within these contexts both regular and irregular forms of the Past Simple are presented. The formation of the question and negative is introduced, but the latter is only minimally practised because it is one of the main grammatical aims of Unit 8. The skills work includes a jigsaw reading task with texts on the first air journey and the first man on the moon which provides further practice of the Past Simple.

Language aims

Grammar – Past Simple 1 The learning of the Past Simple is facilitated by students' knowledge of the Present Simple, in that both tenses use a form of *do* as an auxiliary in the question and negative. It is not such a big leap to learn that the same auxiliary is used in its past tense form, *did*, to make the Past Simple tense, especially as this form remains constant in all persons.

Many of the exercises in this unit provide opportunities to contrast the Present and Past Simple tenses.

> **POSSIBLE PROBLEMS**
> 1 Although students should be helped by their knowledge of the Present Simple (see above), the use of *did* still causes problems and students forget to use it, for example:
> * *Where you went last night?*
> * *When she start school?*
> * *She no liked her job.*
>
> 2 There are a large number of irregular verbs to learn. From now on students should be encouraged to consult the irregular verb list on p142 and learn the irregular verbs as and when needed. You could start setting some to learn for homework and giving short tests on them at the beginning of some lessons!
>
> 3 The different realizations of the pronunciation of *-ed* at the end of regular verbs is a problem. Students always want to pronounce the *-ed* in its entirety – /ed/ – and not the /t/, /d/, /ɪd/ endings, for example:
> cleaned */kliːned/ instead of /kliːnd/
> worked */wɜːked/ instead of /wɜːkt/
> visited */vɪzɪted/ instead of /vɪzɪtɪd/
>
> There is an exercise to help students perceive the different endings, but we suggest you avoid spending too much time getting students to *produce* the endings at this stage so as not to overload them.

Vocabulary and pronunciation Words that go together are focused upon, for example *watch television, drive a car*. Verb and noun combinations, prepositions and compound nouns are introduced and practised.

Everyday English Common social expressions are introduced and practised.

Workbook More irregular verbs are introduced.
There are exercises to revise the Present Simple alongside the Past Simple.
In the vocabulary section, there is an exercise on recognizing parts of speech.
The writing syllabus continues with a piece of narrative writing about *My last holiday*.

Notes on the unit

STARTER (SB p52)

Check comprehension of *great-grandparents*. Students work in pairs and talk about what they know about their grandparents and great-grandparents.

WHEN I WAS YOUNG (SB p52)

Past Simple – regular verbs

1 Focus attention on the photo of Mattie Smith now. Ask students to give you information about her. Pre-teach/check *have a bath*, *clean the house*, *verandah*, *poems*.

T 7.1 [CD 1: Track 53] Ask students to read and listen about Mattie Smith in text A and complete the text. (This text is about Mattie's life now and revises the Present Simple before moving to the introduction of the Past Simple.) Play the recording and then check the answers.

Answers and tapescript
Mattie Smith is 91 years old. She **lives** alone in Atlanta, Georgia. She **starts** her day at 7.30. First she **has** a bath, next she **cleans** the house, and then she **sits** outside on her verandah and **thinks** about her past life. Then she **writes** poems about it.

Ask a few questions about Mattie now.

How old is she?	Ninety-one.
Where does she live?	In Atlanta, Georgia.
Does she live alone?	Yes, she does.
What time does she start her day?	At 7.30.
What does she do every day?	She has a bath, cleans the house, sits outside and thinks about her past life.
What does she write poems about?	Her past life.

2 **T 7.2** [CD 1: Track 54] Establish the answer to this last question clearly and tell your students that they are going to listen to and read about Mattie's past. Play the recording and immediately go through the *Grammar Spot* exercises.

GRAMMAR SPOT

Go through the *Grammar Spot* exercises one by one, establishing the answers after each exercise.

1 Refer students back to text B and get them to find examples of the past of *is* and *can*. Check the answers.

Answers
Mattie **was** never at school. . . . She started work when she **was** eight. . . . She **couldn't** read or write but she **could** think, . . .

2 Students complete the sentence with the correct form of *live*. Check the answers.

Answers
Now she **lives** alone, but when she was a child she **lived** with her mother and sisters.

3 Students work in pairs and find the Past Simple of *start*, *work*, and *create*. Get them to work out the rule for the formation of Past Simple of regular verbs.

Answers
To form the Past Simple of regular verbs, add *-ed* or *-d* to the infinitive.

Read Grammar Reference 7.1 on p129 together in class, and/or ask students to read it at home. Encourage them to ask you questions about it.

3 **T 7.3** [CD 1: Track 55] Check comprehension of *earn*, *die*, and *hate*. Students work in pairs to decide on the past form of the verbs in the box and practise the pronunciation.

Play the recording and let students check their answers. Get students to spell the past forms. Pay particular attention to the change of consonant + *y* to *-ied* in *marry–married*.

Answers and tapescript
/t/ looked worked
/d/ loved learned earned married died
/ɪd/ hated wanted

Play the recording again and get students to repeat.

4 **T 7.4** [CD 1: Track 56] Explain that the next text gives more information about Mattie's past and students have to complete the text using the Past Simple forms of the verbs in the box from exercise 3. You could ask them to try to fill the gaps with the verbs before they listen, then to listen and check their answers with a partner. Or, if you think that it would be too difficult, let them listen to the text and fill in the answers as they go along.

Play the recording without pausing the tape.

Answers and tapescript
I **worked** from 6.00 in the morning until 10.00 at night. Sixteen hours in the cotton fields and I only **earned** $2 a day. I sure **hated** that job but I **loved** the poems in my head. I really **wanted** to learn to read and write. When I was sixteen I **married** Hubert, and soon there were six children, five sons, then a daughter, Lily. Hubert **died** just before she was born. That was sixty-five years ago. So I **looked** after my family alone. There was no time for learning, but my children, they all **learned** to read and write – that was important to me. And when did I learn to read and write? I didn't learn until I was 86, and now I have three books of poems.

Go through the answers as a class, getting students to take turns at reading aloud part of the text. Correct their pronunciation of the past tense verbs in preparation for the exercise on pronunciation in the *Practice* section.

GRAMMAR SPOT

1 Refer students back to the text about Mattie and get them to find a question and negative.

Answers
And when **did I learn** to read and write? I **didn't learn** until I was 86, ...

2/3 Go through the notes on the formation of questions and negatives with the whole class.

Read Grammar Reference 7.2 on p129 together in class, and/or ask students to read it at home. Encourage them to ask you questions about it.

5 This exercise focuses on *wh-* questions in the Past Simple. Students work in pairs to complete the questions about Mattie.

T 7.5 [CD 1: Track 57] Play the recording so that students can check their answers.

Answers and tapescript
1 When **did** she **start** work? When she was eight years old.
2 Where **did** she **work**? In the cotton fields.
3 Who **did** she **live** with? Her mother and sisters.
4 How many hours **did** she **work**? Sixteen hours a day.
5 How much **did** she **earn**? $2 a day.
6 Who **did** she **marry**? Hubert.
7 When **did** Hubert **die**? Sixty-five years ago.
8 When **did** she **learn** to read? She didn't learn until she was 86.

Play the questions from the recording one by one (or say them yourself) and get students to repeat them both chorally and individually. Ask other students to provide the answers. These are all *wh-* questions so encourage natural falling intonation on each one.

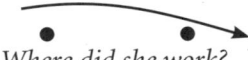

Where did she work?

Students continue practising the questions and answers in pairs.

PRACTICE (SB p54)

Talking about you

1 This activity brings together the past of *be*, *to be born*, and *did* in Past Simple questions, so that students become aware of the difference between the past of the verb *to be* and full verbs. Get students to complete the sentences on their own first and then check in pairs.

Check the answers with the whole class, asking individuals to read out their answers.

Answers
1 Where **were** you born? Where **was** your father born?
2 When **did** you start school?
3 When **did** you learn to read and write?
4 Who **was** your first teacher?
5 What **was** your favourite subject?
6 Where **did** you live when you **were** a child?
7 **Did** you live in a house or a flat?

Drill the questions, reminding students to use falling intonation.

2 If you have room, ask students to get up and walk round the class asking two or three other students the questions, and answering about themselves in return. Or, if you don't mind a lot of movement, ask students to ask each question to a *different* student. Tell them that you are going to see how much they can remember when they sit down.

3 After a few minutes, students sit down and tell you what information they can remember. Remind them to use the third-person singular forms *was* and *was born*.

Sample answer
Saeed was born in Jeddah and his father was born in Riyadh. He started school in 1980. He learned to read and write when he was five. His first teacher was Mr Abdullah. His favourite subject was history. He lived in a flat in Jeddah when he was a child.

You could ask students to write a short paragraph about themselves for homework.

ADDITIONAL MATERIAL

Workbook Unit 7
Exercises 1 and 2 These practise regular verbs, *Yes/No* questions, and short answers in the Past Simple.

Pronunciation

4 **T 7.6** [CD 1: Track 58] Isolate the sounds /t/, /d/, /ɪd/ for your students and get them to listen and repeat them. Play the recording and ask them to put the verbs in the correct column. Get them to check their answers with a partner and then conduct a full class feedback, asking students to practise saying the verbs.

Answers and tapescript

/t/	/d/	/ɪd/
worked	lived	started
finished	married	hated
looked	loved	visited
liked	died	
	cleaned	

T 7.6

worked	finished
lived	looked
started	died
married	visited
loved	cleaned
hated	liked

THE YEAR I WAS BORN (SB p54)

Irregular verbs

Now the theme moves to the more recent past with a focus on life in the year 1996. This provides the context for the introduction of irregular verbs.

1 Refer students to the irregular verb list on p142. Make sure they understand that it is an important resource that they should refer to regularly.

Ask students to work with a partner. Ask them to use their dictionaries to look up new words and check the list to find out which verb is regular and what the irregular forms of the others are.

> **SUGGESTION**
> All these verbs appear at some point later in this unit, so your students need to learn them. You might therefore want to set this exercise for homework prior to the lesson and then go through it in class.

Ask students to read out the correct answers.

Answers

be	was/were	go	went	win	won
begin	began	leave	left	make	made
come	came	have	had	buy	bough
get	got	die	died (regular)	sell	sold
give	gave	become	became		

2 **T 7.7** [CD 1: Track 59] Play the recording (and/or model the verbs yourself) and ask students to listen and repeat. Check pronunciation of the more difficult forms, e.g. *bought* /bɔːt/.

3 Briefly review how to say 19– dates, and if you think your students need to practise dates, ask the class to chant the years from 1990 to 2000. Focus attention on the questions in exercise 3 – they will act as a lead-in to the listening in exercise 4 and help students understand key parts of the recording.

Elicit one or two examples from confident students and then give students time to discuss the questions in pairs.

4 Write *1996* in large numbers on the board and refer students to the photos to elicit ideas about the worlds of politics, sport, and technology. You could put them into groups to do this if you have time and if you feel that your students would respond well. Elicit some examples from the class to set the scene for the recording and James's conversation with his father about 1996.

Let students read the texts first and check for any unknown vocabulary. Encourage students to use the context to help them, but with weaker classes, you could pre-teach/check *election*, *collision*, *champions*, and *record* referring to the photos as appropriate.

Tell students that the recording is in the form of a conversation between James and his father and that the texts in the Student's Book are a summary of what the speakers talk about. Students are required only to select key points to practise certain verbs.

T 7.8 [CD 1: Track 60] Play the recording. Tell your students to listen and complete as much of the texts as they can. After listening for the first time, ask students to work in pairs and compare their answers.

5 Play the recording again so that students can complete or check their answers. Elicit any further information students can remember.

Answers and tapescript
James: left, went, got
World Events: won, made, died, was
Sports and Games: became, came
Technology: had, sold, bought, began, gave

T 7.8

J = James   D = Dad

J Dad, we've got a project at school on the year I was born, so tell me about 1996. That's when you left Qatar, wasn't it?

D Yes. You were born in January, and we left later that year and came to Saudi Arabia. I got a job in Riyadh, my first as an Internet consultant.

J So what was in the news that year?

D Well, there was an election in America that year. Bill Clinton won and got four more years in the White House. And I always remember the news of the Saudi Airlines crash in November.

J What was that?
D It was a mid-air collision between a Saudi Airlines 747, you know, a jumbo, and a Kazakhstan cargo plane, over India. All 349 people on board both planes died.
J No! That's terrible!
D Yes, it was. It was the worst mid-air collision in history – still is. And all because the Kazakhstan pilot couldn't understand the English instructions from the air traffic controller.
J No way!
D And that was one of the first big news stories on the new news channel, Al Jazeera. They made their first broadcast in November 1996.
J And it was an Olympic year, wasn't it?
D That's right. Michael Johnson was the star. He won the 400 metres and then he came first in the 200 metres too. It was a fantastic run – a world record for a long time, until Usain Bolt came along!
J Yes, I remember Johnson was there when Usain Bolt got the new record.
D And it was a great year for Saudi football. Saudi Arabia became champions of Asia again – they won the Asian Cup in the UAE. The final was between Saudi Arabia and the UAE.
J Yes, people still talk about that. And you became an Internet consultant – how big was the Internet in 1996?
D It had about a hundred thousand websites at the beginning of the year, and more than half a million by the end of it.
J Were there any search engines like Google then?
D There were search engines, but they weren't very good. That was the year they began work on Google – but it was called 'Backrub' at first. They gave it the name Google later.
J Computers were really big then, weren't they?
D No, not *really* big! And that was the year Palm sold their first hand-held computers with Internet connection – the Palm Pilot. I bought one, of course. It was very cool for those days!

6 Ask students to give the first question and answer as an example. Ask students to work in pairs and to ask and answer the rest of the questions. Insist on full answers so that students get practice with the irregular past forms. Check for accurate question formation and falling intonation. If students have problems, drill the questions and answers in open pairs and then in closed pairs.

Check the answers with the whole class.

> **Answers**
> 1 When did James and his parents leave Qatar? They left Qatar in 1996.
> 2 Where did his father get a job? He got a job in Riyadh.
> 3 Where did Saudi Arabia win the Asian Cup? They won it in the UAE.
> 4 Who did they play in the final? They played the UAE.
> 5 How many websites did the Internet have at the beginning of 1996? It had about a hundred thousand websites.
> 6 What name did Larry Page and Sergey Brin give to their new search engine? They called it Backrub.

> **SUGGESTION**
> You could ask students to bring in photos of when they were babies to use as a springboard for exercise 7.

7 Give students further examples of key people/events/trends in the year that you were born, e.g. *world leaders*, *sports events*, *science*, *technology*, etc. Write the above categories on the board and get students to find out information about the year they were born for homework. If you have access to online computers, students could do this during class time.

With weaker classes, build a skeleton on the board with the students to help them with the writing task, e.g.

I was born on … in … . In that year … was leader of my country. Other important leaders were … . In sport … won … and … became world champion in … . In science … made … . Millions of people bought a … .

When students have written their summaries, put them into pairs or small groups to exchange information. Elicit any interesting examples during class feedback.

PRACTICE (SB p55)

When did it happen?

1 Set up this activity by giving the class a few cues of major events and getting students to form the question and give the corresponding dates, e.g.
*the Berlin Wall/fall – When did the Berlin Wall fall? In 1989.
the Second World War/end – When did the Second World War end? In 1945.*

Students work in groups and list other major events of the 20th century, both nationally and internationally. They then form questions to 'test' the other groups.

Pre-teach expressions like *in the (1950s), in about (1995)* to enable students to give an answer if they can't give an exact year. Get students to ask their questions to another group. Conduct brief feedback with students saying sentences about the most interesting/popular events.

What did you do?

2 Focus attention on the phrases in the box, pointing out we can't use *last* with parts of a day, except *night*. Check pronunciation and then get students to give a few examples of the phrases in context, e.g. *I went to a football match last night*.

Unit 7 · Then and now 55

3 Drill the questions in the Student's Book chorally and individually and then get students to ask and answer in pairs. You could suggest that they take notes about each other. Go round the class monitoring and helping.

Bring the class together and briefly check the past form of the verbs as students will need these to report back on their partner. Students tell the class what they learned about their partner.

Check it

4 Ask students to do this exercise on their own and then check with a partner before you go through the exercise as a class.

> **Answers**
> 1 He bought some new shoes.
> 2 Where did you go yesterday?
> 3 Did you see Jane last week?
> 4 Did she get the job?
> 5 I went out yesterday evening.
> 6 He studied French at university.
> 7 What did you have for breakfast?
> 8 I was in Riyadh last week.

ADDITIONAL MATERIAL

Workbook Unit 7
Exercises 3–5 These practise irregular verbs in the Past Simple.
Exercise 6 This practises question formation.
Exercise 7 This contrasts Present Simple and Past Simple.

READING AND SPEAKING (SB p56)

Sixty years of flight

> **ABOUT THE TEXT**
> This is another jigsaw reading task, which gives students an opportunity for not only reading practice, but also some freer speaking. The class divides into two groups and each group reads a different, but similar text about a pioneer of aviation. It's important to remind students to read only their text and to get information about the other text via speaking. If necessary and possible, give the instructions for the jigsaw reading in L1.
> The texts continue the theme of keys dates in history with a focus on groundbreaking developments in aviation. They have been chosen to consolidate Past Simple forms and time expressions. The use of a range of numbers in the texts provides for a number referencing task as part of the *Speaking* section.
> **Louis Blériot** /ˈluːi ˈblerɪəʊ/ (1872–1936) was a French aviator, engineer, and inventor. He is best known for his flight over the English Channel, the first crossing of a large body of water in an aircraft, in 1909. The first text in this section is an account of the flight.

> **Louis Blériot** /ˈluːi ˈblerɪəʊ/ (1872–1936) was a French aviator, engineer, and inventor. He is best known for his flight over the English Channel, the first crossing of a large body of water in an aircraft, in 1909. The first text in this section is an account of the flight.
> **Neil Armstrong** /niːl ˈɑːmstrɒŋ/ (1930–) is one of the three astronauts who took part in the Apollo 11 moon mission in 1969. He is best known as the first man to walk on the moon and for his words 'That's one small step for man, one giant leap for mankind.'
> Encourage students to use the context to help them with new vocabulary and to pool knowledge with other students, or use a dictionary. With weaker classes or if you are short of time, ask students to check some of following vocabulary before the lesson:
> **Homework prior to the lesson**
> **Introduction:** *rocket, aviation, phenomenal*.
> **Louis Blériot:** *flight, injury, compass, to take off* (leave the ground), *field, cliff, altitude, foot* (plural *feet*; 1 foot = approximately 30 cm), *fog, to wave a flag, to cut the engine, to crash, pioneer*.
> **Neil Armstrong:** *to lift off, astronaut, to circle, landing, lunar module, to land, to rest, to take a step, leap, mankind, to collect samples, to set up scientific equipment, put up a flag, earth, inscription, peace, exploration*.

1 Focus attention on the photos. Check students recognize the two men and can pronounce their names /ˈluːi ˈblerɪəʊ/ and /niːl ˈɑːmstrɒŋ/. Elicit the answers to the questions in exercise 1 and any additional information students know about the two men.

> **Answers**
> Louis Blériot made the first air journey in 1909.
> Neil Armstrong was the first man on the moon in 1969.

2 Students read the title and introduction. Check the answer to the question.

> **Answers**
> The progress in aviation in the 20th century was phenomenal.

3 Put students into two groups, A and B. (With larger classes, you may need to have multiple sets of the two groups.) Assign a text to each group and remind students to read only their text:

Group A – the first air journey

Group B – the first man on the moon

Get students to read their text quite quickly, asking others in their group for help with vocabulary if you didn't pre-teach the items listed in *About the text* or set them for homework. Monitor and help with any queries.

Give students time to read the questions and deal with any queries. With weaker students, briefly review how to read numbers and years. Get them to work in their groups and answer the questions about their text, noting down the answers to each one. Monitor and help as necessary. The answers for each group are provided below for reference but don't check the answers with the whole class at this stage. Ask students to give full statements where possible in order to practise past forms.

Answers
The first air journey
1 The journey began in Calais in the north of France on July 25, 1909.
2 It took 37 minutes.
3 It was 22 miles.
4 He flew at 40 miles per hour.
5 The journey ended in Dover in the south of England.
6 It was the start of modern aviation.

The first man on the moon
1 The journey began at the Kennedy Space Center in Florida on 16 July, 1969 at 9.30 in the morning.
2 It took three days.
3 It was 250,000 miles.
4 They flew at 21,600 miles per hour.
5 The journey ended on a part of the moon called The Sea of Tranquility.
6 It was the beginning of man's exploration of space.

4 Re-group the students, making sure there is an A and a B student in each pair. Demonstrate the activity by getting a pair of students to talk about the person in their text. Students continue talking about the answers to the questions in exercise 3 and exchanging the information about their person. Monitor and help. Also check for correct use of the present and past of *can* and *be*. Note down any common errors and feed back on them at a later stage. Bring the whole class together to conduct the feedback. Encourage students to expand on their answers where applicable.

5 Students now look at both texts to get further information about each journey. Encourage students to help each other with vocabulary, or use a dictionary. With weaker students, you could pre-teach some of the items listed in *About the text* if you didn't set them for homework.

Students work with the same partner to find the answers to the questions. Monitor and help as necessary.

Check the answers with the whole class, again getting students to give full statements where possible in order to practise past forms.

Answers
Blériot
1 He couldn't swim, he couldn't walk very well because of a leg injury, and he didn't have a compass.

2 No, it was foggy/there was fog.
3 He saw a French newspaper journalist waving a flag.
4 He won £1,000.

Armstrong
5 They were too excited.
6 'That's one small step for man, one giant leap for mankind.'
7 They spent two and a half hours walking on the moon.
8 They left a US flag on the moon.

Speaking

6 **T 7.9** [CD 1: Track 61] Elicit the reference for the first two numbers, *37* and *4.30* (see *Answers.*) Then give students time to complete the task, working in pairs. Monitor and help as necessary.

Play the recording and let students check their answers.

Answers and tapescript
In 1909 Blériot made the first air journey from Calais to Dover.
1 Blériot was just 37 years old when he flew across the Channel. It took him just 37 minutes.
2 He took off from France at 4.30 in the morning.
3 He flew his plane at 40 miles per hour.
4 He flew at 250 feet above the sea.
5 He won a prize of £1,000.

In 1969 Neil Armstrong became the first man to walk on the moon.
6 Three astronauts flew in Apollo 11. The rocket took three days to get to the moon.
7 It circled the moon 30 times.
8 It landed at 8.17 a.m. on 20 July, 1969.
9 Six hundred million people watched the moonwalk on TV.
10 Neil Armstrong said, 'That's one small step for man, one giant leap for mankind.'
11 The astronauts spent 22 hours on the moon.

SUGGESTION
Students can play a memory game based on the facts and figures in the story. Students take it in turns to say a number and their partner guesses what it refers to. Encourage them to use different numbers from those in exercise 6, e.g.
A 9.30 a.m.
B The time Apollo 11 lifted off.
A Yes, that's right.

7 Ask students to close their books. Elicit some information about the start of each of the journeys from a few students.

Students continue retelling the stories in pairs. With weaker students, write key words and dates on the board as prompts. Monitor and help as necessary but don't interrupt or over-correct. Note any common errors for correction at a later stage.

Unit 7 · Then and now

VOCABULARY AND LISTENING (SB p58)

Words that go together

Collocation and word groupings are a key feature of English and it is important that students start to become familiar with them as early in their learning as possible. This vocabulary section focuses on verb + noun collocation, the use of prepositions in a range of high-frequency phrases/structures, and compound nouns (noun + noun combinations).

Verbs and nouns

1 Focus attention on the example sentences from the texts on p57. Explain that in English there are many words which frequently occur together. These sentences show two common verb + noun combinations.

2 Explain that this task has verbs in list A and nouns in list B. Focus attention on the example and then get students to complete the task. Remind them that more than one answer may be possible. Let students check in pairs before checking with the whole class.

Answers
drink tea or coffee	start school
study politics/Spanish	watch television
cook a meal	drive a car
travel the world	buy things in shops
earn a lot of money	speak Spanish
play chess	ride a bike

Focus attention on the example questions and answers in the Student's Book and have students practise them in open pairs. Students continue asking and answering in closed pairs. With weaker classes, elicit other possible questions before the pairwork stage, e.g. *Can you speak Spanish? Do you watch television every day? When did you last ride a bike?*

Prepositions

3 Focus attention on the example and then elicit the preposition for number 2 as a further example. Give students time to complete the task before checking with the whole class.

Answers
1 from	5 in, in	9 of
2 to	6 of, in	10 for
3 to, with	7 at, at	
4 at, on	8 to	

Noun + noun (= compound nouns)

4 Focus attention on the examples and explain or elicit that each is made up of two nouns. Tell students that we call these compound nouns. Point out that some compound nouns are spelled as two words, some as one word. (Some are hyphenated.) Explain that there is no rule for the spelling of these nouns – students just have to learn them!

5 Get students to write their answers to the task, so that they can focus on whether to write them as one or two words. Check the answers with the class, getting students to highlight those that are one word.

Answers
orange juice	bus stop	washing machine
railway station	newspaper	book shop
swimming pool	airport	living room
handbag	credit card	car park

Say the words aloud and get students to say where the main stress usually falls, on the first or second word (*the first word*). Drill the words as necessary.

Focus attention on the examples in the book and get students to say the exchanges in open pairs. Elicit one or two more example definitions and then get students to test each other in pairs.

6 **T 7.10** [CD 1: Track 62] Tell students they will hear four short conversations and that they should listen for the key words which appear in exercise 5.

Answers and tapescript
1 A I can't find my **handbag**.
B Here it is!
A Oh yes, thank you. Where did you find it?
B In the **living room** where you left it!

2 A Would you like some **orange juice**?
B No, thanks, just water for me.
A But I bought this juice for you.
B Did you? I'm sorry! I don't like orange juice.

3 A I have nothing to wear to the **airport**.
B What about your white jeans?
A They aren't clean.
B Well, wash them. You have a **washing machine**, don't you?

4 A Do you want anything from the shops?
B A **newspaper**, please. *The Times*, I think.
A OK.
B Oh, and can you buy a **book** for Alice?
A Sure. There's a new **book shop** in the High Street, isn't there?

SUGGESTION
You can consolidate the verbs and nouns, and compound nouns, with the photocopiable activity on TB p125. Photocopy enough pages for your students to work in pairs. The activity is divided into two sections – a matching activity and a gap-fill to practise the vocabulary. Divide the students into pairs. Give each

pair a set of words and explain that they have to match them to form verb + noun collocations and compound nouns. Elicit an example, e.g. *become a pilot*. If appropriate, do the activity as a race with the fastest students to match the words correctly as winners.

Hand out a copy of the gap-fill to each pair of students. Focus attention on the example, and get students to complete the task. Check the answers, getting students to say which compound noun is written as one word.

Answers
2 railway station
3 drive a car
4 orange juice
5 credit card
6 play chess
7 break a record
8 airport
9 Did ... win a medal
10 ride a bike
11 car park
12 newspaper

EVERYDAY ENGLISH (SB p59)

Social expressions (2)

1 **T 7.11** [CD 1: Track 63] Ask students to look at the pictures and listen to the first lines of the conversations to decide how **B** can reply.

Tapescript
1 We were on holiday in Cairo last month.
2 This is a present for you.
3 Don't forget it's a bank holiday tomorrow, Marco.
4 Why don't we have lunch together tomorrow?
5 Thank goodness it's Friday! Have a good weekend!
6 Excuse me! Can I have the bill, please?
7 Ow! I have a terrible headache!
8 Could you open the door for me?
9 Bye! Have a safe journey!

2 Ask students to write the correct sentence into each conversation.

3 **T 7.12** [CD 1: Track 64] Students listen and check their answers.

Answers and tapescript
1 A We were on holiday in Cairo last month.
  B **Really! Did you have a good time?**
  A Yes, it was great!
  B Was the weather good?
  A It was fantastic! Hot and sunny every day.
2 A This is a present for you.
  B **That's so kind! Thank you very much!**
  A I bought it for you in Cairo. I hope you like it.
  B What is it?
  A Open it and see!
3 A Don't forget it's a bank holiday tomorrow, Marco.
  B **Sorry, what does that mean?**
  A It's a public holiday. Banks and offices are closed.
  B Are any shops open?
  A Oh, yes, a lot of shops and restaurants are still open. They want your money!
4 A Why don't we have lunch together tomorrow?
  B **I'm afraid I'm in a meeting all day. Sorry.**
  A What a pity! Never mind!
  B Another time maybe.
5 A Thank goodness it's Friday! Have a good weekend!
  B **Thanks! Same to you!**
  A Are you doing anything special?
  B I'm playing golf tomorrow, and we're going for a picnic on Sunday.
  A Sounds great! See you next week!
6 A Excuse me! Can I have the bill, please?
  B **Yes, sir. I'll bring it to you.**
  A Thank you very much. I'm in a hurry.
  B Right now, sir, I promise.
7 A Ow! I have a terrible headache!
  B **Poor you! Do you want some aspirin?**
  A Yes, please! And a glass of water too.
  B Sure. Just sit down and take it easy.
8 A Could you open the door for me?
  B **Of course! Can I carry something for you?**
  A No thanks, I can manage.
  B OK.
9 A Bye! Have a safe journey!
  B **Thanks! We'll see you in a couple of days!**
  A Ring us when you arrive!
  B OK. Don't worry! We'll be all right!

4 **T 7.12** Students listen again then practice the conversations with a partner.

Don't forget!

Workbook Unit 7

Exercise 8 Vocabulary of parts of speech, such as *adjective*, *noun*

Exercise 9 Prepositions: *about*, *after*, *for*

Exercise 10 This is the writing activity: describing a holiday. It provides more practice of the Past Simple.

Word list

Remind your students of the Word list for this unit on p138. They could write in the translations, learn them at home, and/or write some of the words in their vocabulary notebook.

8

Past Simple 2 – negatives/*ago*
Forming nouns and adjectives
What's the date?

How long ago?

Introduction to the unit

This is the second unit on the Past Simple tense, and it provides further practice and reinforcement of the input in Unit 7, focusing particularly on the negative. The title of this unit is 'How long ago?' and the topics in the unit lend themselves to practice of the Past Simple. The unifying theme of the unit is how things began, with reading texts on inventions, and listening texts on going abroad for the first time. This main listening exercise is one of the first extensive listening exercises where students do not have the support of the written word.

Language aims

Grammar – Past Simple 2 See the introduction to the Past Simple and problems associated with it on p51 of the Teacher's Book. There is considerable practice of the positive in this unit, but there is also much emphasis on question forms and negatives. These present few problems of concept, but there can inevitably be mistakes of form.

Common mistakes
*When you went home?
*When did you went home?
*Where did go Peter?
*I no went out yesterday evening.

ago *Ago* is an adverb which is used when the point of reference is the present. It means 'before now', and is used only with past tenses, not present tenses or present perfect tenses. *Ago* always comes after an expression of time.

Common mistakes
*I went there ago two weeks.
*I went there before two weeks.
*My cat died for two years.

Time expressions There is a focus on preposition and noun collocations, such as *on Saturday* and *in summer*. These prepositions can cause a lot of confusion and so will need a lot of practice and regular reviewing.

Vocabulary There is quite a lot of vocabulary input throughout the unit. The vocabulary section focuses on the formation of nouns and adjectives by the addition of suffixes. There is also further work on phonetic script.

Everyday English This section introduces and practises ordinals and dates.

> **POSSIBLE PROBLEMS**
>
> The main problem that students face with ordinals is pronunciation. The sound /θ/ always causes difficulty, and there are a lot of consonant clusters, for example, *sixth* /sɪksθ/, *twelfth* /twelfθ/. In rapid speech, sounds are often dropped, for example /twelθ/ instead of /twelfθ/ and /fɪθ/ instead of /fɪfθ/.
>
> Saying dates also causes problems of form. We can begin with the month (*April the third*) or the date (*the third of April*), but in both cases we need to add *the*, which is never written, and in the latter case we need to add *of*, which is also never written.
>
> Note that in American English, *3/8/99* means the eighth of March 1999, whereas in British English it means the third of August 1999.

Workbook In the vocabulary section, there is a focus on words which are both nouns and verbs, e.g. *cook*, and revision and extension of machines and inventions. There is also a section on numbers 100–1,000.

In the writing section, there is further work on linking words, and students are invited to write about an old friend.

Notes on the unit

STARTER (SB p60)

> **POSSIBLE PROBLEMS**
>
> Students often confuse *eat* /iːt/ and its past form *ate* /et, eɪt/, so these will need careful highlighting. The past of *wear* – *wore* /wɔː/ can also present pronunciation problems.
>
> Students may try to look for patterns in the past forms, expecting *take* to work in the same way as *make*, so take the opportunity to remind them that the past forms have to be learned!

Students work in pairs and say the Past Simple of the verbs in the box. If they have problems with the form of any of the irregular verbs, refer them to the irregular verb list on p142.

Check the answers with the whole class, getting students to spell the past forms and making sure they can pronounce them correctly.

> **Answers**
>
> | | |
> |---|---|
> | eat | **ate** |
> | drink | **drank** |
> | drive | **drove** |
> | fly | **flew** |
> | listen to | **listened to** |
> | make | **made** |
> | ride | **rode** |
> | take | **took** |
> | watch | **watched** |
> | wear | **wore** |

FAMOUS INVENTIONS (SB p60)

Past Simple – negatives/*ago*

1 Focus attention on the photographs and get students to name each of the items shown. Check pronunciation carefully, especially of the 'international' words which are the same or very similar in other languages, e.g. *burger* /ˈbɜːɡə/, *Coca-Cola* /ˈkəʊkə ˈkəʊlə/, *jeans* /dʒiːnz/, *television* /ˈtelɪvɪʒn/, and *photograph* /ˈfəʊtəɡrɑːf/.

Students work in pairs and match the verbs from the *Starter* activity to the nouns.

Check the answers with the whole class.

> **Answers**
> 1 **drink** Coca-Cola
> 2 **take** photographs
> 3 **listen to** the radio
> 4 **fly** planes
> 5 **wear** jeans
> 6 **make** phone calls
> 7 **drive** cars
> 8 **eat** burgers
> 9 **watch** television
> 10 **ride** bikes

2
> **SUGGESTION**
>
> You might want to pre-teach *ago*. You could ask questions such as the following to feed this in:
> *When was your last English lesson? (On Tuesday.)*
> *How many days ago was that? (Two days ago.)*
> *When did you last have a holiday? (In June.)*
> *How many months ago was that? (Five months ago.)*
> You could then highlight and explain *ago* (see *Language aims* on p60 of the Teacher's Book). Translation might help.

Model the example question yourself, and get lots of repetition practice. Then practise the question and the three sample answers in open pairs. Do the same for five of the photographs and then ask students to ask and answer questions about the remaining five in closed pairs.

3 Students give you their opinions about what people did and didn't do 100 years ago.

4 **SUGGESTION**
This activity requires students to use the Past Simple passive in the question: *When was/were … invented?* Point out that students will need to use *was* to ask about *Coca-Cola* and *television*. You can drill the question forms, but do not do a full presentation of the passive at this stage.

Get students to ask you about each of the items in the photographs and give them the correct date. Get them to write the dates down and work out how long ago the item was invented. You may get some surprised reactions and even disagreement from students, as there is a big difference between, say, the invention of the car and when cars became generally available.

Answers (The number of years ago will depend on the year you are using the course)
1 Coca-Cola was invented in 1886.
2 The camera was invented in 1826.
3 The radio was invented in 1901.
4 The first plane was invented in 1903. The first flight across the Channel was in 1909.
5 Jeans were invented in 1873, made by Levi Strauss.
6 The phone was invented in 1876.
7 Cars were invented in 1893. A Benz went at 18 miles an hour.
8 Burgers were invented in 1895.
9 The television was invented in 1926.
10 Bikes were invented in about 1840.

GRAMMAR SPOT

Focus attention on the *Grammar Spot* table. Get students to work through the answers orally first. Then check the answers with the whole class, writing the sentences on the board for students to copy.

Answers

Present Simple	Past Simple
He lives in London.	He lived in London.
Do you live in London?	Did you live in London?
Does she live in London?	Did she live in London?
I don't live in London.	I didn't live in London.
He doesn't live in London.	He didn't live in London.

Highlight that *he/she/it* has a different form in the Present Simple from the other persons, but that all forms in the Past Simple are the same.

Read Grammar Reference 8.1 and 8.2 on p129 together in class, and/or ask students to read it at home. Encourage them to ask you questions about it.

PRACTICE (SB p62)

Three inventors

1 Ask students to look at the three photos and say what they can see. Students read the three texts, checking new words in their dictionaries. The following words will probably be new: *cloth, workmen, fashionable, transmitted, workroom, produced, arthritis, best-selling, painkiller, philosopher, century, age* (= era).

Tell students they are going to read the texts again, focusing on the dates. Stress that all three dates in each text are incorrect, and get students to discuss in pairs what the correct dates might be. Remind them that they already have some of the correct dates from *Famous inventions*, exercise 4 and point out that they aren't expected to know the correct dates, just have fun guessing.

T 8.1 [CD 2: Track 2] Students listen, correct the dates, and see if they guessed any of them correctly. You could either play the recording all the way through, or stop it after each text. Ask students to make a negative and a positive sentence about each date. Drill the example sentence in the Student's Book chorally and individually, highlighting the contrastive stress and the use of the pronoun:

They didn't make the first jeans in nineteen twenty-three.

They made them in eighteen seventy-three.

Briefly revise the pronouns *them* and *it* and then get students to continue working in pairs. Check the answers with the whole class, either by getting students to read out the pairs of sentences with the correct stress or asking different students to read the texts aloud with the correct information. Correct any pronunciation mistakes.

Answers and tapescript
They didn't make the first jeans in 1923. They made them in 1873.
Jeans didn't become fashionable for women in 1965. They became fashionable for women in 1935.
Calvin Klein didn't earn $12.5 million a week from jeans in the 1990s. He earned $12.5 million a week from jeans in the 1970s.

Baird didn't transmit the first television picture on 25 November, 1905. He transmitted it on 25 October, 1925.
Baird didn't send pictures from London to Glasgow in 1929. He sent them in 1927.
Baird didn't send pictures to New York in 1940. He sent them in 1928.
Felix Hofman didn't invent Aspirin in 1879. He invented it in 1899.
Aspirin wasn't the best-selling painkiller by 1940. It was the best-selling painkiller by 1950.
The Apollo astronauts didn't take aspirin to the moon in 1959. They took it to the moon in 1969.

T 8.1
JEANS
Two Americans, Jacob Davis and Levi Strauss, made the first jeans in 1873. Davis bought cloth from Levi's shop. He told Levi that he had a special way to make strong trousers for workmen. The first jeans were blue. In 1935 jeans became fashionable for women after they saw them in Vogue magazine. In the 1970s, Calvin Klein earned $12.5 million a week from jeans.

TELEVISION
A Scotsman, John Logie Baird, transmitted the first television picture on 25 October, 1925. The first thing on television was a boy who worked in the office next to Baird's workroom in London. In 1927 Baird sent pictures from London to Glasgow. In 1928 he sent pictures to New York, and also produced the first colour TV pictures.

ASPIRIN
Felix Hofman a 29-year-old chemist who worked for the German company Bayer, invented the drug Aspirin in March 1899. He gave the first aspirin to his father for his arthritis. By 1950 it was the best-selling painkiller in the world, and in 1969 the Apollo astronauts took it to the moon. The Spanish philosopher, José Ortega y Gasset, called the 20th century 'The Age of Aspirin'.

2 Look at the example in the Student's Book and highlight the negative form and the correct answer. Students work on their own and continue the activity.

T 8.2 [CD 2: Track 3] Play the recording and let students check their answers.

Answers and tapescript
1 Two Germans didn't make the first jeans. Two Americans made them.
2 Davis didn't sell cloth in Levi's shop. He bought cloth from Levi's shop.
3 Women didn't see pictures of jeans in *She* magazine. They saw them in *Vogue*.
4 Baird didn't send pictures from London to Paris. He sent pictures from London to Glasgow.
5 Felix Hofman didn't give the first aspirin to his mother. He gave it to his father.
6 A Spanish philosopher didn't call the 19th century, 'the Age of Aspirin'. He called the 20th century 'the Age of Aspirin'.

Play the recording again and get students to practise the stress and intonation.

Did you know that?

3 **T 8.3** [CD 2: Track 4] Pre-teach/check the following vocabulary: *spaghetti*, *really*, *incredible*, *true*, *afraid*, and *believe*. Students read and listen to the conversations. Draw their attention to the wide voice range of the second speaker as he/she expresses incredulity. Practise the conversations in open pairs, and really encourage students to sound surprised!

4 You will need to photocopy the lists of incredible information on p126 of the Teacher's Book. They are repeated to help you save paper.

Divide the class into pairs. Give out the lists of incredible information to Student A and B in each pair. Do an example from Student A's information and one from Student B's. Remember that students will have difficulty in selecting the correct short answer (*wasn't*, *didn't*), so you might want to go through them as a class first. On the other hand, you might decide that as a teacher you can't do everything at once! If students produce a good, wide voice range, and enjoy doing the exercise, maybe that's enough! (This is primarily a pronunciation exercise.)

> **Sample answers**
> Did you know that Buckingham Palace has over 600 rooms?
> **Really? I don't believe it!**
> Did you know that the Rose Rayhaan Hotel in Dubai has 72 floors?
> **Really? That's incredible!**
> Did you know that Shakespeare spelled his name in eleven different ways?
> **He didn't! Really? That's incredible!**
> Did you know that in 1979 it snowed in the Sahara Desert?
> **Really?**
> Did you know that the American President George Washington had wooden false teeth?
> **He didn't!**
> Did you know that it took 1,700 years to build the Great Wall of China?
> **It didn't!**
> Did you know that King Henry VIII of England had six wives?
> **Really? He didn't!**
> Did you know that your heart beats over 100,000 times a day?
> **Really?**
> Did you know that Shakespeare and the Spanish novelist Cervantes both died on the same day, 23 April 1616?
> **They didn't! Really?**
> Did you know that, in Belgium, 172,000 tons of chocolate are made every year?
> **I didn't!**

ADDITIONAL MATERIAL

Workbook Unit 8
Exercises 1–4 Past Simple, regular and irregular
Exercise 5 Past time expressions
Exercise 6 *ago*

Time expressions

5   Ask students to identify the correct preposition for the time expressions. Some they will know, some will be new. Give them these rules to help:
on + day/day of the week plus part of the day, e.g. *on Saturday morning*
in + part of the day (except *night*)/month/season/year/century
at + time

This leaves only *at night* and *at weekends* that do not fit any of the categories. Check the answers.

> **Answers**
> **at** seven o'clock
> **in** the morning
> **on** Saturday
> **on** Sunday evening
> **at** night
> **in** September
> **at** weekends
> **in** summer
> **in** 1994
> **in** the twentieth century

6   Demonstrate the activity by getting students to practise the examples in the Student's Book in open pairs. Students continue in closed pairs asking questions with *when*, and answering the questions in the two different ways. Monitor and check that the questions are well formed, and that the voice starts high. Feed back on any common errors in grammar or pronunciation.

7   Get students to tell the class about their day so far. If you have a small group and sufficient time, you could ask each student to give their example. If you have a lot of students, you could get students to work simultaneously in small groups, making sure the students who worked together in exercise 6 talk to different students.

VOCABULARY AND PRONUNCIATION (SB p63)

Forming nouns

The aim of these activities is to focus on common noun endings.

1   Read the instructions and the example as a class. Students work in pairs to complete the nouns.

> **Answers**
> 1 television, dinner
> 2 number, meeting
> 3 application, reception
> 4 arrival, passengers
> 5 information, computer
> 6 summer, experience
> 7 wedding, flowers
> 8 exhibition, drawings
> 9 daughter, teenager
> 10 shopping, sweater

2   Students look at the words in phonetic script. Tell them not to panic as all the words have been taken from exercise 1, so they should recognize most of them! Students work in pairs and practise saying the words. Monitor and check pronunciation, particularly of the more difficult words – *reception, exhibition*.

Answers and tapescript
1 computer
2 shopping
3 passenger
4 reception
5 flowers
6 exhibition
7 daughter
8 arrival

T 8.4 [CD 2: Track 5] Students listen and check.

Forming adjectives

3 Students work in pairs to complete the adjectives using the endings in the box.

Check answers with the class and draw the students' attention to the difference between *exciting* and *excited*.

Answers
1 delicious, expensive
2 happy, friendly
3 dangerous, careful
4 famous, noisy
5 wonderful, enormous
6 lovely, sunny
7 comfortable, excellent
8 excited, fantastic
9 important, useful
10 exciting, different

4 Once again, the words are from the previous exercise, so students should recognise them. Get students to work in pairs to practise saying the words aloud. Monitor and check their pronunciation.

Answers and tapescript
1 famous
2 important
3 exciting
4 delicious
5 enormous
6 different
7 excited
8 fantastic

T 8.5 [CD 2: Track 6] Students listen and check.

LISTENING AND SPEAKING (SB p64)

The first time I went abroad

The build-up to this activity is quite controlled, with careful preparation of the questions and possible answers. The same questions are then used by students while listening to the two interviews.

1 Students work in pairs or small groups to add ideas to the boxes.

Sample answers

What's good	What's not so good
It's exciting.	Perhaps you don't speak the language.
You can see new places.	Everything is strange.
You can meet new people.	The food is different.
You can lean a new language.	You can get ill.
You can try new food.	You aren't at home with your parents.
You can do different things.	You don't make new friends.

2 Students work in pairs to put the questions in A in the right order, then match an answer in B. Be careful with the question *How long did the journey take?* This use of *take* is idiomatic, and is unlikely to be translated by the same word in students' own language.

Answers
1 A How old were you?
  B I was eight.
2 A Where did you go to?
  B To France.
3 A Who did you go with?
  B With my family.
4 A How did you travel?
  B By plane.
5 A How long did the journey take?
  B About four hours.
6 A Where did you stay?
  B In a hotel.
7 A What did you do?
  B We travelled around.
8 A Did you enjoy it?
  B Yes, it was great.

You could practise the questions and answers across the room in open pairs.

3 **T 8.6** [CD 2: Track 7] Students listen and write the extra comments that B makes.

Answers and tapescript

1. **A** How old were you when you first went abroad?
   B I was eight. **I was very excited.**
2. **A** Where did you go to?
   B To France. **My parents had friends there.**
3. **A** Who did you go with?
   B My family. **And my grandparents.**
4. **A** How did you travel?
   B By plane. **It was really exciting.**
5. **A** How long did the journey take?
   B About four hours. **It wasn't long, but I was tired.**
6. **A** Where did you stay?
   B In a hotel. **It was really comfortable.**
7. **A** What did you do?
   B We travelled around **and visited friends.**
8. **A** Did you enjoy it?
   B Yes, it was great. **I had a fantastic time.**

4 **T 8.7** **[CD 2: Track 8]** Students listen to Peter and Yasmina and answer questions 1–8. Ask students to listen first to Peter, then check the answers as a class before listening to the second interview.

Answers and tapescript
Part one
1 Fourteen.
2 To Hungary, to a small town fifty miles from Budapest.
3 With other students and teachers from school.
4 By train and boat and train again.
5 Ages – about fourteen hours.
6 With a Hungarian family.
7 He played football, visited friends, went to the zoo, and had lots of picnics.
8 He had a wonderful time.

Part two
1 Ten.
2 To England, to West London.
3 With her father, mother, and two brothers.
4 By plane.
5 Nine or ten hours.
6 In her uncle's house in Acton.
7 She played with her cousins and visited lots of places in London, for example Buckingham Palace and the London Eye.
8 It was fantastic. She loved it.

T 8.7
Part one
I = interviewer   P = Peter
I How old were you when you first went abroad?
P I was 14. Quite old really.
I Where did you go to?
P I went to Hungary, to a small town 50 miles from Budapest.
I Who did you go with?
P Well, it was a school exchange, so I went with other students and teachers from school.
I How did you travel?
P By train and boat, then train again. We didn't fly because that was too expensive.
I How long did the journey take?
P Ages! About 14 hours. We left England at six in the morning, and we arrived at eight in the evening.
I Where did you stay?
P Well, with a Hungarian family. They were there at the station when we arrived, and it was very difficult because I didn't speak Hungarian, and they didn't speak any English. So we couldn't say much.
I What happened then?
P We drove back to their house, and there were about 40 friends and relatives to meet me. I wanted to go to bed because I was so tired, but we all sat down for dinner. The meal didn't finish until midnight.
I What did you do in Hungary?
P Well. I lived with the family, and they were really nice. I really liked my exchange student, Josef. He was 15. We played football and visited his friends. And his parents took me to the zoo. We had lots of picnics. The weather was lovely.
I Did you enjoy it?
P I had a wonderful time. Josef's parents were really friendly, especially his mother. And I loved Hungarian food!

Part two
I = interviewer   Y = Yasmina
I How old were you when you first went abroad?
Y I was ten.
I And where did you go to? Can you remember?
Y Oh, yes. Of course I can. I went to England to visit my uncle who lives in West London.
I And who did you go with?
Y My father, mother, and two brothers. One of my brothers was just a baby.
I How did you travel? By plane, I suppose.
Y Yes. We flew into Heathrow Airport. But when we arrived, there was a problem. We couldn't find my uncle and aunt because our plane was late. We looked everywhere and waited and waited. Then after an hour we found them.

I So how long did the journey take?
Y Well, it was about ... nine or ten hours.
I Where did you stay?
Y In my uncle's house in Acton. When we arrived, there was a party for all our relatives and Egyptian friends. We had lots of Egyptian food and mint tea. I remember I didn't go to bed until ten o'clock.
I What did you do in England?
Y Well, my uncle has three children, so I played with my cousins. We visited a lot of places in London. Buckingham Palace, the London Eye ... but it was very cold. It was March, so the weather wasn't very good.
I Did you enjoy it?
Y Oh, yes! It was fantastic! London is enormous! There is so much to see and do! I loved it.

EVERYDAY ENGLISH (SB p65)

What's the date?

1 Students work in pairs to put the correct ordinal next to the numbers.

Answers

1st	first	13th	thirteenth
2nd	second	16th	sixteenth
3rd	third	17th	seventeenth
4th	fourth	20th	twentieth
5th	fifth	21st	twenty-first
6th	sixth	30th	thirtieth
10th	tenth	31st	thirty-first
12th	twelfth		

T 8.8 [CD 2: Track 9] Students listen and practise saying the ordinals. Stop the recording after each one and drill them around the class, correcting carefully.

2 Students ask and answer questions about the months of the year. You don't need to let this go on for very long.

3 Focus attention on the Caution Box and highlight the different ways of writing and saying the dates. Students practise saying the dates both ways. Students often have a lot of difficulties saying dates, for the reasons explained on p61 of the Teacher's Book, so do the activity as a class and correct mistakes very carefully.

T 8.9 [CD 2: Track 10] Students listen and check.

Answers and tapescript
1 The first of April
  April the first
2 The second of March
  March the second
3 The seventeenth of September
  September the seventeenth
4 The nineteenth of November
  November the nineteenth
5 The twenty-third of June
  June the twenty-third
6 The twenty-ninth of February, nineteen seventy-six
7 The nineteenth of December, nineteen eighty-three
8 The third of October, nineteen ninety-nine
9 The thirty-first of May, two thousand
10 The fifteenth of July, two thousand and ten

4 **T 8.10** [CD 2: Track 11] Students listen and write down the dates they hear. Tell them there are seven dates in total. Let them check in pairs before you give the answers.

Answers and tapescript
1 4 January
2 7 May, 1997
3 15 August, 2001
4 13 July
5 30 June
6 23 April, 1564
  23 April, 1616

T 8.10
1 The fourth of January.
2 May the seventh, 1997
3 The fifteenth of August, 2001
4 A It was a Friday.
  B No, it wasn't. It was a Thursday.
  A No, I remember. It was Friday the thirteenth. The thirteenth of July.
5 A Oh no! I forgot to book tickets for the cup final. I hope it hasn't sold out.
  B There might be a few tickets left. When is it?
  A It's next Saturday, isn't it? The thirtieth. June the thirtieth.
6 A Hey! Did you know that Shakespeare was born and died on the same day?
  B That's not possible!
  A Yes, it is. He was born on April the twenty-third fifteen sixty-four and he died on April the twenty-third, sixteen sixteen.

5 Students work in pairs to answer the questions about dates. Monitor and feed back on any common errors before checking the answers with the whole class.

> **Answers**
> 1, 2, 4, 5 Student's own ideas.
> 3 21st century
> 6 23 September

Don't forget!

Workbook Unit 8
Exercise 8 A vocabulary exercise on words that are both nouns and verbs
Exercise 9 A puzzle activity on machines and inventions.
Exercises 10–12 Revision of numbers 100–1,000
Exercises 13 and 14 The writing syllabus continues with a further exercise on linking words, *because*, *when*, and *until*. Students are invited to write about an old friend.

Word list
Remind your students of the Word list for this unit on p138. They could write in the translations, learn them at home, and/or write some of the words in their vocabulary notebook.

> **EXTRA IDEAS UNITS 5–8**
> On p127 of the Teacher's Book there is an additional reading activity. If you have time and feel that your students would benefit from this, you can photocopy it and use it in class. The reading exercise revises Units 5–8 and could also be done for homework. Activities to exploit the reading are provided, and the answers are on p155.

9

Count and uncount nouns
I like/I'd like • *much/many*
Food • Polite requests

Food you like!

Introduction to the unit

The theme of this unit is food and drink, which lends itself to the presentation and practice of the target items – count and uncount nouns with a review of the determiners *some* and *any* (in Unit 5 they were introduced with countable nouns only) and a focus on *much/many*. The verb *like* is contrasted with *would like*, and the *Everyday English* focus *Polite requests* carries through the food and drink theme. The skills material includes a reading text about food around the world, and an invitation to discuss eating habits in different countries. There is also a *Listening and Speaking* section on *My favourite national food*.

Language aims

Grammar – count and uncount nouns Students often need help with the concept of count and uncount nouns, and need regular practice with the articles and determiners that can be used with them. Students also need to understand that a lot of nouns can be both countable and uncountable, depending on the context in which they are used, e.g.
Two coffees, please. (countable and meaning two cups of coffee)
Coffee is expensive. (uncountable and meaning coffee in general)
Students also have to get to grips with interference from their own language where some nouns which are uncount in English are countable. This can lead to misuse, e.g.
*They gave me advices.
*I'd like some informations.

like and would like *Would like* is introduced for the first time, and this is the first time that students have seen the modal verb *would*. It is easy for students to confuse these two forms. Here are some common mistakes.
*Do you like a coffee?
*I like a cup of tea, please.
*Are you hungry? *You like a sandwich?
It is relatively easy for students to perceive the difference between a general expression of liking and a specific request, but you can expect many mistakes for a long time as students confuse the two forms, especially the two auxiliary verbs *do* and *would*.

some/any *Some* and *any* were first introduced in Unit 5, but only with count nouns. This unit introduces them with uncount nouns as well.

The often-repeated rule that *some* is used in positive sentences and *any* in questions and negatives is not entirely true, but it's still useful at this level. However, in this unit the use of *some* in requests and offers is also introduced. It is quite a subtle concept for students to grasp that *some* can be used in questions when there is no doubt about the existence of the thing requested or offered. The use of L1 might help to clarify this.

As in Unit 5, we do not suggest that you explore the use of *any* to mean *it doesn't matter which*, as in *Take any book you want*.

much/many The focus on indefinite quantities is extended with a focus on *much/many*. The question forms *How much … ?* and *How many … ?* are also practised.

Vocabulary There is quite a heavy vocabulary load in this unit, largely to do with food and drink. Words to do with food and drink are introduced as part of the presentation of count/uncount nouns, and there is more lexis to do with food in the language practice and skills work. For this reason, there is no separate *Vocabulary* section.

Everyday English Polite requests with *Can/Could you ...?* and *Can/Could I ...?* are introduced and practised.

Workbook There are exercises on count and uncount nouns, *I like/I'd like*, and *some/any*, *much/many*.

The vocabulary of the unit is recycled and extended through a menu and related activities.

In the writing section, there is the second focus on formal letters, and students are invited to write a letter to a hotel.

Notes on the unit

STARTER (SB p66)

1 Check comprehension of *to be a fussy eater*. Answer the questions in exercise 1 about yourself, writing examples of food you didn't like on the board. Ask students to write down their own examples. Then elicit a range of answers from the class, checking and drilling pronunciation as necessary. Revise the alphabet by getting students to spell key words. Build up a vocabulary list on the board and get students to copy it into their vocabulary notebooks. With weaker students, you could brainstorm food vocabulary with the class at the start of the activity and write key words on the board before looking at the questions.

2 **T 9.1** [CD 2: Track 12] Elicit one or two examples with the class. Students match the food and drink in columns **A** and **B** with the pictures.

Play the recording and get students to listen and follow in their books. Students then say the list aloud. Drill the pronunciation of any words students find difficult, highlighting the word stress as necessary.

> **Answers and tapescript**
> **A**
> l tea   w ice-cream
> p coffee   k apple juice
> j mineral water h bread
> v cheese   u milk
> n yoghurt   o chocolate
> d pasta   s broccoli
>
> **B**
> i bananas   e onions
> a apples   c tomatoes
> f strawberries q eggs
> t potatoes   b biscuits
> r carrots   g crisps
> x peas   m chips

3 Ask students to identify which list (**A** or **B**) has plural nouns (list **B**). Put students into pairs to complete the sentences with *is* or *are*. Check the answers and elicit that we can't count *broccoli* or *apple juice*, but we can count *tomatoes* and *apples*.

Read Grammar Reference 9.1 on p130 together in class and/or ask students to read it at home. Encourage them to ask you questions about it.

> **Answers**
> Broccoli **is** good for you.
> Tomatoes **are** good for you.
> Apple juice **is** delicious.
> Apples **are** delicious.

WHO'S A FUSSY EATER? (SB p67)

Count and uncount nouns – *some, any, a lot of ...*

The aim of this section is to revise count and uncount nouns and provide practice of *some*, *any*, and *a lot of*.

1 **T 9.2** [CD 2: Track 13] Focus attention on the photos. Explain that Duncan and Nick are flatmates and that they are talking about what they like and don't like to eat and drink, and what they liked and didn't like as children.

Pre-teach/check *kid* (informal for *child*), *green vegetables*, and *fruit*. Play the recording as far as *Ah – you were a fussy eater!* Elicit who was a fussy eater (*Duncan*). Play the full recording and ask students to note down the foods that Duncan did and didn't like when he was a child.

Give students time to check in pairs before checking with the class.

Elicit the answer to the question about where Duncan and Nick go to eat.

> **Answers and tapescript**
> Duncan is the fussy eater.
> He didn't like green vegetables, other vegetables (apart from potatoes), bananas, coffee, or tea.
> He liked chips, fruit juice, ice-cream, chocolate, crisps, biscuits, and pasta.
> They go to Romano's to eat.
>
> **T 9.2**
> D = Duncan N = Nick
> N Oh, good, we have some tomatoes.
> D Sorry, Nick. I don't like them.
> N Come on, Duncan! Tomatoes are really good for you. I didn't like them much when I was a child, but I love them now.
> D Hmm. I didn't like a lot of things when I was a kid.
> N Ah – you were a fussy eater! What didn't you like?
> D I didn't like any green vegetables.
> N Did you like any vegetables at all?
> D Only potatoes. I loved chips.
> N What about fruit? Did you like fruit?
> D I liked some fruit, but not all. I didn't like bananas. I liked fruit juice. I drank a lot of apple juice.
> N And now you drink lots of tea!
> D Yeah – and coffee. But I didn't like coffee or tea when I was a kid.

N So what were your favourite foods?
D I liked ice-cream, chocolate, crisps, biscuits especially chocolate biscuits. Er, you know, I liked all the usual things kids like.
N All the unhealthy things!
D I liked pasta too. Pasta with tomato sauce. I love that!
N Tomato sauce!? But you don't like tomatoes.
D Tomato sauce is different. Hey, let's not eat in tonight. Let's go out to Romano's.
N Romano's – a great idea! It's my favourite Italian restaurant.

2 **T 9.2** [CD 2: Track 13] With weaker classes, give students time to read the gapped lines and try to remember some of the answers before they listen. Focus attention on the example. Play the recording and get students to complete the lines. Check the answers with the class.

> **Answers**
> 1 Oh, good, we have **some** tomatoes.
> 2 I didn't like a **lot** of things when I was a kid.
> 3 I didn't like **any** green vegetables.
> 4 Did you like **any** vegetables at all?
> 5 I liked **some** fruit, but not all.
> 6 I drank a **lot** of apple juice.
> 7 I liked **all** the usual things kids like.

GRAMMAR SPOT

Look at the examples and question as a class. Allow students time to think about their answers before checking with the class.

> **Answer**
> We use *some* in positive sentences with both singular uncount nouns (*juice*) and plural count nouns (*tomatoes*). We use *any* in negative sentences and questions with both singular uncount nouns (*water*, *coffee*) and plural count nouns (*bananas*, *apples*).

Read Grammar Reference 9.2 on p130 together in class and/or ask students to read it at home. Encourage them to ask you questions about it.

EXTRA ACTIVITY

Give some examples of your own likes and dislikes, now and as a child. Students look at the lists of food and drink on p66 and decide what they liked and didn't like as a child, and what they like and don't like now. They then work in pairs and talk about their likes and dislikes. Monitor and check. Get students to feed back briefly, e.g. *Ana likes fruit, but I don't.*

I like . . . and *I'd like . . .*

3 **T 9.3** [CD 2: Track 14] Focus attention on the photo of Duncan and Nick in the Italian restaurant. Pre-teach/check *spaghetti Bolognese* (spaghetti with a thick tomato and minced meat sauce), *sparkling/still/tap water*. Play the recording through once and get students to follow in their books.

4 Give students time to answer the true-false questions, working in pairs.

> **Answers**
> 1 True
> 2 False. He really likes spaghetti.
> 3 False. Only Nick would like a salad.
> 4 True
> 5 False. They ask for some water.
> 6 False. He orders some tap water.

5 Students work in their pairs to practise the conversation in exercise 3. Monitor and check. If students have problems with pronunciation, play the recording again and drill difficult lines as a class.

Students work with a new partner and practise the conversation again, changing the things they order.

GRAMMAR SPOT

1 Look at the *Grammar Spot* questions as a class. This section is intended to guide students to the difference between *I like* and *I'd like*. Do not attempt to go into a full presentation of the uses of *would* at this stage, just introduce it as a polite way of making requests and offers.

> **Answer**
> *Would you like some ice-cream?* and *I'd like some ice-cream* mean *Do you want . . .* and *I want . . .*

Point out that when we talk about things in general, we do not use an article/determiner with plural count nouns or with uncount nouns. You could write these examples on the board:

I like biscuits. (NOT **I like some biscuits.*)

I don't like tea very much. (NOT **I don't like any tea very much.*)

Do you like Chinese food? (NOT **Do you like any Chinese food?*)

2/3 These sections demonstrate the special use of *some* in requests and offers, and *any* in other questions and negatives. Read the notes as a class.

Read Grammar Reference 9.3 on p130 together in class, and/or ask students to read it at home. Encourage them to ask you questions about it.

PRACTICE (SB p68)

Would/Do you like...?

1 **T 9.4** [CD 2: Track 15] Elicit the answer to question 1 as an example with the whole class. Students work in pairs or small groups to choose the correct form.

Play the recording and let students listen and check. Students practise the conversations in pairs. Monitor and check for accurate pronunciation. Drill any difficult lines with the class as necessary.

> **Answers and tapescript**
> 1 A Excuse me, are you ready to order?
>   B Yes. **I'd like** a steak, please.
> 2 A **Would** you like a sandwich?
>   B No, thanks. I'm not hungry.
> 3 A **Do** you like Ella?
>   B Yes. She's very nice.
> 4 A **Would** you like a cold drink?
>   B Yes, please. Do you have any apple juice?
> 5 A Can I help you?
>   B Yes. **I'd like** some stamps, please.
> 6 A What sports do you do?
>   B Well, **I like** skiing very much.

2 **T 9.5** [CD 2: Track 16] Play the first question and elicit the correct reply as an example. Students listen to the rest of the questions and complete the exercise. (See *Answers and tapescript* below for the questions.)

T 9.6 [CD 2: Track 17] Play the recording for students to listen and check their answers. Then get them to practise the conversations in pairs.

> **Answers and tapescript**
> 1 A What kind of juice do you like?
>   B **I like orange juice, especially fresh orange juice.**
> 2 A Would you like a cheese and tomato sandwich?
>   B **Just cheese, please. I don't like tomatoes.**
> 3 A Who's your favourite author?
>   B **I like books by Patricia Cornwell.**
> 4 A Is everything OK in your new office?
>   B **Yes, but I'd like a new computer.**
> 5 A Do you have any pets?
>   B **No, but I'd like a cat.**
> 6 A Do you want some ice-cream for dessert?
>   B **No, thanks. I don't like ice-cream.**

a or *some*?

3 The aim of this exercise is to consolidate the concept of count and uncount nouns and practise the use of *a/an* and *some*. Use the section to check how well students have grasped the concept and be prepared to explain further, using L1 if possible.

Focus attention on the examples. Students then work in pairs to write *a*, *an*, or *some* before the nouns.

> **Answers**
> 1 a banana   7 **an** apple
> 2 **some** fruit   8 **some** toast
> 3 **an** egg   9 **some** sandwiches
> 4 **some** bread   10 **some** biscuits
> 5 **some** milk   11 **a** cup of coffee
> 6 **some** meat   12 **some** apple juice

ADDITIONAL MATERIAL

Workbook Unit 9
Exercises 1–2 Count and uncount nouns
Exercises 3–5 *I like...* and *I'd like...*
Exercise 6 *like* or *would like*?

EATING IN (SB p68)

some/any, much/many

The aim of this section is to practise *some/any* and introduce *(not) much/many* with both count and uncount nouns. The question forms *How much ...?* and *How many ...?* are also practised.

1 Focus attention on the photo and ask students what they can remember about Duncan and Nick (*They are students and flatmates. They both like Italian food*, etc.). Ask *Who do they want to cook for?* (Nick's friends).

Focus attention on the photo of the cottage pie. Explain that this is a traditional dish often served as a family meal. Give students time to read the list of ingredients. Deal with any vocabulary queries, using the photos to help. Cheddar cheese is a type of hard yellow cheese, originally from the village of Cheddar in the county of Somerset, south-west England. Check pronunciation of *thyme* /taɪm/ and that students recognize the abbreviations *tbsp* (*tablespoon*), *g* (*gram*), and *ml* (*millilitre*).

Elicit the ingredients needed for the dish, as listed in the recipe.

2 Focus attention on the photo of the ingredients on the worktop. Read the examples with the class. Drill the pronunciation if necessary, highlighting the weak pronunciation of *some* /səm/.

Put students in pairs to continue talking about the ingredients for the recipe. Monitor and check carefully for correct use of *many* with count nouns and *much* with uncount nouns. If students have major problems, go through the *Grammar Spot* with the class, then get them to repeat the pairwork.

Check the answers with the class. Correct any mistakes carefully. With weaker students, drill the sentences again by saying the ingredients in random order and getting students to say the sentences, e.g. *potatoes – there aren't many potatoes.*

Answers
These are given in the same order as the ingredients in the recipe.
There are some onions.
There isn't any minced beef.
There isn't much oil.
There aren't any carrots.
There aren't many tomatoes.
There isn't much thyme.
There isn't any salt and pepper.
There aren't many potatoes.
There isn't much butter.
There isn't much cheese.
There's some milk.

3 **T 9.7** [CD 2: Track 18] Explain that Duncan and Nick are talking about the ingredients they have and don't have for the Cottage Pie. Pre-teach/check *herbs, to be left (in the bottle).*

Read the first four lines as a class, including the example. Ask *Who can cook?* (Nick). Give students time to complete the conversation, working individually. Let students check in pairs before playing the recording as a final check. If students query the use of *ones* in lines 9 and 12 of the conversation, elicit the food items that it refers back to each time (*potatoes, tomatoes*).

Put students in pairs to practise the conversation. Monitor and check. If students have problems with pronunciation and intonation, play the recording again and get students to repeat key sentences before practising the conversation again.

Answers and tapescript
N = Nick   D = Duncan
N This recipe for Cottage Pie looks easy.
D But I can't cook at all.
N Don't worry. I really like cooking. Now, vegetables – do we have any onions? Are there **any** carrots or potatoes?
D Well, there are **some** onions, but there aren't **any** carrots, and we don't have **many** potatoes. How **many** do we need?
N Four big ones.
D OK, put potatoes on your list.
N And how **many** tomatoes are there?
D Only two small ones. Put them on the list too.
N OK. How **much** milk is there?
D There's a lot, but there isn't **much** cheese or butter.
N OK, cheese and butter. What about herbs? Do we have **any** thyme?

D Yeah, that's fine. But don't forget the minced beef. How **much** do we need?
N 500 grams. Now, is that everything?
D Er – I think so. Do we have oil? Oh, yeah, there's **some** left in the bottle.
N OK, first shopping, then I'll give you a cooking lesson!
D I'd like that. I hope your friends like Cottage Pie.
N Everyone likes Cottage Pie!

GRAMMAR SPOT

1/2 Read the Grammar Spot as a class. Also point out to students the use of *many* with the plural verb *are* and *much* with the singular verb *is*.

3 Explain to students that *a lot of* is used with both count and uncount nouns. It describes a large quantity or amount of something.

Read Grammar Reference 9.4 on p130 together in class, and/or ask students to read it at home. Encourage them to ask you questions about it.

PRACTICE (SB p69)

much or *many*?

1 Pre-teach/check *petrol*. Focus attention on the example. Ask *Why 'much', not 'many'?* (*toast* is an uncount noun). Students work in pairs to complete the questions using *much* or *many*.

Answers
1 How much toast would you like?
2 How **much** yoghurt do we have left?
3 How **many** people were at the wedding?
4 How **much** money do you have in your pocket?
5 How **much** petrol is there in the car?
6 How **many** children does your brother have?
7 How **many** days is it until your holiday?
8 How **much** time do you need for this exercise?

2 **T 9.8** [CD 2: Track 19] Pre-teach/check *slice* and *raspberry*. Focus attention on the example. Students choose an answer for each question in exercise 1.

Play the recording and let students check their answers. Put students in pairs to practise the questions and answers. If students have problems with pronunciation, drill some of the exchanges chorally and individually.

Answers and tapescript
a 4   b 7   c 1   d 2   e 8   f 6   g 3   h 5
1 A How much toast would you like?
  B Just one slice, please.
2 A How much yoghurt do we have left?
  B Not a lot. Just one strawberry and one raspberry.

Unit 9 • Food you like!   73

> 3 A How many people were at the wedding?
>   B About 150.
> 4 A How much money do you have in your pocket?
>   B Just 50p.
> 5 A How much petrol is there in the car?
>   B It's full.
> 6 A How many children does your brother have?
>   B Two. A boy and a girl.
> 7 A How many days is it until your holiday?
>   B It's tomorrow!
> 8 A How much time do you need for this exercise?
>   B Two more minutes.

Check it

3 Students work in pairs to complete the task.

Elicit a range of answers from the class for each sentence. If there is disagreement, write the relevant sentences on the board and get students to explain the reason for their choice. Encourage students to correct each other where possible.

> **Answers**
> 1 How many **eggs** do you need?
> 2 We don't have much **cheese** left.
> 3 I'm hungry. I'd like a **sandwich**, please.
> 4 I'd like **some** fruit, please.
> 5 I don't like **broccoli**.
> 6 Would you like some **tea**?
> 7 How many **cousins** do you have?
> 8 We have **no** homework today.

Speaking

4 Demonstrate the verbs in the box with simple mimes. Focus attention on the example and then elicit possible ways of continuing the recipe.

Put students into groups of three or four. Remind them to refer to the ingredients list to make sure they have included everything. Monitor and help, writing up any additional cooking verbs on the board as necessary.

Project

Make sure students have brought along their notes for their recipe. Put students into groups of three. In a multilingual class, ask students from different countries to work together to encourage an exchange of information.

Students take it in turns to talk about their recipe. Make sure they use their notes just as a reference and don't read out the complete text of their recipe. Encourage the other students to ask questions. Monitor and help as necessary. Check for accurate use of *some/any*, *much/many*, food vocabulary, and cooking verbs. Note down any common errors but don't feed back on these until after the groupwork.

Ask students to choose their favourite recipe from their group and give reasons for their choice.

ADDITIONAL MATERIAL

Workbook Unit 9
Exercise 7 *some* or *any*?
Exercise 8 *How much … ?* or *How many … ?*

READING AND SPEAKING (SB p70)

Food around the world

> **SUGGESTION**
> You might want to set some vocabulary for homework prior to this lesson – the pictures on the page can then be used to check vocabulary in the lesson.
>
> move on   environment   sardines
> pick up (food)   farm (v.)   depend on
> course (of a meal) transport (v.)   land (n.)
> noodles   chopsticks   control (v.)
> herrings   fingers

1 In a monolingual group, answer the questions as a whole-class activity. In a multilingual group, students can work in pairs or small groups and exchange information about their country.

2 Focus attention on the photographs. Ask students to name the places or nationalities represented by the food.

> **Answers** (clockwise from top left)
> Saudi Arabia – desert family sharing meal
> China – rice harvest
> Venezuela – strawberries
> Sudan – rice
> Japan – sushi and tempura
> China – noodles

3 Get students to read the text through quickly and match the correct headings to paragraphs 2, 3, and 4. Encourage students to focus on just matching the headings and tell them not to worry about new vocabulary at this stage. (If they have done the above homework task, they should not have too many difficulties.) You might want to set a time limit to encourage students to read extensively.

> **Answers**
> Paragraph 2: WHAT DO WE EAT?
> Paragraph 3: HOW DO WE EAT?
> Paragraph 4: WHERE DOES OUR FOOD COME FROM?

4 Students read the text again more slowly and answer the questions. Get them to check in pairs before checking answers with the whole class.

> **Answers**
> 1 About 1 million years ago.
> 2 Yes, they do.
> 3 Because they live by the sea.
> 4 Because they live away from the sea.
> 5 Germany and Poland.
> 6 Only one.
> 7 They use their fingers and bread to pick up the food.
> 8 Because it is possible to transport them from Chile or Spain.

Speaking

5 Read through the questions as a class. Quickly revise the meaning and pronunciation of *breakfast*, *lunch*, and *dinner* and check comprehension of *main meal*.

Students work in small groups and discuss the questions. This will obviously be a very productive activity in a multilingual group, but students in a monolingual group can also discuss food habits in their own country and their own family, and compare with other countries they have visited.

Conduct a brief feedback session with the whole class, encouraging students to highlight different eating habits in different countries.

Writing

6 Students write a short paragraph about meals in their country. This can be given as a homework activity if you do not have time to do it in class. When you correct this, don't correct too harshly. The idea is to give students an opportunity for some freer writing, and they will inevitably make a lot of mistakes.

LISTENING AND SPEAKING (SB p72)

My favourite national food

1 Focus attention on the photographs. Students work in pairs and decide which of the dishes they like. They match them with the countries.

> **Answers**
> Bruschetta – Italy
> Bife de chorizo – Argentina
> Sachertorte – Austria
> Full English breakfast – England

2 Tell the students to look carefully at the photos and find the food items.

> **Answers**
> Bruschetta – tomatoes, onions
> Bife de chorizo – tomatoes, chilli, onions, beef
> Sachertorte – chocolate
> Full English breakfast – mushrooms, tomatoes, egg

3 **T 9.9** [CD 2: Track 20] Tell students they are going to hear the four people in the photographs talking about their favourite food. Ask them to identify the nationalities of the people and match them to the food in the photographs. When you have checked answers with the class, elicit some of the things they say about the dishes.

> **Answers and tapescript**
> Hans: Austrian, Sachertorte
> Graham: English, Full English breakfast
> Sergio: Italian, Bruschetta
> Alberto: Argentinian, Bife de chorizo
>
> **T 9.9**
> **Hans**
> One dish that is very famous in my country is 'Sachertorte'. It is a kind of chocolate cake and you eat it with cream. I love it! The famous Café Sacher is in the centre of Vienna. They say a chef called Franz Sacher invented it there. When I am in Vienna, I always go to Café Sacher for some of their cake and a nice black coffee.
> **Graham**
> Now in my job, I travel the world, and I like all kinds of food ... but my favourite, my favourite is ... er ... I always have it as soon as I come home ... is a full English breakfast. Eggs, mushrooms, tomatoes, and of course toast. I love it, not every day but when I'm at home we have it every Sunday. Mmm! I'd like it right now – delicious.
> **Sergio**
> We love eating in my country! One of my favourite national dishes is called 'bruschetta'. This is actually toast, but you make it with special bread. You can eat it with a lot of things, but my favourite bruschetta has tomatoes, garlic, and olive oil on it. In my town there is a 'bruschetteria'. This is a small café – selling only toast! It is my favourite place to go.
> **Alberto**
> One kind of food that my country is very famous for is meat, especially beef. Everybody eats a lot more meat here. My family eats beef three or four times a week. There are a lot of different beef dishes, but my favourite is 'bife de chorizo'. This is a big steak! My mum cooks it with tomatoes and chilli. Delicious!

4 Focus attention on the questions about the people in exercise 3 and the things they say. Students work in pairs and answer as many questions as they can. If necessary, play the recording again to let students complete their answers. Check the answers with the whole class.

> **Answers**
> 1 Graham travels a lot.
>   Hans and Sergio go to cafés to eat their favourite food.
>   Hans likes sweet things.
>   Graham and Alberto eat their favourite food at home.
> 2 Café Sacher is in the centre of Vienna.
> 3 A chef at Café Sacher called Franz Sacher invented it.

Unit 9 · Food you like! 75

> 4 As soon as he comes home from travelling and on Sundays when he is at home.
> 5 You toast a special kind of bread and put things like tomatoes, garlic, and olive oil on top.
> 6 The small bruschetteria in his town.
> 7 Three or four times a week.
> 8 His mother.

What do you think?

Students discuss the questions in pairs and then feed back to the rest of the class.

ADDITIONAL MATERIAL

Workbook Unit 9
Exercise 9 Food vocabulary; ordering a meal in a restaurant.

EVERYDAY ENGLISH (SB p73)

Polite requests

> **POSSIBLE PROBLEMS**
> This section introduces *Can I ... ?/Could I ... ?* and *Can you ... ?/Could you ... ?* for the first time. If you think your students will not be familiar with it, present it yourself, using the classroom to illustrate meaning: *Aziz, can you open the window, please? Samira, could you clean the board, please? Hassan, could I borrow your pen, please?* etc.
> You could tell students that *Can I ... ?* and *Could I ... ?* mean the same, but *could* is usually more polite. Point out that although *could* looks like the past tense, the concept is in fact present. However, if you think your class is strong enough, you could use the situations in the Student's Book as a vehicle for presentation.

1 Look at the photograph and get students to say what they can see.

2 Pre-teach/check *pass* (the salt), *fizzy/still* (water). Ask students to match the questions and responses, using the singular and plural forms, e.g. *It's/They're delicious* to help them.

T 9.10 [CD 2: Track 21] Students listen and check their answers.

> **Answers and tapescript**
> 1 Would you like some more carrots?
>   Yes, please. They're delicious.
> 2 Could you pass the salt, please?
>   Yes, of course. Here you are.
> 3 Could I have a glass of water, please?
>   Do you want fizzy or still?
> 4 Does anybody want more dessert?
>   Yes, please. I'd love some. It's delicious.
> 5 How would you like your coffee?
>   Black, no sugar, please.
> 6 This is delicious! Can you give me the recipe?
>   Yes, of course. I'm glad you like it.
> 7 Do you want help with the washing-up?
>   No, of course not. We have a dishwasher.

Students practise the questions and responses in pairs. Monitor and check pronunciation mistakes.

Read the information in the caution box as a class.

3 Students look at the requests and complete them, using *Can/Could I ... ?* or *Can/Could you ... ?*

> **Answers**
> 1 **Can/Could I** have a cheese sandwich, please?
> 2 **Can/Could you** tell me the time, please?
> 3 **Can/Could you** take me to school?
> 4 **Can/Could I** see the menu, please?
> 5 **Can/Could you** lend me some money, please?
> 6 **Can/Could you** help me with my homework, please?
> 7 **Can/Could I** borrow your dictionary, please?

4 Students work in pairs to practise the requests in exercise 3 and give an answer.

T 9.11 [CD 2: Track 22] Play the recording and get students to compare their answers with those on the tape.

> **Tapescript**
> 1 Can I have a cheese sandwich, please?
>   Yes, of course. That's £2.50.
> 2 Could you tell me the time, please?
>   It's just after ten.
> 3 Can you take me to school?
>   Jump in.
> 4 Can I see the menu, please?
>   Here you are. And would you like a drink to start?
> 5 Could you lend me some money, please?
>   Not again! How much would you like this time?
> 6 Can you help me with my homework, please?
>   What is it? French? I can't speak a word of French.
> 7 Can I borrow your dictionary, please?
>   Yes, if I can find it. I think it's in my bag.

Don't forget!

Workbook Unit 9
Exercise 10 Formal letters 2. Students are invited to write a letter to a hotel.

Word list
Remind your students of the Word list for this unit on p139. They could write in the translations, learn them at home, and/or write some of the words in their vocabulary notebook.

10

Comparatives and superlatives • *have got*
City and country • Directions 2

Bigger and better!

Introduction to the unit

This unit is unusual in that it has three presentation sections, each one revising the grammar of the one before.

The theme is describing places: cities, the countryside, and hotels. These are useful contexts to practise comparatives and superlatives. Now we introduce *have got* (see *Note* in Unit 3, p18 of the Teacher's Book) in a direct comparison with *have* (for possession), which students are already familiar with. The skills section includes a jigsaw reading about three megacities and provides further practice of the grammatical aims.

Language aims

Grammar – comparative and superlative adjectives The following aspects of comparatives and superlatives are introduced:
- the use of *-er/-est* with short adjectives, such as *cheap, cheaper, cheapest*.
- the use of *-ier/-iest* with adjectives that end in *-y*, such as *noisy, noisier, noisiest*.
- the use of *more/most* with longer adjectives, such as *more expensive, most expensive*.
- irregular adjectives such as *good, better, best*.

The presentation of these is staged. In the first presentation, pairs of opposite adjectives are revised/introduced and this leads to the introduction of comparative forms. These forms are then revised in the second presentation when *have got* is introduced. Finally, superlatives are introduced in the third presentation and at the same time comparatives and *have got* are revised.

Students usually experience little difficulty with the concept of comparatives and superlatives but experience more difficulty in producing and pronouncing the forms because of all the different parts involved. Utterances often sound very laboured and unnatural because equal stress is given to each word and syllable. For this reason we practise natural-sounding connected speech.

Common mistakes
*She's more tall than me.
*He's the most tall student in the class.
*She's taller that me.
*He's tallest student in the class.

have got The verb *have* for possession was introduced in Unit 3. We purposely have delayed the introduction of *have got* for possession until now because of the complications of production it causes if introduced alongside the Present Simple of *have*, particularly in the question and negative. (See the *Note* in the *Language Aims* of Unit 3, p18 of the Teacher's Book.)

In this unit there are many exercises that contrast *have* and *have got*.

Vocabulary and pronunciation Pairs of opposite adjectives are introduced as part of the presentation of comparative adjectives.

In the vocabulary section, city and country words are introduced and practised in contexts which provide an opportunity to review comparatives and superlatives.

There is further practice in recognizing phonetic script.

Everyday English There is further practice of getting and giving directions, and prepositions of movement such as *along* and *down* are introduced.

Workbook There is further practice on comparatives and superlatives, and *have got*.

In the vocabulary section, compound nouns to do with towns are introduced such as *town centre, railway station*.

The writing syllabus includes work on relative pronouns. Then students study a model text about London before being guided to write a short piece about *their* capital city.

Notes on the unit

STARTER (SB p74)

> **POSSIBLE PROBLEMS**
> This activity aims to remind students of the concept of comparatives and to help you assess how well students can cope with simple comparative statements. It is also intended to be good fun, so don't worry too much if students slip into mistakes like **more tall* or if the pronunciation is a little stilted. Students will get plenty of practice in the activities that follow.

Demonstrate the activity by standing next to one of your students who is taller or shorter and highlighting the difference in height. Then ask the same student *How old are you?* and get him/her to ask you the same question. Write the ages on the board and then give a full example, e.g. *I'm smaller and older than (Reza). (He) is taller and younger than me.*

Students work in pairs and compare heights and ages. Encourage students who are of a similar height to stand next to each other or back to back to check.

CITY LIFE (SB p74)

Comparative adjectives

> **SUGGESTION**
> You could set exercise 1 for homework if you need to save class time. If you do, begin the lesson by going through the answers and practising the pronunciation of each word.

1 If students haven't done this exercise as homework (see *Suggestion* above), put your students into pairs and get them to match the adjectives with their opposites. Check the answers and the pronunciation first before students categorize the words into 'city' and 'country'.

Be prepared for students to want to pronounce the *ie* of *friendly* separately */frɪendli/ and make sure they say it correctly, /frendli/.

Answers
In these pairs of words the opposite of *old* is *modern* (it could also be *new*) not *young*, because in the context of the presentation the adjectives are being used to talk about buildings not people.

fast	/fɑːst/	slow	/sləʊ/
big	/bɪg/	small	/smɔːl/
dirty	/ˈdɜːti/	clean	/kliːn/
dangerous	/ˈdeɪndʒərəs/	safe	/seɪf/
noisy	/ˈnɔɪzi/	quiet	/ˈkwaɪət/
modern	/ˈmɒdən/	old	/əʊld/
unfriendly	/ʌnˈfrendli/	friendly	/ˈfrendli/
exciting	/ɪkˈsaɪtɪŋ/	boring	/ˈbɔːrɪŋ/
expensive	/ɪkˈspensɪv/	cheap	/tʃiːp/

Ask students to think about which words describe life in the city and life in the country. You could put the headings CITY and COUNTRY on the board and write in your students' suggestions as to which adjectives belong where, or you could ask individual students to come up to the board to write in the suggestions themselves. Be prepared for some debate and discussion as there are obviously no prescribed right answers. A lot is to do with personal opinion and experience. Welcome any freer speaking that results.

2 This exercise focuses on the main target language for this section, so make it clear to your class that this is an important moment and that this is the structure in English that compares things. If necessary and possible, use translation to do this.

Ask students to look at the chart and to work in pairs to make sentences comparing life in the city and country. (You may need to point out the use of *more* with longer adjectives, but don't go into the rules in too much detail at this stage. They are dealt with more fully later on.)

At this stage, don't worry too much about pronunciation as long as students understand the meaning of the structure, just let them try to produce sentences that express their opinions. Get some feedback from the whole class.

3 **T 10.1** [CD 2: Track 23] Now is the moment to concentrate on the pronunciation. Ask your students to look at the example sentence in the Student's Book and say it in chorus either using yourself or the recording as a model. Focus particularly on the /ə/ sound at the end of the comparative and in the pronunciation of *than* /ðən/. Isolate *safer* and *than* and then drill them together as connected speech:

cheaper than /ˈtʃiːpəðən/
safer than /ˈseɪfəðən/

Drill the other sentences from the recording or by saying them yourself. If necessary, break up the sentences to drill them, particularly the comparative forms + *than*.

Try to get a natural 'flow' in the repetition of the sentences as on the recording.

Tapescript
The country is cheaper and safer than the city.
The city is noisier and dirtier than the country.
The city is more expensive than the country.
The city is more exciting than the country.

4 Get students to discuss their opinions in pairs. Monitor and check for accurate use of comparatives and acceptable pronunciation.

Students share their opinions with the rest of the class. If most of your students had problems with the comparative forms, write their sentences on the board including the mistakes and get students to correct them as a class. Major problems with pronunciation can be dealt with by drilling the students' sentences with the whole class.

GRAMMAR SPOT

1 This is to reinforce and make clear to your students the rules governing the formation of comparative adjectives. Get students to work individually to complete the comparative sentences and try to formulate any rules they can. They may have got a clear idea from doing exercise 2 or they may need a bit of prompting and guiding, but try not to just give them the rules. You could write the rules up on the board as you go along.

Answers
I'm **older** than you.
Your class is **noisier** than my class.
Your car was **more expensive** than my car.

-er is used with short adjectives such as *old, older*.
-ier with adjectives that end in *-y* such as *noisy, noisier*.
more . . . is used with longer adjectives such as *expensive, more expensive*.

2 Students work in pairs to write the comparative forms of the adjectives in exercise 1, using dictionaries to help them if appropriate. Some of the comparative forms have already been given in exercise 2.

Check the answers with the whole class, getting students to spell the comparative forms. Highlight *bigger* as an example of the doubling of the consonant in short adjectives with a short vowel sound. (You don't need to go into this rule in detail, but do check that they have noticed the doubling of the consonant.)

Answers

fast	faster	slow	slower
big	bigger	small	smaller
dirty	dirtier	clean	cleaner
dangerous	more dangerous	safe	safer
noisy	noisier	quiet	quieter
modern	more modern	old	older
unfriendly	unfriendlier*	friendly	friendlier
exciting	more exciting	boring	more boring
expensive	more expensive	cheap	cheaper

*This is the comparative usually given by dictionaries, but more unfriendly is also often used.

3 Ask students for the irregular forms of *good* and *bad*, and check the pronunciation of *worse* /wɜːs/ carefully.

Answers
good **better**   bad **worse**

Read Grammar Reference 10.1 on p131 together in class, and/or ask students to read it at home. Encourage them to ask you questions about it.

PRACTICE (SB p75)

Much more than . . .

1 This exercise is also good for stress and intonation practice. Put the conversations in a context and tell your students that two people are discussing different cities that they know.

NOTE
In this exercise we bring in the use of *much* to emphasize comparatives. The students are only asked to recognize it at first, and not produce it until later.

Do the example with your students to illustrate the activity. Then ask them to work in pairs to complete the conversations. Point out that the students have to fill in the opposite adjectives in B's comments to those A uses.

T 10.2 [CD 2: Track 24] Play the recording and get students to check their answers. Tell them to also focus on the pronunciation, particularly the stress and intonation.

Answers and tapescript
1 A Life in the country is **slower than** city life.
   B Yes, the city's much **faster**.
2 A Moscow is **safer than** London.
   B No, it isn't. Moscow is much **more dangerous**.
3 A Paris is **bigger than** Madrid.
   B No, it isn't! It's much **smaller**.

Unit 10 · Bigger and better! 79

> 4 **A** Hong Kong is **more expensive than** Rome.
>   **B** No, it isn't. Hong Kong is much **cheaper**.
> 5 **A** The buildings in Mecca are **more modern than** the buildings in Riyadh.
>   **B** No, they aren't. They're much **older**.
> 6 **A** The Underground in London is **better than** the Metro in Paris.
>   **B** No! The Underground is much **worse**.

Get individual students to practise the conversations across the class in open pairs. Encourage the Bs to sound really indignant when they disagree with A. Give them exaggerated models yourself or play the recording again to make clear that you want them to produce good stress and intonation and connected speech:

Examples

A *Moscow is safer than London.*

B *No, it isn't. Moscow is much more dangerous.*

A *Paris is bigger than Madrid.*

B *No, it isn't. It's much smaller.*

2 This is the personalization stage. Decide on two cities that you and all, or most, of the students know and demonstrate the activity. Students continue in pairs and decide which city they prefer. Monitor and check for accurate use of comparative forms and pronunciation.

Get a few students to feed back to the rest of the class. Highlight any common mistakes in grammar or pronunciation from the pairwork stage.

ADDITIONAL MATERIAL

Workbook Unit 10
Exercises 1 and 2 consolidate the work on comparatives.

COUNTRY LIFE (SB p75)

have got

In this presentation, comparatives are revised and *have got* is introduced in the context of a telephone conversation where someone has moved from the city to the country.

Read the introduction about Jim and Alan aloud to the class to set the scene. You could ask your students *Why do you think Jim moved to Seacombe?*

1 **T 10.3** [CD 2: Track 25] Tell students they are going to read and listen to the telephone conversation between Jim and Alan. For the moment, don't focus on the examples of *have got* in the text – just tell students to complete the conversation with the missing adjectives. Make it clear that some of them are comparatives and some are not.

Play the recording through once and then ask students to check their answers in pairs. Play the recording again for students to add in any answers they missed. Check the answers with the whole class.

> **Answers and tapescript**
> **Alan** Why did you leave London? You had a **good** job.
> **Jim** Yes, but I've got a **better** job here.
> **Alan** And you had a **big** flat in London.
> **Jim** Well, I've got a **bigger** flat here.
> **Alan** Really? How many bedrooms has it got?
> **Jim** Three. And it's got a garden. It's **nicer** than my flat in London and it's **cheaper**.
> **Alan** But you haven't got any friends!
> **Jim** I've got a lot of friends here. People are much **friendlier** than in London.
> **Alan** But the country's so **boring**.
> **Jim** No, it isn't. It's much **more interesting** than London. And Seacombe has got lots of shops, a library, and some fantastic cafés. And the air is **cleaner** and the streets are **safer**.
> **Alan** OK. Everything is **wonderful**! So when can I visit you?

GRAMMAR SPOT

This *Grammar Spot* highlights the form and use of *have got* compared with *have*.

1 Read through the notes with the whole class. You will need to highlight the fact that the *have* in *have got* contracts but that it doesn't in *have* for possession. Students may have trouble saying the contracted and negative forms, especially next to the following consonant, so practise saying the examples in the box. You could drill them chorally and individually.
   I've got a computer.   /aɪv gɒt ə kəmpjuːtə/
   He's got a car.   /hiːz gɒt ə kɑː/
   Have you got a computer?   /hæv (həv) juː gɒt ə kəmpjuːtə/
   Has she got a car?   /hæz (həs) ʃiː gɒt ə kɑː/
   They haven't got a flat.   /ðeɪ hævnt gɒt ə flæt/
   It hasn't got a garden.   /ɪt hæznt gɒt ə gɑːdn/

2 Highlight the past of *have* and *have got*. Elicit a few examples from the class of things they had when they were younger, e.g. *I had a bike.*

3 Ask your students to study the conversation and underline all the examples of *have got* and *had*.

Make it clear that they are looking for questions and negatives and not just the positive. Ask students to check in pairs, and then check with the whole class.

> **Answers**
> *have got*
> I**'ve got** a better job here.
> I**'ve got** a bigger flat here.
> How many bedrooms **has it got**?
> And it**'s got** a garden.
> But you **haven't got** any friends!
> I**'ve got** a lot of friends here.
> Seacombe **has got** shops . . .
> *had*
> You **had** a good job in London.
> And you **had** a big flat in London.

Read the Grammar Reference 10.2 on p131 together in class, and/or ask students to read it at home. Encourage them to ask you questions about it.

2 Ask students to work in pairs and take the parts in the dialogue to practise *have got*. If necessary, play the recording again and let students listen and repeat, before practising in pairs.

You can then ask students to go through the dialogue again and encourage them not to follow the dialogue exactly, but to replace the adjectives with others that are suitable. If they have the confidence, encourage them to improvise completely without their books.

PRACTICE (SB p76)

have/have got

This is a very straightforward transformation exercise designed to focus students' attention solely on the difference in form between *have* and *have got* for possession. It is worth bearing in mind that focusing on the form of *have got* at this stage should help students when they meet the Present Perfect Simple in Unit 14.

1 We suggest that you refer students back to Grammar Reference 10.2 on p131 as they do the exercise. Ask them to do the exercise on their own, writing the contracted forms where possible. Then get students to check with a partner, before you conduct a full class feedback.

> **Answers**
> 3 I've got a lot of homework tonight.
> 4 Have you got any homework?
> 5 Our school has got a library, but it hasn't got any computers.
> 6 My parents have got a new car.
> 7 Has your sister got a computer?
> 8 I haven't got a problem with this exercise.

I've got more than you!

> **NOTE**
> You will need to photocopy the information about the multi-millionaires' possessions on p128 of the Teacher's Book.

2 This roleplay should be a fun (and not very realistic!) activity. Ask your students to look at the pictures of the two millionaires. Ask *What have millionaires usually got?* and elicit a few suggestions from the whole class.

> **Possible answers**
> money   horses
> (big) houses   boats
> (fast) cars   servants
> planes

Say the first line yourself and then in open pairs. Encourage exaggerated stress and intonation as students boast about their possessions!

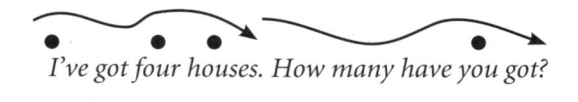

I've got four houses. How many have you got?

Five. I've got two in France, one in Miami,

one in the Caribbean, and a castle in Scotland.

Ask your students to work in pairs. Give out the rolecards on p129 of the Teacher's Book and get students to exchange information about their possessions. Go round the class checking grammar and pronunciation. Only correct where absolutely necessary, in order to encourage fluency. Then get feedback as to who is the richer! (Millionaire B is.)

ADDITIONAL MATERIAL

Workbook Unit 10
Exercises 3–5 These give further practice of *have got*.
Exercise 6 This brings together comparatives and *have got*.

THE WORLD'S BEST HOTELS (SB p76)

Superlative adjectives

This presentation of superlative adjectives includes revision of comparatives and *have got*.

1 Ask students to look at the pictures of the hotels and read the information about each of them. Ask them to tell you which they like and why. Here they could be revising *have got*, but don't insist on this, as the main

aim here is to generate interest in the theme and to take in some of the information about the hotels.

2 This exercise has been specially designed so that *all* the true sentences contain examples of superlative adjectives, thereby providing a means of highlighting the new structure. The false sentences contain examples of comparatives and *have got*.

Focus attention on the examples, pointing out the superlative example *the cheapest* but not going into detail at this stage. Students work in pairs to decide which sentences are true and which are false, and to correct the information in the false ones.

POSSIBLE PROBLEMS

1 In sentence 4, make sure students are clear about which opposite of *old* students need to use (*new*).
2 You will have to draw attention to *the* in superlatives. It is common for students to omit this.
3 Point out that the superlative *the furthest* is irregular – the adjective is *far* and the comparative is *further*.
4 Draw students' attention to the prepositions in sentences 10 and 11: *the nearest to*, and *the furthest from*.

Check the answers with the whole class.

Answers
3 Claridge's is the most expensive hotel. ✔
4 Al Bustan Palace is older than the Mandarin. ✘
 No, it isn't. It's newer.
5 Claridge's is the oldest hotel. ✔
6 The Mandarin Oriental is the biggest hotel. ✔
7 Claridge's is smaller than Al Bustan Palace. ✘
 No, it isn't. It's bigger.
8 Claridge's has got a swimming pool. **No, it hasn't.** ✘
9 Claridge's is nearer the airport than the Mandarin. ✘
 No, it isn't.
10 The Mandarin is the nearest to the airport. ✔
11 Al Bustan Palace is the furthest from the airport. ✔

Get students to work in pairs and focus on the six correct sentences. Ask your class what they notice about all these sentences. Students should highlight the *-est* endings in the short adjectives and *the most* form with longer adjectives, but be prepared to prompt them if necessary. (Do not go into a full explanation of the rules, as this is the focus of the *Grammar Spot* activity on p77.)

3 Check comprehension of *best* as the superlative of *good*. Get students to discuss which is the best hotel near where they live and to describe what it has got.

GRAMMAR SPOT

1 Students complete the superlative sentences and try to supply the rules. Prompt and guide them if they need it. Write the rules up on the board as students work them out, taking the opportunity to remind them of the comparative forms.

Answers
The Oasis is the **cheapest** hotel in Kuwait City.
The Sheraton Kuwait is the **most expensive**.
– *the . . .-est* is used with short adjectives such as *cheap, (cheaper), the cheapest*.
– *the most* is used with longer adjectives such as *expensive, (more expensive), the most expensive*.

2 Students focus on the irregular forms and the dictionary entry for *good*. Elicit what information the dictionary gives (phonetic script, word category, and irregular comparative and superlative forms). Students complete the irregular forms for *bad* and *far*, using their dictionaries if appropriate.

Answers
bad   **worse, the worst**   far   **further, the furthest**

Read the Grammar Reference 10.1 on p131 together in class, and/or ask students to read it at home. Encourage them to ask you questions about it.

PRACTICE (SB p77)

The biggest and best!

This is another activity which integrates pronunciation work on stress and intonation.

1 Demonstrate the activity by reading the example aloud to the class. Then ask students to work on their own to complete the sentences.

T 10.4 [CD 2: Track 26] Play the recording and ask your students to check their answers. Also tell them to listen carefully to the rhythm/stress and intonation of the sentences.

Answers and tapescript
1 That house is very old.
 Yes, **it's the oldest house** in the village.
2 Claridge's is a very expensive hotel.
 Yes, **it's the most expensive hotel** in London.
3 Tehran is a very big city.
 Yes, **it's the biggest city** in Iran.
4 New York is a very cosmopolitan city.
 Yes, **it's the most cosmopolitan city** in the world.
5 Kabsa is a very popular dish.
 Yes, **it's the most popular dish** in Saudi Arabia.

6 Richard is a very funny boy.
  Yes, **he's the funniest boy** in our class.
7 Lulwah is a very intelligent student.
  Yes, **she's the most intelligent student** in the university.
8 This is a very easy exercise.
  Yes, **it's the easiest exercise** in the book.

2 **T 10.5** [CD 2: Track 27] Now ask students to close their books. Play the first lines again, pausing after each one so that your students can produce the reply. You could do this in chorus with the whole class, or ask individuals to respond, or mix the two approaches.

Really work hard to encourage good (probably exaggerated) stress and intonation in the replies, with the main stress on the superlative adjective.

Student(s): *Yes, it's the oldest house in the village.*

Yes, it's the most expensive hotel in London.

The more you work on the stress and intonation, the more fun the activity becomes!

Talking about your class

This is a freer speaking activity, which should be good fun, provided you warn students to be careful not to offend other people! Give them enough time to describe one or two other people, but do not let the activity go on too long.

You could put some other cues on the board to prompt comparative and superlative sentences: *lives near to school/lives far from school; has a big bag*, etc.

3 Read the examples with students, then put them into small groups and ask them to make sentences about the other students.
  Get the class to give you comments about each other.

4 Students write the name of their favourite holiday destination and then tell the rest of the class. Write the names of the holiday destinations on the board and keep a score for each one. Students work in pairs and compare the places, e.g. *(Dubai) is more popular than (Paris)*. Then get students to say which is the most popular holiday destination in the class.

Check it

5 Ask students to work in pairs or small groups to tick the correct sentence. Ask them to work quite quickly, then conduct a full class feedback on which are the correct answers. Try to get students to correct each other and explain any mistakes they hear.

Answers
1 Yesterday was hotter than today.
2 She's taller than her brother.
3 I'm the youngest in the class.
4 Last week was busier than this week.
5 He hasn't got any sisters.
6 Do you have any bread?
7 My homework is the worst in the class.
8 This exercise is the most difficult in the book.

ADDITIONAL MATERIAL

Workbook Unit 10
Exercises 7–9 These practise comparatives and superlatives together.

READING AND LISTENING (SB p78)

Megacities

> **NOTE**
> At the end of this section, there is a project activity on megacities. You will need to build in time for students to do some research and make notes on a megacity, probably for homework. Students then give a short presentation about their chosen city to the class. In larger groups, you may need to stage the presentations across a series of lessons or get students to give their presentations in groups.

1 **T 10.6** [CD 2: Track 28] This exercise aims to generate some interest in the topic of megacities, and hopefully provide some motivation to read the texts.

Give students time to read the exercise and number the cities, working individually. Students then compare their answers in pairs and briefly justify their order.

Give students time to read the questions in exercise 1. Pre-teach/check *inhabitants* and *rural*. Then play the recording through once and check the answers to the order of the cities. If necessary, play the recording again and check the answers to the questions.

Answers and tapescript
3 Mumbai   5 Shanghai   1 Tokyo   4 New York
2 Mexico City
A megacity is a city with more than ten million people. In 2008, for the first time in the history of the world, more people on earth lived in cities than in rural areas.

T 10.6
A megacity is a city with more than ten million inhabitants. The largest megacity is in fact Tokyo. The next biggest is Mexico City. Third is Mumbai. Fourth is New York, with about 22 million people. And last, the smallest is Shanghai,

which has about 18.4 million. Some time in 2008, for the first time in the history of the world, more people on earth lived in cities than in rural areas.

2 Focus attention on the photos and elicit a brief description of each city. Use this opportunity to feed in key words from the texts. Focus attention on the headings and elicit the answers to the questions in exercise 2.

Answers
Tokyo is very fast.
Mexico City has a mix of cultures.
Mumbai has a lot of poverty.

3 Put students into three groups, A, B, and C. (With larger classes, you may need to have multiple sets of the three groups.) Assign a text to each group and remind students to read only their text:

Group A – Tokyo

Group B – Mumbai

Group C – Mexico City

Get students to read their text quite quickly. Monitor and help with any queries.

Check comprehension of the headings. Give students time to write down the headings to make recording their answers easier. Remind students to write their answers in note form. Get students to work in their groups and make notes.

Answers
Tokyo
The city and its people
largest and most expensive city in the world; one of the most exciting – everything moves fast; on east coast of Japan; huge but one of safest cities in the world; mysterious – difficult for foreigners to understand; 35 million people; wear latest fashions and have most up-to-date phones
Money and business
people earn highest salaries and spend most money
Buildings and history
not many old buildings – 1923 earthquake and Second World War; architecture very modern but also many Shinto shrines + public baths; originally small fishing village called Edo; name changed in 1868 when Emperor moved there
Climate
summers hot and humid; most beautiful time of year spring, when cherry blossom on trees
Transport
one of the biggest and busiest railway systems in world; 11 million commuters use it

Mumbai
The city and its people
India's largest city; both old and modern, rich and poor; on west coast; because of poverty can be difficult place to live, but experience unique; 22.8 million people; streets full of people doing business, selling snacks and clothes or just living; 60% live with no running water/electricity/sanitation
Money and business
India's most important commercial centre; most important businesses + banks have headquarters here; also important centre for IT industry
Buildings and history
modern skyscrapers + new shopping malls next to slums; best at sunrise and sunset – colour of stone buildings changes; part of British Empire until independence in 1947; called Bombay until 1995; renamed after Hindu goddess Mumba Devi for political reasons
Climate
wet season June to September; November to February a little cooler and dryer
Transport
cheapest and easiest transport by bus; trains crowded and dangerous

Mexico City
The city and its people
largest city in North and South America; offers variety of experiences; in valley in south central area, surrounded by mountains; air quality not good; visitors need to be careful, but city offers rich cultural mix; 23.4 million people; busy markets selling Mexican food + Indian handicrafts
Money and business
richest city in Latin America; elegant shops selling high-class goods, expensive restaurants, supercool cafés; also many people in poor houses
Buildings and history
in main square, modern skyscraper; European squares + colonial houses; Aztecs called it Tenochtitlan; already important city when Spanish invaded in 1521; became independent in 1821
Climate
rainy season June to October; warmest months April and May
Transport
largest and cheapest subway system in Latin America; traffic slow – often faster to walk

4 Re-group the students, making sure there is an A, a B, and a C student in each group. Demonstrate the activity by getting a group of students to talk about their city. Encourage students to discuss the cities using comparative and superlative forms and *have/have got* where possible, e.g.
Tokyo has got the biggest population.
Mexico City is more multicultural than the other cities.

Students continue exchanging the information about their city. Remind them to use their notes, rather than read sections directly from their text. Monitor and help as necessary. Check for correct use of the present and past tenses, and for comparative and superlative forms. Note down any common errors but feed back on them at a later stage.

Listening

5 **T 10.7** [CD 2: Track 29] Tell students they are going to hear three people talking about their city, first Makiko from Tokyo, then Vimahl from Mumbai, and finally Carmen from Mexico City. Play the recording.

> **Tapescript**
> **Makiko from Tokyo**
> The first thing to say about Tokyo is that it is very safe. Women can walk everywhere anytime, day or night. Little children walk to school. You can leave something on the table in a restaurant while you go out for a minute and nobody will take it. Tokyo is also very clean, and it is very easy to travel around. All the trains and buses run on time. Personally, my favourite time of year is spring, when it's dry and the cherry blossom is out. Tokyo is a very exciting city, because there are always new things to do, new places to go, new things to eat. It changes very quickly!
>
> **Vimahl from Mumbai**
> I have two strong impressions of Mumbai. First, it is a city that is so full of activity! It is busy busy busy all day long and all night long! It's a city that doesn't sleep much. The day begins early because it is so hot. It's a noisy place. There are cars going beep beep, auto rickshaws by the thousand, fast trains rushing past, vendors shouting and trying to get you to buy their food, their drinks, their clothes. And people, people everywhere trying to get to work. The second thing to say is that the people are very, very enthusiastic. Life isn't easy in Mumbai for a lot of people, but we really work hard and we really want to do our best. Every new day brings new possibilities! The future is exciting for us!
>
> **Carmen from Mexico City**
> There are three things I like about living in Mexico City. First, the weather. It is warm and sunny most of the year. The second is the fresh fruit and vegetables – the markets are wonderful, the colours and smells are great! And the third is that I'm never bored because there is so much to see and do! We have museums, parks, restaurants, cafés ... everything!
> My favourite time of year in Mexico City is the end of December, from the 16th to the 31st. The city is full of lights, and we eat and drink and give presents. Everyone's really happy! I love it!

Project

See *Note* at the start of this section. Ask students to use their notes in exercise 3 to help them do the research and organize their notes. If appropriate, encourage them to bring some visuals to support their presentation, e.g. a map and photos. If you have access to computers, students can give their talk with the support of a presentation program.

When students give their presentation, ask them to come to the front of the class. Allow students to refer to their notes but don't let them read the information from a script. Encourage the class/groups to ask questions to the presenter.

VOCABULARY AND PRONUNCIATION (SB p80)

City and country words

1 Students work in pairs and put the words into the correct columns. They can use their dictionaries and/or they can ask you about words they don't know.

> **Answers**
>
> | City | Country | Both |
> |---|---|---|
> | hospital | wood | park |
> | port | farm | museum |
> | factory | field | school |
> | library | lake | bridge |
> | | village | car park |
> | | mountain | hill |
> | | cottage | building |
> | | river bank | |
> | | tractor | |

Go through the columns with the whole class. Ask individuals to read out what they have in their columns and see if the others agree. Be prepared for some debate about such things as *library* and *lake* which could go in the *Both* column. Correct pronunciation as you go.

2 This exercise aims to consolidate the vocabulary in exercise 1 and review superlative and comparative forms. Do this exercise quickly with the whole class. Ask students for suggestions and when you have established the correct answer and practised saying it, ask them to complete the sentences. Make sure students realize that numbers 2 and 5 require the same word, but that students should decide which one needs a capital letter.

> **Answers**
> 1 mountain   4 port
> 2 Bridge, bridge   5 Building, building
> 3 lake   6 hill

3 This exercise gives more practice on phonetic transcription, again using words that students have already seen. Always encourage your students to consult

the phonetic symbols chart on p143 when they do an exercise like this. Ask them to do it on their own and then check answers with a partner.

T 10.8 [CD 2: Track 30] Play the recording and get students to check their answers. Play the recording again and get students to listen and repeat, looking at the phonetic transcription as they do so.

> **Answers and tapescript**
> wood
> library
> farm
> village
> factory
> cottage
> field
> museum

4 This is a fun activity to give further practice with the city and country vocabulary. Demonstrate the activity by getting students to say the examples in the Student's Book chorally and individually. Encourage them to deliver the sentences rhythmically. Give a new sentence with five or six examples to demonstrate 'list' intonation, e.g.

… *and I saw a farm, some cows, a wood, a cottage,*

a field, and a lake.

Get students to divide themselves into a 'country' and a 'city' group, according to which they prefer. If you have one group with a lot more students than the other, you may have to ask some students to switch. Get each set of students to play the game. The group that can continue the longest without forgetting a word is the winner.

ADDITIONAL MATERIAL

Workbook Unit 10
Exercise 10 This is a vocabulary exercise which introduces and revises compound nouns connected with city life, such as *post office* and *railway station*.
Exercises 11 and 12 There are two writing exercises. The first introduces simple relative pronouns. The second provides a model text about London and gives guidance for students to write a similar piece about their own capital city.

EVERYDAY ENGLISH (SB p81)

Directions 2

The listening text and the pictures provide the context for the introduction of prepositions of movement.

1 **T 10.9** [CD 2: Track 31] Briefly revise *left* and *right*. Focus attention on the map and get students to find Park Road. Play the recording and tell students to mark the route to the lake with a pencil (or a finger).

Now ask them to work with a partner to fill in the gaps. Play the recording again for a final check.

> **Answers and tapescript**
> Drive **along** Park Road and turn **right**. Go **under** the bridge and **past** the school. Turn **left** up the hill, then drive **down** the hill to the river. **Turn right** after the farm and the lake is **on the right**. It takes twenty minutes.

2 Focus attention on the pictures of Norman and his wife and ask students to briefly describe the situation. Complete the first three sentences as a class, using the prepositions from the box (see Answers below). Students work in pairs to complete the rest of the text, using the information in the pictures.

T 10.10 [CD 2: Track 32] Students listen to the recording and check.

> **Answers and tapescript**
> Norman drove **out of** the garage, **along** the road, and **under** the bridge.
> Then he drove **past** the school, **up** the hill, and **down** the hill.
> Next he drove **over** the river, **through** the hedge, and **into** the lake!
>
> **T 10.10**
> Well, I drove out of the garage, along the road, and under the bridge. Then I drove past the school, up the hill, and down the hill. But then I drove over the river, and then – it was terrible – I went through the hedge, and into the lake!

3 Get students to cover the text, look at the pictures, and tell Norman's story in pairs.

As an alternative or extension to students telling the story in the third person, it can be fun to ask them to pretend to be Norman.

4 If you want to you can demonstrate the activity by giving some directions to a few places near your school and getting students to call out when they think they know the answer.

Students continue working in pairs. Go round and help and check as they do it.

Don't forget!

Word list
Remind your students of the Word list for this unit on p139. They could write in the translations, learn them at home, and/or write some of the words in their vocabulary notebook.

11

Present Continuous • *Whose?*
Clothes • Words that rhyme
In a clothes shop

Looking good!

Introduction to the unit

This is the first unit where students encounter the Present Continuous. The Present Simple was introduced and practised much earlier in *New Headway Plus Special Edition Elementary* because it is used far more frequently, but by this stage of the course students should be ready to compare and contrast the two present tenses.

The theme of this unit is describing people, and there is a lot of related vocabulary input. The unit also practises *Whose … ?* in conjunction with possessive pronouns.

Language aims

Grammar – Present Continuous In this unit, we aim to teach the Present Continuous as though the present participle were just another adjective used after the verb *to be*, for example,
She's tall, pretty, hungry ➙ *She's working, cooking, thinking*.

> **POSSIBLE PROBLEMS**
> The Present Continuous has no equivalent form in many other languages, which use the present tense to convey the two concepts of 'action which relates to all time' and 'activity happening now'.
>
> Students not only confuse the two concepts of the Present Simple and the Present Continuous, they also confuse the forms. When they have seen the *am/is/are* in the Present Continuous, they tend to try to use it in the Present Simple.
>
> The use of Present Continuous for activities happening in the near future can seem strange, so the unit also highlights and practises this use.
>
> **Common mistakes**
> **She's come from Spain.*
> **She's coming from Spain.*
> **I'm come to school by bus.*
> **What does he doing?*
> **Does he wearing a suit?*

Whose is it? It's mine.

> **POSSIBLE PROBLEMS**
> The question *Whose … ?* and possessive pronouns present few problems of concept, but learners do confuse *who's* and *whose*. Possessive pronouns simply have to be learned. They are practised in this unit in conjunction with *Whose … ?* and there is also a complete overview of subject and object pronouns, and possessive adjectives and pronouns in the *Grammar Spot* on p85.

Vocabulary There is a lot of vocabulary to do with describing people – colours, clothes, adjectives. There is also an exercise on words that rhyme and further practice of the phonetic script.

Everyday English Language used in a clothes shop is introduced and practised, as is the use of *will* to express a spontaneous decision.

Workbook There is a section on the Present Continuous, and the Present Simple and the Present Continuous are further compared and contrasted. The spelling of the present participle is practised.

Whose … ? and possessive pronouns are further practised.

In the vocabulary section, some names for parts of the body are taught. In the writing section, there is more work on linking words, and students are invited to write about someone in their family.

Notes on the unit

STARTER (SB p82)

1 Ask students to look around the classroom and try to find the items of clothing. You might need to bring in pictures of the items that might not be present in the classroom, e.g. a suit, a hat.

Focus attention on the words *trousers, jeans, shorts, shoes, trainers*, and *boots*. Ask students what they notice about these words (they are all plural in English).

Drill the pronunciation of the words and briefly revise colours. Ask students to make sentences such as *It's a white T-shirt, They're black shoes*, but avoid the Present Continuous at this stage.

2
> **NOTE**
> Exercise 2 aims to give initial practice in the Present Continuous with just one simple sentence. Do *not* go into a full presentation of the tense at this stage.

Drill the examples in the Student's Book. Get students to give two or three examples in open pairs to practise the *I* and *you* forms. Students continue in closed pairs and then get a few students to tell the whole class about themselves.

DESCRIBING PEOPLE (SB p82)

Present Continuous

1 Pre-teach/check *pretty* and *fair/dark/grey* (hair). Focus attention on the photo of Becca and on the description of her. Elicit one or two other descriptions from the whole class and then drill the sentences around the class. Students continue in pairs.

> **Sample answers**
> 1 Anna's got dark hair.
> 2 Nadia's got brown eyes.
> 3 Rudi's got short, dark hair.
> 4 Hassan is tall. George has got very short hair.
> 5 Tom is tall, and he's got short hair.
> 6 Juan isn't very tall. He's got short, dark hair.
> 7 Edna and Violet have got grey hair.
> 8 Miles has got fair hair and blue eyes. He's handsome.
> 9 Becca's got blue eyes and fair hair.

2 Pre-teach/check the verbs in the list. Use mime to demonstrate the verbs if necessary. Ask the questions for the examples in the Student's Book and get students to read the answers, *Anna's smiling* and *Tom's running*. Ask the students each of the questions in the list and get them to reply using the contracted form of the third person of the Present Continuous.

Drill the questions and answers. Students ask and answer the questions in the list in pairs.

> **Sample answers**
> 1 Lucy, Mary and Anna are smiling.
> 2 Nadia's sitting down/writing.
> 3 Rudi's sitting down/cooking.
> 4 Hassan and George are standing up. Hassan's smiling.
> 5 Tom's running.
> 6 Juan's playing.
> 7 Edna and Violet are laughing/sitting down.
> 8 Miles is writing/smiling/sitting down.
> 9 Becca's eating.

3 Say the names of two or three people in the photos and get students to describe what they are wearing. Drill the sentences and then get students to continue in pairs. Get students to continue practising the *he/she* form by talking about the other students, e.g. *Ahmad's wearing jeans and a black T-shirt*.

GRAMMAR SPOT

1 Read the notes with the whole class. Elicit other examples, by pointing to people and objects in the class, e.g. *He's tall. It's new. We're happy*, etc.

2 Read the notes with the whole class and then get students to complete the table, using contracted forms. Check the answers with the whole class.

Answers		
I	'm (am)	
You	're (are)	learning English.
He/She	's (is)	sitting in a classroom.
We	're (are)	listening to the teacher.
They	're (are)	

Name the tense and then get students to work out the negative and question forms. Get students to do this in pairs and then write up the answers on the board, or refer students to Grammar Reference 11.1 and 11.2 on p132.

Answers
Negatives

I	'm not	
You	aren't	learning English.
He/She	isn't	sitting in a classroom.
We	aren't	listening to the teacher.
They	aren't	

Questions

Am	I	
Are	you	learning English?
Is	he/she	sitting in a classroom?
Are	we	listening to the teacher?
Are	they	

3 Focus attention on the sentences. Get students to work out the difference between the two tenses. Make sure they understand that Present Simple describes things that are always true, or true for a long time, and that Present Continuous describes activities happening now and temporary activities. (Do not overload students by focusing on the use of Present Continuous for activities happening in the near future. This is covered later in the unit.)

You could put sentences on the board to discuss with the whole class, e.g.

Present Simple	**Present Continuous**
She usually wears jeans.	*She's wearing a dress today.*
He works in a bank.	*He's working in the garden today.*
They speak French.	*They're speaking English at the moment.*
I like ice-skating.	Not possible: **I'm liking ice-skating ... .*

Read Grammar Reference 11.1 and 11.2 on p132 together in class, and/or ask students to read it at home. Encourage them to ask you questions about it.

PRACTICE (SB p83)

Who is it?

1 Make sure that students are clear what *Yes/No* questions are. Demonstrate the activity by drilling the question forms chorally and individually and correcting any mistakes.

Ask a student to think of someone in the room, and ask a few *Yes/No* questions yourself. Drill these questions as much as necessary. When you feel students are ready, ask them to work in pairs. Remind them not to ask questions that are too personal!

2 This activity aims to practise the Present Continuous in a personalized way. Demonstrate the activity by giving two or three examples about yourself. Get students to work individually and write their answers.

Get students to work in pairs and exchange their answers. Monitor and check for correct use of the Present Continuous and for appropriate linking, e.g. *I'm not wearing a jacket.* If necessary, drill pronunciation before eliciting a range of answers from students.

Sample answers
2 I'm not wearing trainers, I'm wearing shoes.
3 I'm not standing up, I'm sitting down.
4 I'm not looking out of the window, I'm looking at my book.
5 It's raining.
6 The teacher isn't writing.
7 We're working hard.
8 I'm chewing gum.

Who's at the conference?

3 **T 11.1** [CD 2: Track 33] This activity aims to practise the difference between the two present tenses, first in a recognition exercise, then in a productive one. Pre-teach/check the following vocabulary items: *computer scientist*, *physics*.

Read the instructions with the whole class. Students listen and write the names next to the correct people.

Answers and tapescript
From left to right:
Ziyad Barry Jeffrey Pierre Fiona Susan

T 11.1
O = Oliver   M = Mike
O Mike, I don't know any of these people. Who are they?
M Can you see that man over there? He's sitting down. That's Jeffrey Mason. He's a Computer Scientist. He works in a research department in L.A.
O Sorry? Where?
M You know, L.A., Los Angeles.
O Oh, yes.
M And he's talking to Pierre Alain. He's wearing a blue shirt. He teacher Physics at a private university in France.
O Oh, yes, I met one of his students earlier.
M And over on the right, that's Fiona McCarthy. She's wearing a blue dress. Fiona's a professor at Central College here in London.
O What's her subject?
M Nuclear Physics, I think. She writes paper on that, I know. She's talking to Susan Camfield. Susan's drinking a cup of coffee. She's a lecturer at the same college.
O And who are those two over there? They're eating cake.

Unit 11 · Looking good! 89

M Oh, that's Ziyad Al Zimal and Barry Gardner. They work in my department. Barry's Australian but he lives in London now. Barry's the one in the green shirt, Ziyad's wearing a pink shirt. Ziyad's over here for six months.

O So, er . . . that's Jeffrey Mason, and Pierre . . . er . . . Oh, it's no good, I can't remember all these names! It's good we all have name badges!

4 Focus attention on the table and on the names of the guests in the first column. Play the recording again as far as *He works in LA* and get students to read the example in the table.

Ask students to work in pairs to complete the table. Play the recording again to check before you provide the answers.

Answers

	Present Continuous	Present Simple
Pierre	He's wearing a blue shirt.	He teaches Physics.
Fiona	She's wearing a blue dress. She's talking to Susan.	She writes papers on Nuclear Physics.
Susan	She's drinking a cup of coffee.	She works at a college.
Ziyad and Barry	They're eating cake.	They work in Mike's department.

> **SUGGESTION**
> You might want to get some further practice of the two present tenses from this exercise. You could ask questions such as the following:
> *Where is Jeffrey sitting? Where does he work?*
> *What is Pierre wearing? Where does he teach Physics?*
> *What is Fiona wearing? What does she write?*
> *What is Susan drinking? Where does she work?*
> *What are Ziyad and Barry doing? Where do they work?*
>
> You could begin by asking a few questions yourself, and then encourage students to ask and answer the other questions in open and/or closed pairs.

5 You will need to photocopy the pictures on p129 of the Teacher's Book, enough for half of the class to have picture A and the other half to have picture B. Students should be familiar with such information gap activities by now, but still be careful with instructions. Use L1 if necessary. You could set the activity up by doing one or two examples with the class first.

You may need to give students some vocabulary before the exercise, or, if the class is small enough, let them ask you for words when the need arises. (That way you won't give away clues as to what may be missing or different in the pictures beforehand!)

Answers
The eight differences in the pictures:
Picture A
Three people are cooking.
The girl with pigtails is wearing a white dress.
The boy with the cap is drinking some water.
There's a boy using a camcorder.
There's a girl wearing sunglasses.
There are two boys playing football.
There's a man sitting down reading a newspaper.
There's a boy with very short hair wearing shorts.
Picture B
Four people are cooking.
The girl with pigtails is wearing a black dress.
The boy with the cap is eating a sandwich.
There's a boy taking a photo.
There's a girl wearing glasses.
There are three boys playing football.
There's a man standing up reading a newspaper.
There's a boy with very short hair wearing trousers.

ADDITIONAL MATERIAL

Workbook Unit 11
Exercises 1–5 Present Continuous
Exercises 6–7 Present Continuous and Present Simple

A DAY IN THE PARK (SB p84)

Whose is it?

> **SUGGESTION**
> You might choose to introduce *Whose is it?* and possessive pronouns using the classroom situation and use the coursebook material for further practice and consolidation.
>
> Take some personal possessions from the students and put them on the floor where everyone can see them. Hold something up and ask *Whose is this? Is it Samir's? Is it Reza's?* The aim is to convey the concept of possession.
>
> You could use the board and write up the question *Whose is this?*, pointing out that *whose* is not the same as *who's*. Then hold up a possession of your own, and ask *Whose is this?* Teach *It's mine.* Write this on the board. Then do the same for the other possessive pronouns, *yours, his, hers, ours,* and *theirs.*

1 Focus attention on the picture. Students work in pairs and locate the items in the scene. Drill the pronunciation of the words chorally and individually.

2 If you haven't presented *Whose?* using the classroom situation, do so now using the technique in the *Suggestion* above. Do not present all the possessive pronouns, as this can be done from the book. Just focus on *Whose is this?*, making sure students understand the concept by translating into L1 if possible.

T 11.2 [CD 2: Track 34] Play the recording. Students listen to the questions and then complete the answers with *his*, *hers*, or *theirs*.

Answers
1 Whose is the baseball cap?   It's his.
2 Whose are the flowers?   They're hers.
3 Whose is the football?   It's theirs.

Drill the questions and answers from the recording. Demonstrate the singular and plural question forms, using words from the box in exercise 1, e.g. *Whose is the bike? Whose are the sunglasses?* Students ask and answer questions about the other things in exercise 1.

Answers
Whose is the bike?   It's hers.
Whose are the trainers?   They're his.
Whose is the baby?   It's theirs.
Whose are the sunglasses?   They're hers.
Whose is the radio?   It's his.
Whose is the skateboard?   It's his.
Whose is the umbrella?   It's his.
Whose are the flowers?   They're hers.

3 Get students to give you some objects that belong to them. Practise questions with *Whose?* in open pairs, making sure that the objects will generate each of the possessive pronouns in the box. Do the questions and answers as a class, with you giving models for repetition, drilling, and correction. Then ask students to continue the activity in pairs.

GRAMMAR SPOT

1 Make sure students understand the different categories in the table by putting simple sentences on the board and asking students to highlight the key word, e.g.
   We speak English. (subject pronoun)
   They are helping *us*. (object pronoun)
   Our classroom is large. (possessive adjective)
   Those books are *ours*. (possessive pronoun)

Answers

Subject	Object	Adjective	Pronoun
I	me	my	mine
You	you	**your**	**yours**
He	**him**	his	his
She	**her**	her	hers
We	use	our	**ours**
They	them	**their**	**theirs**

2 Read the notes with the whole class. Point out that there are two ways of asking the question, *whose* + noun + *is this*, or *whose* + *is this* + noun, and that possessive pronouns replace possessive adjectives + noun.

3 Highlight the difference between *Who's* = *Who is* and *Whose?* for possession. Tell students that the pronunciation is the same, but the meaning is different.

Read Grammar Reference 11.3 on p132 together in class, and/or ask students to read it at home. Encourage them to ask you questions about it.

PRACTICE (SB p85)

who's or *whose*?

1 Students work individually and choose the correct word. Get students to compare with a partner before checking the answers with the whole class.

Answers
1 your
2 Our, theirs
3 their, ours
4 My, hers
5 Who's, your
6 mine, yours
7 Whose, his
8 Who's
9 Whose, our

2 **T 11.3** [CD 2: Track 35] Read the instructions. Students shout out 1 if they think the word is *Whose ... ?* and 2 if they think it is *Who's ... ?* This is not an easy exercise, so take it slowly, and if a lot of students find it difficult, repeat each sentence as often as necessary.

Answers and tapescript
T 11.3
1 Who's on the phone? **2**
2 I'm going to the park. Who's coming? **2**
3 Wow! Look at that sports car. Whose is it? **1**
4 Whose dictionary is this? It's not mine. **1**
5 There are books all over the floor. Whose are they? **1**
6 Who's the most intelligent in our class? **2**
7 Who's got my book? **2**
8 Do you know whose jacket this is? **1**

What a mess!

> **NOTE**
> This exercise introduces the use of the Present Continuous to refer to arrangements in the near future. You might decide that this use merits a full presentation from you, but you could also decide to downplay it. Students are introduced to the *going to* future in Unit 12. The area of future forms and the concepts that they express in English is very complex, and we do not suggest that you explore it at this level.
>
> It is not such a leap for students to be told that the Present Continuous can be used to describe activities happening in the near future, even though in their own language this concept may be expressed by the equivalent of the Present Simple. You can also mention that to express an arrangement in the near future, the Present Continuous usually needs a future time reference, e.g. *I'm doing my homework (now)* versus *I'm doing my homework tonight*.

3 **T 11.4** [CD 2: Track 36] Students listen and complete the conversation. Check the answers.

> **Answers and tapescript**
> A **Whose** is this tennis racket?
> B It's **mine**.
> A What's it doing here?
> B I'm **playing** tennis this afternoon.

Read the information in the Caution Box as a class. Use L1 to translate and explain if you can.

4 **T 11.4** Play the recording of the conversation again. Get students to listen and repeat. (It can be good fun to practise the intonation of an exasperated person tidying up!)

Students work in pairs to make similar dialogues. Do the first couple as an example with the whole class.

> **Answers**
> 1 Whose are these football boots?
>   They're John's.
>   What are they doing here?
>   He's playing football later.
> 2 Whose are these notes?
>   They're Mary's.
>   What are they doing here?
>   She's writing a report this evening.
> 3 Whose is this suitcase?
>   It's mine.
>   What's it doing here?
>   I'm going on holiday tomorrow.
> 4 Whose is this coat?
>   It's Jane's.
>   What's it doing here?
>   She's going for a walk soon.
> 5 Whose is this plane ticket?
>   It's Jo's.
>   What's it doing here?
>   She's flying to Rome this afternoon.
> 6 Whose are all these plates?
>   They're ours.
>   What are they doing here?
>   We're having a picnic this afternoon.

Follow up the activity by getting students to tell the class what they are doing at the following times: *this afternoon, this evening, tomorrow, later, soon*.

Check it

5 Students work individually and correct the mistakes and then check their answers in pairs. Then check the answers with the whole class.

> **Answers**
> 1 Noor is tall and she's got long, black **hair**.
> 2 **Whose** boots are these?
> 3 I'm wearing **jeans**.
> 4 Look at Roger. He's **standing** next to Jeremy.
> 5 He **works** in a bank. He's the manager.
> 6 What's **Suzie** drinking?
> 7 **Who's** that man in the garden?
> 8 Where **are** you going this evening?
> 9 What **are you doing** after school today?

ADDITIONAL MATERIAL

Workbook Unit 11
Exercise 8 Auxiliary verbs
Exercises 9 and 10 *Whose … ?* and possessive pronouns
Exercise 11 This is an error-correction exercise based on the target language of the unit.

LISTENING AND SPEAKING (SB p86)

What a wonderful world!

1 Look out of the window and give a brief description of what you can see. If possible, include examples of the Present Continuous to describe what people are doing.

Get students to look out of the window and describe what they can see (from a different vantage spot if possible!) Encourage them to be as detailed as possible and include colours and other adjectives in their description.

> **NOTE**
> If you have a large group, you will have to choose just three or four students to do this activity. With a smaller group, you could do this as a pairwork activity, with Student A describing the scene and Student B with his/her back to the window and listening.
> If you have a classroom with no windows, you can still do this activity by getting students to imagine the scene.

2 Do the first two collocations with the whole class as an example – *shake hands* and *babies cry*. Students continue the activity in pairs. If students have access to dictionaries, encourage them to use them. If students do not find the collocations as a separate dictionary entry, encourage them to look at any example sentences for the words as these may help.

Check the answers with the whole class.

> **Answers**
> shake hands
> babies cry
> sunny day
> starry night
> blue skies
> red roses
> white clouds
> green trees
> flowers bloom
> colours of the rainbow

Students use the phrases to talk about the photos. Encourage them to do this in a meaningful way, rather than just pointing and saying the phrases, e.g. *There is a baby crying. The sun is shining and there are some white clouds in the sky.*

3 Get students to work in pairs and try to complete the lines from the poem, using the words from exercise 2 where they can.

4 **T 11.5** [CD 2: Track 37] Play the recording. Students check their answers and complete the poem with any words they couldn't guess.

> **Answers and tapescript**
> **What a wonderful world!**
> I see **trees** of green
> red **roses** too
> I see them **bloom** for me and you
> and I think to myself
> what a wonderful world.
> I see **skies** of blue
> and **clouds** of white
> the bright **sunny** day
> and the dark **starry** night
> and I think to myself
> what a wonderful world.
> The **colours** of the rainbow
> so pretty in the sky
> are also on the **faces**
> of the people going by.
> I see friends shaking **hands**
> saying 'How do you do?'
> They're really saying
> 'I **love** you.'
> I hear **babies** cry
> I watch them grow.
> They'll **learn** much more
> than you'll ever know
> and I think to myself
> what a wonderful world.
> Yes, I think to myself
> what a wonderful world.

You could point out that the way of describing the things in the poem differs from how they would be described in normal spoken English, e.g. *I see trees of green* would be *I (can) see green trees.* Similarly, *How do you do?* has the meaning of *How are you?* in the poem. Explain that poetry often uses a different form of expression, but don't go into too much detail as this may spoil the enjoyment of having listened to and understood the poem.

What do you think?

Students write of things that they think are wonderful lists and then compare in pairs. Elicit a few interesting or surprising examples in a short feedback session with the whole class.

VOCABULARY AND PRONUNCIATION (SB p88)

Words that rhyme

> **SUGGESTION**
> You could do this exercise as it is in the book, or you could put the words in their columns on the board and ask students to do the exercise in pairs or small groups. This makes a nice warmer to do at the beginning of a lesson, as the whole class is focused on the board, and students don't have their 'noses' in the book.
>
> **POSSIBLE PROBLEMS**
> Students find the different pronunciations of the spelling *ea* difficult.
> *mean* /iː/
> *near* /ɪə/
> *wear* /eə/
> The following words often cause problems, too.
> *laugh* (*gh* pronounced as /f/)
> *bought* (silent *gh*)
> *half* (silent *l*)

1 The aim of this exercise is to show students once again that English spelling is not phonetic, and so the same sound can be spelled in different ways. Most or all of the vocabulary should be known, but check comprehension before students start matching.

Students work in pairs or small groups to match the words that rhyme. Do one or two as a class as an example. Again the pronunciation in the book and on the cassette recording are based on English RP. If, as a native speaker teacher, your accent differs (and some of the pairs don't rhyme for you) then you can point this out to your students.

Students check their answers.

Answers

red	said	white	night
hat	that	near	here
missed	list	they	pay
green	mean	hair	wear
laugh	half	rose	knows
whose	shoes	ours	flowers
short	bought		

Ask students to practise the words in rhyming pairs. Do this first as a class so that you can monitor pronunciation. Correct mistakes very carefully! Then students can practise the words again in pairs.

2 Students categorize two of the words according to the vowel sound. Check first that they know the symbols. They can use the phonetic symbols chart on p143. Note that the symbols are in three groups – single sounds, long sounds, and diphthongs.

T 11.6 [CD 2: Track 38] Students listen and check.

Answers
Vowels
1 /e/ red said
2 /æ/ hat that
3 /ɪ/ missed list
4 /iː/ green mean
5 /ɑː/ laugh half
6 /uː/ whose shoes
7 /ɔː/ short bought

Diphthongs
1 /aɪ/ white night
2 /ɪə/ near here
3 /eɪ/ they pay
4 /eə/ hair wear
5 /əʊ/ rose knows
6 /aʊ/ ours flowers

3 Students work in pairs and think of more words to add to the lists. If students have access to dictionaries, they could check their suggestions as they go along. Build up a set of answers on the board.

Sample answers
Vowels
1 /e/ bread, head, when, again, ten
2 /æ/ jam, cat, sat, stamp, map
3 /ɪ/ fish, give, lived, his, it
4 /iː/ meat, feet, leave, see, be
5 /ɑː/ heart, part, start, dark, card
6 /uː/ boot, suit, you, true, blue
7 /ɔː/ ball, door, caught, floor, or

Diphthongs
1 /aɪ/ buy, light, right, shy, die
2 /ɪə/ cheer, dear, clear, real, hear
3 /eɪ/ say, way, main, game, shake
4 /eə/ where, fair, care, pear, rare
5 /əʊ/ clothes, soap, hope, no, show
6 /aʊ/ hour, shower, now, how, cow

Tongue twisters

4 **T 11.7** [CD 2: Track 39] Read the instructions with the whole class. Check comprehension of the vocabulary in the tongue twisters and then play the recording. Students listen and repeat.

Students work in pairs and say the tongue twisters to each other. Make sure students try to say them quickly, rather than read each word off the page.

5 Students learn two of the tongue twisters and say them to the rest of the class. You could introduce a little light-hearted competition and get students to vote for the 'tongue twister champion'. Allow students to 'get their own back' by asking you to say a tongue twister from their language! If you have a multilingual group, just choose one or two examples from the languages represented by the class.

EVERYDAY ENGLISH (SB p89)

In a clothes shop

> **SUGGESTION**
> The final activity in this section works best if you have some props! Try to bring in some clothes so that students can actually try them on.

1 Students look at the lines of a conversation in a clothes shop and decide who says them.

You could perhaps do this as a class so that you can sort out any unknown vocabulary. Point out that *I'm afraid* can also mean *I'm sorry*, as it does in this exercise. This is the first time that students may have come across the use of *will* for spontaneous decisions.

> **Answers**
> a SA Can I help you?
> b C Oh yes. I like that one much better. Can I try it on?
> c SA £39.99. How do you want to pay?
> d C Yes, please. I'm looking for a shirt to go with my new suit.
> e C Blue.
> f SA Yes, of course. The changing rooms are over there.
> g C OK. I'll take the white. How much is it?
> h C Can I pay by credit card?
> i SA What colour are you looking for?
> j C No, it isn't the right blue.
> k C No, it's a bit too big. Have you got a smaller size?
> l SA That's the last blue one we've got, I'm afraid. But we've got it in white.
> m SA Well, what about this one? It's a bit darker blue.
> n SA What about this one? Do you like this?
> o SA Is the size OK?
> p SA Credit card's fine. Thank you very much.

2 Students try to match some of the lines in the conversation. Get them to practise any sets of lines that work but not to recreate the whole conversation at this stage.

3 Students work in pairs and try to put all the lines of the conversation in the correct order.

T 11.8 [CD 2: Track 40] Students listen and check their order against the recording. They might find other lines that match, so do go through and check their alternatives with them after they have listened to the recording.

> **Answers and tapescript**
> SA = shop assistant C = customer
> SA Can I help you?
> C Yes, please. I'm looking for a shirt to go with my new suit.
> SA What colour are you looking for?
> C Blue.
> SA What about this one? Do you like this?
> C No, it isn't the right blue.
> SA Well, what about his one? It's a bit darker blue.
> C Oh yes. I like that one much better. Can I try it on?
> SA Yes, of course. The changing rooms are over there.
> (*pause*)
> Is the size OK?
> C No, it's a bit too big. Have you got a smaller size?
> SA That's the last blue one we've got, I'm afraid. But we've got it in white.
> C OK. I'll take the white. How much is it?
> SA £39.99. How do you want to pay?
> C Can I pay by credit card?
> SA Credit card's fine. Thank you very much.

4 Students practise the conversation with a partner and then make similar improvised conversations. Use the props! Some interesting dialogues might ensue!

Don't forget!

Workbook Unit 11
Exercise 12 Vocabulary of parts of the body
Exercises 13 and 14 There is a writing exercise on linking words and students are invited to write about a member of their family.

Word list
Remind your students of the Word list for this unit on p140. They could write in the translations, learn them at home, and/or write some of the words in their vocabulary notebook.

12

going to future
Infinitive of purpose
The weather • Making suggestions

Life's an adventure!

Introduction to the unit

The theme of this unit is planning the future. We focus on the *going to* future for plans and intentions. We do not at the same time introduce and contrast the Future Simple with *will* (this rather complex distinction is for a later stage of learning), but in the *Everyday English* section we do focus on *shall* for suggestions and revise *will* for immediate decisions. The second presentation in the unit is the infinitive of purpose, which is relatively simple to operate in English but is often realized differently in other languages. The skills work includes a jigsaw reading about dangerous sports – sky-diving and motor racing. This highlights the theme of adventure and provides opportunities to revise the grammar not only of this unit but also of previous units (Past Simple and comparatives/superlatives).

Language aims

Grammar – *going to* The learning of the *going to* future is facilitated by the fact that students already know the present forms of the verb *to be*, both on its own and as part of the Present Continuous, which they met in the previous unit, Unit 11. These are, of course, intrinsic parts of this structure. Also, as this is the first future they have encountered (apart from the Present Continuous with future meaning touched on briefly in Unit 11), the problem of when to use it in relation to other future forms (always an area of difficulty for students) is deferred for the time being, and they can simply concentrate on this one. The two uses of *going to* are introduced in the unit: plans and intentions, such as *I'm going to be a photographer*, and making predictions based on present evidence, such as *It's going to rain./He's going to fall*.

> **POSSIBLE PROBLEMS**
>
> 1 With the verbs *go* and *come* we often avoid using the full *going to* future form, and just use the Present Continuous.
>   *She's going to go to Cairo next week.* → *She's going to Cairo next week.*
>
> 2 The Present Continuous can be used for future arrangements and is often interchangeable with the *going to* future.
>   *I'm going to see the doctor tomorrow./I'm seeing the doctor tomorrow.*

The infinitive of purpose The infinitive of purpose answers the question *why* in place of *because I wanted to*, e.g. *Why did you go to the shops? Because I wanted to buy a newspaper./To buy a newspaper.*

There is often a problem for learners when they attempt to translate this item from their own language and insert *for* which is wrong in English.

Common mistakes
*I went to the shops for to buy a newspaper.
*I went to the shops for buy a newspaper.
*I went to the shops for buying a newspaper.

Vocabulary Vocabulary to do with weather is introduced, such as *It's sunny/windy/rainy*. The question for description *What … like?* is presented and practised in dialogues, but only in connection with weather: *What's the weather like?*

Everyday English Two of the most common functional exponents for asking for and making suggestions are introduced:
What shall we do?

Workbook There are exercises to consolidate the uses of *going to* and the infinitive of purpose. All of the auxiliary verbs covered so far – *am/is/are* and *do/does/did* – are brought together and practised.

The vocabulary section focuses on word stress and phonetic transcription of a range of words students are already familiar with.

There is also an exercise on the prepositions *from, like, than*.

The writing syllabus continues with work on writing postcards, and provides an opportunity to bring together *going to* with other tenses.

Notes on the unit

STARTER (SB p90)

1 Focus attention on *I'm going to Malta* and *I went to Malta*. Establish the overall time reference by asking *past, present, or future?* about each sentence. Students should recognize *went* as the past of *go* but make sure that they realize *going to* refers to the future. (Do not go into a full presentation of the tense at this stage.)

Pre-teach/check the meaning of *retire*. Students work in pairs and make sentences using the time references in the second box. Check the answers with the whole class.

> **Answers**
> I'm going to Malta soon/next month/in a year's time/when I retire.
> I went to Malta when I was a student/two years ago.

2 Demonstrate the activity by giving similar sentences about yourself, e.g. *I'm going to (London) soon. I went to (South America) when I was a student*, etc. Drill the sentences in the Student's Book and then get students to continue the activity in pairs.

Elicit any interesting or surprising examples in a short feedback session with the whole class.

FUTURE PLANS (SB p90)

going to

1 The context for the presentation of *going to* is future plans not only of a young girl but also of an older woman who is about to retire.

Ask your students to look at the photographs of Jack and his sports teacher Danny Carrick. Elicit a few suggestions about what their future plans might be.

Pre-teach/check the meaning of *grow up* and *retire*.

> **POSSIBLE PROBLEM**
> The *when* clauses with *grow up* and *retire* require the Present Simple. Sometimes students find it strange that the Present Simple is used to talk about future events; they might want to say *When I will grow up …* . However, try not to go into this at this stage.

Make it clear that students are going to read about Jack's and Danny Carrick's future plans, therefore what they are looking at is a future tense. Put students into pairs to discuss the sentences and put J or D according to who they think is speaking. Tell them that sometimes Jack and Danny both have the same plan, so they must write J and D next to the sentence.

T 12.1 [CD 2: Track 41] Play the recording of both Jack and Danny right through, asking students to listen carefully and check if they are right. At the end ask *Were all your answers right? Were there any surprises?*

> **Answers and tapescript**
> J   1 I'm going to be a footballer.
> J, D 2 I'm going to travel all over the world.
> J, D 3 I'm going to train very hard.
> D   4 I'm going to try new things.
> J   5 I'm going to play for Manchester United.
> J   6 I'm not going to marry until I'm very old.
> D   7 I'm not going to stay at home and watch TV.
> D   8 I'm going to lean to scuba-dive.
> D   9 I'm going to write a book.
> J   10 I'm going to be famous.
>
> **T 12.1**
> **Jack (aged 11)**
> When I grow up I'm going to be a footballer – a really good one. I'm in the school team and I play three times a week. But I'm going to train very hard, every day, so I can be really, really good. First I'm going to play for Manchester United, then Inter Milan, and then Real Madrid. Those are my favourite teams. I'm going to travel all over the world and I'm going to be famous. I'm not going to marry until I'm very old – about 25. Then I want to have two sons. I'm going to play football until I'm 35 – that's a very long time. And I'm going to teach my sons to play. I want them to be famous footballers, too!
>
> **Danny Carrick (aged 58)**
> When I retire next year … I'm going to retire early … I'm not going to stay at home and watch TV. I'm going to try lots of new things. First I want to go mountain-climbing. In fact, I want to climb Mount Everest, so I'm going to train very hard for that. I'm going to learn to scuba-dive, too, because I want to go scuba-diving in Australia. There are so many things I want to do! I'm going to travel all over the world, then I'm going to write a book about my adventures. I want to call it 'Life begins at 60!' In my book, I'm going to tell other retired people to try new things, too. You are only as old as you feel!

2 This exercise moves from first person to third person, still practising positive and negative sentences only. First ask individuals to give you some of Jack's and Danny's plans. Focus on the pronunciation of *going to*: /ˈɡəʊɪŋtə/ or /ˈɡəʊɪŋtʊ/. Practise it in isolation first, and then as part of a full sentence, drilling the examples in the book.

Now put your students into pairs, one to tell the other about Jack's plans, and the other about Danny's focusing on the plans they have in common, using *They're both going to …* . Monitor as they do this, checking for correct use and pronunciation of *going to*.

> **Answers**
>
> **Jack**
> Jack's going to be a footballer.
> Jack's going to play for Manchester United.
> Jack's isn't going to marry until he's very old.
> Jack's going to be famous.
>
> **Danny Carrick**
> Danny's going to try new things.
> Danny isn't going to stay at home and watch TV.
> Danny's going to learn to scuba-dive.
> Danny's going to write a book.
>
> **The two plans that are the same**
> They're both going to travel all over the world.
> They're both going to train very hard.

3 **T 12.2** [CD 2: Track 42] Now we focus on the formation and pronunciation of the question, which should not cause your students too much difficulty because they are already familiar with the Present Continuous.

Play the recording and ask students to repeat the questions and answers. Encourage them to use falling intonation for *wh-* questions.

> **GRAMMAR SPOT**
>
> Highlight that the form of *going to* builds on what students already know by getting the class to chorus first the positive and then the negative forms of the verb *to be*. (Conjugating verbs may be deemed 'old-fashioned' in these communicative days, but it is an effective way of consolidating grammatical forms!)
>
> 1 Read the notes with the whole class and then get students to complete the table using contracted forms. Check the answers with the whole class.
>
> **Answers**
>
> | I | 'm | |
> |---|----|--|
> | You | 're | |
> | He/She | 's | going to leave tomorrow. |
> | We | 're | |
> | They | 're | |
>
> Get students to work out the question and negative forms in pairs, and then write the answers on the board or refer students to the Grammar Reference on p133.

> **Answers**
>
> **Negatives**
>
> | I | 'm not | |
> |---|--------|--|
> | You | aren't | |
> | He/She | isn't | going to leave tomorrow. |
> | We | aren't | |
> | They | aren't | |
>
> **Questions**
>
> | Am | I | |
> |----|---|--|
> | Are | you | |
> | Is | he/she | going to leave tomorrow? |
> | Are | we | |
> | Are | they | |

This may be a good opportunity to draw students' attention again to the two realizations of the negative of *to be*. Remind them that this is possible in all persons except the first person singular.

2 Focus attention on the uses of the Present Continuous for future and *going to*. Establish that there is little difference between the two sentences.

Read Grammar Reference 12.1 on p133 together in class, and/or ask students to read it at home. Encourage them to ask you questions about it.

PRACTICE (SB p91)

Questions about Jack

1 Students work in pairs to form the questions about Jack and then match the answers.

> **Answers and tapescript**
>
> 1 e Why is he going to train very hard? Because he wants to be a footballer.
> 2 a How long is he going to play football? Until he's 35.
> 3 d When is he going to marry? Not until he's very old – about 25!
> 4 b How many children is he going to have? Two.
> 5 c Who is he going to teach to play football? His sons.

2 **T 12.3** [CD 2: Track 43] Play the recording and get students to check their answers. Then ask them to practise saying the questions and answers in pairs. Go round and help and check as they do this. If students have problems with the falling intonation of the *wh-* questions, get them to listen and repeat the questions from the recording and then continue asking and answering in pairs.

Questions about you

3 Now we move away from Jack and Danny Carrick and get students to talk about themselves. Drill the example in the Student's Book individually and chorally. Get one or two students to demonstrate question 2 in open pairs. Then get students to work in closed pairs, asking and answering the rest of the questions. Go round and monitor as they do this, checking for correct use and pronunciation of the *Yes/No* questions.

4 Ask students to tell the class about themselves and their partner, thereby practising third person singular and first person singular and plural.

I'm going to sneeze!

Here we introduce the second use of *going to*, when we can see now that something is sure to happen in the future. Read the Caution Box with the whole class. If possible and necessary, use L1 to explain.

5 Ask students to look at the pictures and write a sentence for each picture using *going to* with *it, you, I*, etc. If students have access to dictionaries, get them to look up new words, or they can ask you. Students can work in pairs so that they can help each other with vocabulary.

Check through the answers with the class as a whole. Ask individuals to read a sentence aloud.

> **Answers**
> 1 It's **going to rain**.
> 2 I'm **going to sneeze**.
> 3 He's **going to win the race**.
> 4 He's **going to jump**.
> 5 You're **going to be late**.
> 6 It's **going to turn left**.
> 7 They're **going to buy a new house**.
> 8 He's **going to fall**.

6 Students work on their own or in pairs to fill the gaps, using sentences from exercise 5.

T 12.4 [CD 2: Track 44] Play the recording and get students to check their answers. There are some useful little expressions included in the sentences: *Look at the time! Oh dear! Bless you!* Illustrate the meaning of these when you go through the exercise and get the class to repeat them. It can also be interesting and fun to discuss what is said in the students' own language(s) when someone sneezes.

They can then practise saying the sentences with a partner and have fun practising the stress and intonation in the expressions.

> **Answers and tapescript**
> 1 Take an umbrella. **It's going to rain.**
> 2 Look at the time! **You're going to be late** for the meeting.
> 3 Rob's running very fast. **He's going to win the race.**
> 4 Look! Jack's on the wall. **He's going to fall.**
> 5 Look at that man! **He's going to jump.**
> 6 **They're going to buy a new house.** They want to live in the country.
> 7 Follow that car! **It's going to turn left.**
> 8 'Oh dear. **I'm going to sneeze.** Aaattishooo!'
> 'Bless you!'

ADDITIONAL MATERIAL

Workbook Unit 12
Exercises 1–5 These consolidate and practise all aspects of the *going to* future.

I WANT TO SEE THE WORLD (SB p92)

Infinitive of purpose

1 The aim of this activity is to set the scene and check the vocabulary needed for the presentation dialogue in exercise 2.

First ask your students to look at the photos and ask them which places they recognize. The photos will also help to check some of the vocabulary needed for the matching exercise. Briefly check the pronunciation of the names of the places, focusing on *Nepal* /nɪˈpɔːl/, *Hawaii* /həˈwaɪjiː/, and *China* /ˈtʃaɪnə/ in particular.

Students work in pairs to match a place with a photo, and then with an activity. Then check quickly through the exercise with the whole class. Point out the silent letters in *climb* /klaɪm/ and *whale* /weɪl/ and check students' pronunciation.

> **Answers**
> Nepal – climb Mount Everest (photo h)
> Brazil – visit the rainforest (photo d)
> The Great Barrier Reef – go scuba-diving (photo f)
> China – walk along the Great Wall (photo c)
> Hawaii – go surfing (photo g)
> Alaska – watch whales (photo b)
> the USA – fly over the Grand Canyon (photo a)
> Kenya – take photographs of the lions (photo e)

2 In this activity, students meet Danny again. Ask students what they remember about him (he's going to retire soon and he's going to travel around the world). He is now planning all the places he is going to visit on his travels.

> **SUGGESTION**
> Danny's dialogue with his friend, Harold, incorporates revision of *going to* but some additional information is introduced: the fact that with the verb *go* we do not usually say *going to go*, but simply use the Present Continuous. The notes in the *Grammar Spot* spell this out in more detail. You could read this with your students either after they first read the dialogue, or after they have listened to check the answer.

Go through the dialogue with the whole class. Ask one student to read Danny's lines and another Harold's. See if they can complete Danny's final line.

T 12.5 [CD 2: Track 45] Play the recording for your students, not only to check the line, but also to familiarize them with the stress and intonation patterns in the dialogue. Students practice the conversation in pairs.

> **Answers and tapescript**
> D = Danny, H = Harold
> **D** First I'm going to Nepal.
> **H** Why?
> **D** To climb Mount Everest!
> **H** Oh my goodness! What are you going to do after that?
> **D** Well, then I'm going to Kenya to **take photographs of the lions**.

3 Ask students if they would like to try any of the activities and/or elicit any other adventures students would like to go on.

> **GRAMMAR SPOT**
> 1 Read through the notes with the class (if you have not done so earlier) and point out the use of *going/ coming* rather than *going to go/going to come*.
> 2 Focus attention on the sentences and get students to decide if they mean the same.
>
> > **Answer**
> > Yes, the sentences do mean the same.
>
> Explain, in L1 if possible, that the infinitive can be used in answer to a *Why ... ?* question and focus on the example in the Student's Book.
>
> Read Grammar Reference 12.2 on p133 together in class, and/or ask students to read it at home. Encourage them to ask you questions about it.

PRACTICE (SB p93)

Roleplay

1 This is a controlled practice roleplay, where students work in pairs and take the roles of Danny and Harold, and ask and answer questions about the places on p92. Do the example in the book in open pairs across the class to illustrate the activity. Encourage students to sound surprised when delivering the line *Oh my goodness!* Then put your students into closed pairs to complete the activity.

2 This is an extension of the previous activity, so you could move on to the next activity if you are short of time.

Put students into groups of four so that the activity can be completed quite quickly. Ask them to take turns to tell part of Danny's planned journey. Remind them to use the adverbs *first, then, next, after that, finally*.

> **Sample answer**
> **Student 1**: First he's going to Nepal to climb Mount Everest. Then he's going to Brazil to visit the rainforest.
> **Student 2**: Next he's going to The Great Barrier Reef to go scuba-diving, then to China to walk along the Great Wall, and after that to Hawaii to go surfing.
> **Student 3**: After that he's going to Alaska to watch whales, and then to the USA to fly over the Grand Canyon.
> **Student 4**: Finally, he's going to Kenya to take photographs of the lions.

Why ...? and When ...?

3 This activity personalizes the infinitive of purpose. It also moves away from practising the structure with *going to*, and revises the Past Simple. Encourage students to follow the highlighted stress patterns in the examples. Model the pattern for them if necessary.

You could introduce the activity by just going through the examples in the Student's Book, but it is much more interesting if you say some names of places you visited in the past and then get students to ask you why you went there and when, for example:

Teacher *I went to Milan.*
Student(s) *Why did you go to Milan?*
Teacher *To visit a friend and to practise my Italian.*
Student(s) *When did you go?*
Teacher *Eighteen months ago.*

Ask students to write down the names of some places they visited in the past – countries, cities, villages, or any places of interest. Then put them into pairs to ask each other questions about the places. Let this go on for as long as students are interested if you have time.

Round the activity off by asking one or two individuals to give feedback to the class about their partner.

4   This activity follows the same procedure as exercise 3, but focuses on the future. Remind students of the expressions of future time that they can use, e.g. *soon, next week/month/year, in a few weeks' time*, etc. Again, you can use the examples in the Student's Book or give examples about places you are going to visit.

    Students work in pairs and ask each other questions about the places. Ask one or two individuals to give feedback to the class about their partner.

Check it

5   This exercise brings together the key structures from this unit. Ask your students to do it on their own as quickly as possible, then check their answers with a partner before you conduct feedback with the whole class.

> **Answers**
> 1 It's going to rain.
> 2 Are you going to wash your hair this evening?
> 3 She's going to have lunch.
> 4 I'm going to the post office to buy some stamps.
> 5 I'm going home early this evening.
> 6 I opened the window to get some fresh air.

ADDITIONAL MATERIAL

Workbook Unit 12
Exercises 6 and 7 These consolidate and practise the infinitive of purpose.

READING AND SPEAKING (SB p94)

Living dangerously

1   This activity pre-teaches some of the collocations that appear in the texts. Get students to work in pairs and match the verbs with the nouns or phrases. Check the answers with the whole class.

> **Answers**
> have an accident   feel sick   get top marks
> win a race   float in water

2   This activity is to set the scene for the reading task and hopefully motivate students to read about the dangerous sports.

    First, ask your students to work on their own and number the list according to which sports they think are the most dangerous. Make it clear that *1* is the *most* dangerous. Obviously, there are no right or wrong answers to this.

    Students compare their ideas with a partner. Encourage them to give reasons for their choices.

    Get students to compare their ideas with the whole class. Again, encourage them to justify their answers (with luck some free speaking might result if there is disagreement across the group!). Finally, establish with everyone where *motor racing* and *sky-diving* came on their lists.

3   Establish who does which sport (Clem = sky-diving and Sue = motor racing). Ask students which sport they would most like to try and why. Ask if anyone does either of these sports and to briefly describe their reasons and/or any experiences they had doing the sport.

    Then divide the class into two groups. Tell Group A to read about Clem and Group B to read about Sue. Students should read and answer the questions about their person. Each group has the same questions to work on. If they have access to dictionaries, allow students to check new words. Otherwise, they can ask you for help or ask other students in their group.

    Students check their answers with others from the same group. Then check the answers with Group A students and Group B students separately.

> **Answers**
> **Clem Quinn**
> 1 He tried to fly by jumping off the garden shed.
> 2 He worked as a taxi driver.
> 3 He did a parachute jump and loved it.
> 4 Because the world looks so good – you can see blue sky, green fields, and white clouds. You float through the air and it's like floating in water. The views are fantastic. You can forget all your worries.
> 5 No, he says it's safer than football.
> 6 Yes, he's a full-time teacher of sky-diving.
> 7 He's going to do a sky-dive with 100 people from six planes.
> 8 Never.
> 9 5 – Clem's age when he jumped off the garden shed
>   6 – the number of planes he's going to use for his record dive
>   20 – the number of years ago that he did his first jump
>   100 – the number of people who are going to do the record dive with Clem
>
> **Sue Glass**
> 1 She had a car accident so she didn't like driving.
> 2 She worked in a car company.
> 3 She met Julian Swayland. He drove her around Brands Hatch racing circuit and she loved it.
> 4 Because she loves the excitement of motor racing.
> 5 Yes, and she says she's always very frightened. She felt sick before a race because she was so nervous.
> 6 No, but she's going to teach other people to drive.
> 7 She's going to open a driving school next year.
> 8 She stopped a year ago.

9 5 – the number of men on the motor racing course with Sue
   6 – the number of years ago that she met Julian Swayland
   20 – the number of competitors in her first championship race
   100 – the speed she drove around corners at the racing circuit

4 Tell each student to find a partner from the other group and to compare Clem and Sue, using their answers from exercise 3. Encourage them to exchange information in a meaningful way, rather than just read their answers, e.g.
   A Clem tried to fly by jumping off the garden shed. What about Sue?
   B She had a car accident so she didn't like driving. What job did Clem do?
   A He was a taxi driver. And Sue?
   B She worked in a car company.

Interviews

1 Put students back into the A and B groups they were in for the reading task. Ask the As to get together in small groups to prepare the questions they are going to ask about Sue, and the Bs to get together in small groups to prepare the questions they are going to ask about Clem. Make sure students understand they have to use a range of tenses in the questions.

Check the answers with Group A and B students separately.

Answers
Group A
1 Why didn't you like driving?
2 Why did Julian Swayland take you to Brands Hatch?
3 Why did you do well on the motor racing course?
4 Why did you stop motor racing?
5 What are you going to do next year?

Group B
1 What did you do when you were five?
2 When did you do your first parachute jump?
3 Why did you move to the country?
4 Why do you love sky-diving?
5 What are you going to do next July?

2 Students work with a partner from the other group and ask each other the questions. Make sure they work with a different partner from the reading stage. Monitor and help where necessary.

Finally, ask a couple of pairs to act out their interview to the whole class. It would be a great idea to tape some of the roleplays if possible and play them back to the whole class for them to comment on and correct. Students often find this very productive and satisfying.

VOCABULARY AND SPEAKING (SB p96)

The weather

1 Ask your students to look at the weather symbols. Elicit words for symbols students already know and then get them to continue working in pairs to match the remaining symbols and words. If students have access to dictionaries, get them to look up words they don't know.

Go through the answers with the class.

Answers
1 foggy 2 snowy 3 windy 4 rainy 5 sunny 6 cloudy

The next part of this exercise is to practise which pairs of adjectives commonly go together to describe weather. This will vary in different countries according to the climate, for example it can be warm and windy in many climates but is only rarely so in Britain.

Ask your class to give you their ideas about British weather. (Everyone always has something to say about British weather!)

CULTURAL NOTES
1 Despite London's reputation, the last big fog/smog (smoke + fog) was in 1957 when the Clean Air Act was passed!
2 There are lots of jokes about British weather. Can your students understand this one?
   If you don't like English weather, wait ten minutes!

You could have a mini-discussion comparing which pairs they think will often go together in Britain and which for the climate of their own country.

Sample answers (for Britain)
cool and cloudy	cold and windy
cool and rainy	warm and sunny
cool and windy	hot and sunny
cold and cloudy	cold and foggy
dry and cloudy	cold and rainy
wet and windy	cold and snowy

Also you often hear the pairs *warm and dry, cold and wet* together.

2 **T 12.6** [CD 2: Track 46] Get students to look out of the window at the weather conditions. Either play the recording or model the questions yourself.

102 Unit 12 · Life's an adventure!

POSSIBLE PROBLEM

What … like? for descriptions always creates some difficulty because of the different use of *like*. You need to make two things very clear to your students:

1 It has nothing to do with the verb *like*. The *Caution Box* will help you do this.
2 The answer does not contain the word *like*.
   What's the weather like? It's sunny.
   NOT *It's like sunny.*

Ask your students to listen and write in the weather for today, yesterday, and tomorrow. Check their answers.

Answers and tapescript
A What's the weather like today?
B It's **snowy** and it's very **cold**.
A What was it like yesterday?
B Oh, it was **cold** and **cloudy**.
A What's it going to be like tomorrow?
B I think it's going to be **warmer**.

Read through the *Caution Box* with the students (see *Possible problem* above).

Practise the questions and answers about where you are in open pairs. Drill the pronunciation as necessary, encouraging falling intonation in the *wh-* questions.

3 This is an information-gap activity. Ask your students to work in pairs. Tell Student A to look at the World Weather information on p96 of the Student's Book and give Student B the information you have copied from p130 of the Teacher's Book.

Briefly check the pronunciation of the cities, focusing in particular on *Edinburgh* /ˈedɪnbrə/ and *Los Angeles* /lɒsˈændʒəlɪz/. Illustrate the activity by doing the first question and answer about Athens across the class. This is a good time to feed in the modifier *quite*, if you feel your students can cope with it. (Make sure they realize that this is yesterday's weather and therefore they need to use *was* in the questions and answers.)

Get students to continue the activity in closed pairs. Monitor and check as they do it.

Check the answers with the whole class. Get students to read out their answers as complete sentences, e.g. *It was sunny and (quite) warm in Athens yesterday. 18 degrees.*

Answers
World weather: noon yesterday

		°C	It was:
Athens	S	18	sunny and warm
Berlin	R	7	wet/rainy and cold
Bombay	R	31	wet/rainy and hot
Edinburgh	C	5	cloudy and cold
Geneva	C	12	cloudy and cool
Hong Kong	S	29	sunny and hot
Lisbon	C	19	cloudy and warm
London	R	10	wet/rainy and cool
Los Angeles	Fg	21	foggy and warm
Luxor	S	40	sunny and very hot
Milan	Fg	19	foggy and warm
Moscow	Sn	–1	snowy and very cold
Oslo	Sn	2	snowy and cold

S = sunny **C = cloudy** **Fg = foggy**
R = rainy **Sn = snowy**

4 Get students to answer the questions about the weather report in pairs before checking with the whole class.

Answers
Luxor was the hottest. (Ask your students if they know where this is. It's in Egypt.)
Moscow was the coldest.
The month is in fact March. (Encourage a bit of discussion about this – it could be other months, but clearly, in Europe anyway, the season is either winter or early spring.)

ADDITIONAL MATERIAL

Workbook
Exercise 13 Writing postcards fits nicely after this vocabulary as it includes information about the weather. It could be done in class or for homework.

EVERYDAY ENGLISH (SB p97)

Making suggestions

> **NOTES**
> In order not to overload students, we have restricted the exponents in this section to: *shall* to ask for suggestions and make suggestions, and *Let's* to make a suggestion for everyone.
> We also revise *will* for spontaneous decisions, which was introduced in the previous unit.

1 Focus attention on the two examples and then elicit a few more activities for good weather (*go for a walk, play tennis, do gardening*, etc.) and some for bad weather (*read a book, do a jigsaw, play chess*, etc.) Students continue the two lists on their own and then compare their lists with a partner. Ask for some feedback from the whole class and tell students that they will need their lists later.

2 **T 12.7** [CD 2: Track 47] Tell students that they are going to hear the beginnings of two conversations, one for good weather and one for bad. Ask them to read and listen at the same time and complete the suggestions.

> **Answers and tapescript**
> 1 A It's a lovely day! What shall we do?
>   B Let's **play tennis**!
> 2 A It's raining again! What shall we do?
>   B Let's **stay at home** and **watch TV**.

Then get students to listen and repeat in chorus. First focus on the question, and then practise the answer. Encourage good stress and intonation.

What shall we *do*?   /wɒt ʃəl wi duː/
*Let's play ten*nis.   /lets pleɪ tenɪs/

Ask students to practise the conversations in pairs.

Read through the *Caution Box* with the whole class. In a monolingual class, you could ask students to translate the sentences.

3 Ask your students to work in pairs. Ask them first to find the 'good weather' lines and then the 'bad weather' lines. Then ask them to put each set in order to complete the conversations from exercise 2, marking 1 or 2 in the first column to show which conversation the lines come from.

T 12.8 [CD 2: Track 48] Play the recording and get students to listen and check their answers.

> **Answers and tapescript**
> 1b Well, let's go swimming.
> 2c OK. Which exhibition do you want to see?
> 1a Oh no! It's too hot to play tennis.
> 2a Oh no! We watched TV last night.
> 1c OK. I'll get my swimming costume.
> 2b Well, let's go to a museum.
>
> **T 12.8**
> 1 A It's a lovely day! What shall we do?
>   B Let's play tennis!
>   A Oh no! It's too hot to play tennis.
>   B Well, let's go swimming.
>   A OK. I'll get my swimming costume.
> 2 A It's raining again! What shall we do?
>   B Let's stay at home and watch TV.
>   A Oh no! We watched TV last night.
>   B Well, let's go to a museum.
>   A OK. Which exhibition do you want to see?

4 Students continue to work in pairs. Ask them to look at the lists they made in exercise 1. Demonstrate the activity by asking for examples of a good weather and a bad weather activity and building the dialogues with the whole class. Get students to continue in pairs, using the activities in their lists. Monitor and check.

To round off the activity, you could either ask a couple of pairs to do their dialogues for the whole class, or record a few dialogues and play them for the class to correct any mistakes in the language and the pronunciation.

Don't forget!

Workbook Unit 12
Exercises 8 and 9 These bring together all the auxiliary verbs covered so far.
Exercises 10 and 11 These revise many items of vocabulary covered so far. They focus on word stress and phonetic transcription.
Exercise 12 Prepositions *from*, *like*, and *than*.
Word list
Remind your students of the Word list for this unit on p140. They could write in the translations, learn them at home, and/or write some of the words in their vocabulary notebook.

13

Question forms • Adverbs and adjectives
Describing feelings • Catching a train

How terribly clever!

Introduction to the unit

Question forms are the main target language of this unit. This is not a particularly new language area, as question forms have been introduced and practised throughout the book, but focusing on question forms allows a lot of language areas, especially tenses, to be pulled together and revised.

The theme of the unit is general knowledge, and reading stories. In the reading and listening section, students read the story of the businessman and the fisherman. If you haven't already encouraged your students to read outside the coursebook, now is the time to start! Reading is one of the easiest, cheapest, and most pleasurable ways of learning a foreign language and there is a big range of simplified stories available in series of readers such as the *Oxford Bookworms*.

Language aims

Grammar – question forms All the *wh-* questions (*when, where, who, what, why, which*) except *whose*, and questions with *how* + adjective (e.g. *How old ... ?*) and *how* + adverb (e.g. *How far ... ?*) are revised. *What* + noun (*What languages ... ?/What sort of ... ?*) is also practised.

We 'drop in' some subject questions, *Who won ... ?, Who wrote ... ?* and *Who started ... ?* in the quiz in the first presentation. The first of these is 'dropped in' in case students want to make such a question in exercise 3, where they are asked to think up some general knowledge questions of their own. We suggest that you do not embark on a detailed presentation of the difference between subject and object question forms. If students wonder (very sensibly) why *do/does/did* is not used in these questions, try to satisfy them with a quick explanation.

Adverbs and adjectives There are exercises to highlight the difference between adjectives and adverbs, and regular and irregular adverbs are presented and practised.

Vocabulary The vocabulary section focuses on describing feelings and highlights adjectives with both *-ed* and *-ing* endings. Students often find these confusing and so choose the wrong form.
Common mistakes
**I'm interesting in sport.*
**I was very boring.* (when the student meant to say *I was very bored*!)
**The problem is very worried.*

Everyday English The language used when catching a train is practised.

Workbook Question words are further consolidated and the question *Which one ... ?* is introduced and practised.
There is further practice on adverbs and adjectives.
Noun and adjective suffixes are introduced, and *-ed* and *-ing* adjectives (*interested/interesting*) are further practised.
In the writing section, adjectives and adverbs are further practised, and students are invited to write a story.

Notes on the unit

STARTER (SB p98)

This activity provides a quick review of the question words students have already met, without making them form complete questions. It also acts as a preview to the focus on stories later in the unit.

1 Demonstrate the activity with the whole class by asking students to match *When ... ?* and *Where ... ?* with the appropriate answer (*When ... ? – Last week, Where ... ? – The hospital*). Students work in pairs and continue the activity.

Check the answers with the whole class.

> **Answers**
> When ... ? – Last week.   Which ... ? – The red ones.
> Where ... ? – The hospital.   How ... ? – By bus.
> What ... ? – Some roses.   How much ... ? – £25.
> Who ... ? – My aunt.   How many ... ? – Six.
> Why ... ? – Because she was ill.

2 Students look at the answers again and say what the story is. You could encourage students to make up a short story.

Sample story: *Last week John went to the hospital by bus because his aunt was ill. He bought her six red roses. The roses cost £25.*

A QUIZ (SB p98)

Question words

1 Students work in groups to answer the general knowledge quiz. Encourage discussion if/when students disagree about the answers. Elicit a range of answers to the quiz questions but do not confirm or reject students' ideas at this stage.

2 **T 13.1** [CD 2: Track 49] Students listen and check their answers.

> **Answers and tapescript**
> 1 When did the first man walk on the moon?
>   In 1969.
> 2 Where is Mount Everest?
>   In the Himalayas.
> 3 Who started A1 Grand Prix motor racing?
>   Sheikh Maktoum.
> 4 Who won the World Cup in 2010?
>   Spain.
> 5 How many bones are there in the human body?
>   206.
> 6 How much does an African elephant weigh?
>   5–7 tonnes.
> 7 How much of the earth's surface is desert?
>   30%.
> 8 What sort of literature did Al-Mutanabbi write?
>   Poems.
> 9 What languages do Swiss people speak?
>   German, French, Italian, and Romansch.
> 10 What did Marconi invent in 1901?
>   The radio.
> 11 Who wrote the world's first computer program?
>   Ada Lovelace.
> 12 Which city is on two continents?
>   Istanbul.
> 13 Who was Ibn Battuta?
>   A traveller.
> 14 Why do birds migrate?
>   Because the winter is cold.
> 15 Which was the first country to have TV?
>   Britain.
> 16 Which language has the most words?
>   English.

Play some of the questions again and ask students to focus on the intonation of the questions. Ask them whether the voice rises or falls at the end (the voices falls because these are all questions with a question word). If necessary, highlight this on the board by writing up the first two questions and adding the stress marks and intonation arrows:

When did the first man walk on the moon?

Where is Mount Everest?

Drill the questions chorally and individually.

> ### GRAMMAR SPOT
>
> 1 Ask students to underline the question words in the quiz. Remind them that some question words consist of two words. Check the answers.
>
> > **Answers**
> > 1 When ... ?   9 What ... ?
> > 2 Where ... ?   10 What ... ?
> > 3 Who ... ?   11 Who ... ?
> > 4 Who ... ?   12 Which ... ?
> > 5 How many ... ?   13 Who ... ?
> > 6 How much ... ?   14 Why ... ?
> > 7 How much ... ?   15 Which ... ?
> > 8 What ... ?   16 Which ... ?

2 This exercise extends the focus on question formation to include *Yes/No* questions. Read the example with the whole class and then get students to continue making the questions working on their own. Tell them to use contracted forms where possible and not to write the answers at this stage. Students who finish early can check in pairs. Check the answers with the whole class.

> **Answers**
> 1 What's she wearing?
>   Is she wearing jeans?
> 2 Where does she work?
>   Does she work in the bank?
> 3 When's he leaving?
>   Is he leaving tomorrow?
> 4 Who did you visit?
>   Did you visit your aunt?
> 5 How did you come?
>   Did you come by taxi?
> 6 Why are they going to have a meeting?
>   Are they going to have a meeting?

3 Elicit the short answers for the two types of question in number 1 (*Jeans.* and *Yes, she is./No, she isn't.*) Students continue writing the answers, giving both a positive and negative answer to the *Yes/No* questions. Check the answers with the whole class.

> **Answers**
> 1 Jeans.
>   Yes, she is./No, she isn't.
> 2 In the bank.
>   Yes, she does./No, she doesn't.
> 3 Tomorrow.
>   Yes, he is./No, he isn't.
> 4 My aunt.
>   Yes, I did./No I didn't.
> 5 By taxi.
>   Yes, I did./No I didn't.
> 6 Because there is a problem. (*sample answer*)
>   Yes, they are./No they aren't.

Read Grammar Reference 13.1 on p133 together in class, and/or ask students to read it at home. Encourage them to ask you questions about it.

3 Students work in groups to write some more general knowledge questions. Allow adequate time for this. It might take students a while to get started. Go round the groups to ensure that the questions are well formed.

When they have a reasonable number of questions, ask the groups to put the questions to the rest of the class. You could make this activity into a team game and allocate points if time allows.

PRACTICE (SB p99)

Questions and answers

1 Demonstrate the activity by getting students to give you the correct question and answer, matching the question word and answer in A and C and choosing the correct question from B. (*Where did you go? To the shops.*) Explain that students will have to use some of the questions in B more than once. Students continue the activity, working in pairs.

Ask students for their answers before giving them the correct versions. This will allow you to see where students are going wrong.

> **Answers**
> Where did you go? To the shops.
> What did you buy? A new jacket.
> When did you go? This morning.
> Who did you go with? A friend from work.
> Why did you go? To buy some new clothes.
> Which one did you buy? The black, leather one.
> How did you go? We drove.
> How much did you pay? £120.99.
> How many did you buy? Only one.

If students have made a lot of mistakes, go back over the question words and how they relate to the answers. Then drill the questions and answers in open pairs, getting students to repeat in closed pairs if necessary.

> **POSSIBLE PROBLEM**
> If students get confused by the use of *one* in *Which one … ?*, *The black leather one* and *Only one*, explain that we say *Which one … ?* and *The black leather one* to avoid repeating the word *jacket*, and that *Only one* refers to the number one. This point is further practised in exercise 4 in the Workbook.

Listening and pronunciation

2 **T 13.2** [CD 2: Track 50] Students listen and tick the sentence they hear. Let students check in pairs before you give the answers.

> **Answers and tapescript**
> 1 Why do you want to go?
> 2 Who is she?
> 3 Where's he staying?
> 4 Why didn't they come?
> 5 How old was she?
> 6 Does he play tennis?
> 7 Where did you go at the weekend?

Asking about you

3 Demonstrate the activity by getting students to put the words in number 1 in the correct order (*Do you like learning English?*). Students continue the activity in pairs. Check the answers with the whole class.

> **Answers**
> 2 What did you do last night?
> 3 How many languages does your mother speak?
> 4 When did you last go shopping?
> 5 Which football team do you support?
> 6 Did you come to school by car today?
> 7 How much do you weigh?
> 8 Who do you usually sit next to in class?
> 9 Why do you want to learn English?

4 Drill the questions around the class. Make sure that students use the correct intonation – falling on the *wh-* questions and rising on the *Yes/No* questions.

In pairs, students ask and answer the questions about themselves. Remind them that they can use short answers where appropriate. Monitor and check for correct intonation and for acceptable short answers.

> **Sample answers**
> 1 Yes, I do.
> 2 I went to a restaurant.
> 3 Two (Arabic and French).
> 4 A week ago.
> 5 Al-Hilal.
> 6 No, I came by bus.
> 7 60 kilos.
> 8 Sara.
> 9 Because I need it for my job.

ADDITIONAL MATERIAL

Workbook Unit 13
Exercises 1–5 Question forms including *What (sort)?*, *How (old)?*, *Which (one)?*

DO IT CAREFULLY! (SB p100)

Adverbs and adjectives

1 Focus on the first pair of sentences as an example. Elicit the answers (*bad* – adjective, *badly* – adverb). Students then work in pairs. Check the answers with the whole class.

> **Answers**
> 1 *bad* – adjective
>   *badly* – adverb
> 2 *carefully* – adverb
>   *careful* – adjective
> 3 *easy* – adjective
>   *easily* – adverb
> 4 *well* – adverb (point out that *well* is the irregular adverb of *good*)
>   *good* – adjective
> 5 *hard* – adjective
>   *hard* – adverb (This question is difficult, as *hard* is irregular.)

GRAMMAR SPOT

1 Read the sentences and the explanation about adjectives and adverbs as a class.

2 If necessary, put some adjectives that have regular adverbs on the board, e.g. *quick*, *bad*, *careful*. Include an example of an adjective ending in -*y*, e.g. *easy*. Elicit the adverbs and get students to tell you the rule.

> **Answers**
> We make regular adverbs by adding -*ly* to the adjective. If the adjective ends in -*y*, it changes to -*ily*.

3 Ask students to look back at exercise 1 and find the irregular adverbs. Check the answers.

> **Answers**
> *well* and *hard* are irregular.

Read Grammar Reference 13.2 on p133 together in class, and/or ask students to read it at home. Encourage them to ask you questions about it.

2 This activity focuses on adverbs that collocate with common verbs and phrases. Elicit adverbs that can go with *get up* as an example (*get up slowly/quietly/early/quickly*).

Students work in pairs and continue the activity. Remind them to decide which adverbs in the box are irregular. Check the answers with the whole class.

> **Answers**
> get up slowly/quietly/early/quickly
> walk slowly/quietly/fast/quickly/carefully
> work slowly/quietly/carefully/hard/fast/quickly
> run slowly/fast/quickly
> speak slowly/quietly/fast/quickly
> speak English slowly/fluently/fast/quickly
> pass the exam easily
> do your homework slowly/carefully/easily/fast/quickly
>
> *hard* and *fast* are irregular.

PRACTICE (SB p100)

Order of adjectives/adverbs

1 Students put the word in brackets in the correct place in the sentences, changing the adjective to an adverb if necessary. Tell them that sometimes more than one answer is possible. Students can work in pairs, or alone and then check with a partner.

> **POSSIBLE PROBLEM**
> We do not overtly give the rules for the order of adverbs (front position, mid position, end position), because the rules are rather complicated. We do not suggest that you try to go into them at this stage. You could perhaps point out that adverbs usually follow the verb and object if there is one, whereas adjectives go before the noun (unlike many other languages). Otherwise let students see how they get on without rules, and simply correct any mistakes.

> **Answers**
> 1 We had a holiday in Turkey, but unfortunately we had **terrible** weather.
> 2 Maria cooks **well**.
> 3 When I saw the accident, I phoned the police **immediately** (or I **immediately** phoned . . .).
> 4 Don't worry. Samir is a **careful** driver.
> 5 Carlos is a **typical** Brazilian. He loves food, and football.
> 6 Please speak **slowly**. I can't understand you.
> 7 We had an **easy** test today.
> 8 We all passed **easily**.
> 9 You speak **good** English./You speak English **well**.

Telling a story

2 Focus on sentence 1 as an example with the whole class. Elicit a range of endings that will fit with the adverb *fortunately*, e.g. *I had a umbrella./we were inside./the rain didn't last long.*

Students continue working in pairs. Monitor and check if their answers fit with the adverbs given. Where possible, elicit a range of answers for each sentence that highlight the meaning of the adverb.

> **Answers**
> 1 Fortunately, I had a umbrella./we were inside./the rain didn't last long.
> 2 Unfortunately, I couldn't go./I was ill./I was on holiday.
> 3 . . . suddenly the phone rang./I heard a loud noise./the doorbell rang.
> 4 Immediately, I called the police.

If you want to double-check that students have understood the adverbs, explain or translate them. You could get them to look up the definitions in dictionaries.

3 **T 13.3** [CD 2: Track 51] Students listen to the story and number the adverbs in the correct order. Check the answers.

> **Answers and tapescript**
> 8 quickly   3 carefully
> 4 quietly   1 suddenly
> 2 slowly   7 fortunately
> 5 immediately   6 really

> **T 13.3** It was about two o'clock in the morning, and . . . suddenly I woke up. I heard a noise. I got out of bed and went slowly downstairs. There was a light on in the living room. I listened carefully. I could hear two men speaking very quietly. 'Burglars!' I thought. 'Two burglars!' Immediately I ran back upstairs and phoned the police. I was really frightened. Fortunately the police arrived quickly. They opened the front door and went into the living room. Then they came upstairs to find me. 'It's all right now, sir,' they explained. 'We turned the television off for you!'

4 In pairs, students retell the story either one sentence at a time each, or one student first, then the other. Remind them to use the order of adverbs to help them.

Check it

5 Students work in pairs to correct the mistakes.

> **Answers**
> 1 Where does Anna's sister live?
> 2 The children came into the classroom noisily.
> 3 What does *whistle* mean?
> 4 I always work hard.
> 5 Can you help me, please?
> 6 When is Peter going on holiday?

ADDITIONAL MATERIAL

Workbook Unit 13
Exercises 6 and 7 Adverbs

VOCABULARY (SB p101)

Describing feelings

1 Demonstrate the activity by getting students to find the correct picture for *bored* (5). Students match the rest of the feelings to the pictures.

Check the answers with the whole class.

> **Answers**
> bored 5   excited 3
> tired 1   annoyed 2
> worried 6   interested 4

Drill the pronunciation of the feelings, making sure that students pronounce *bored* and *tired* as one syllable – /bɔːd/, /taɪəd/.

2   If you want to you can demonstrate the activity by getting students to find the correct reason for *bored* (*I am bored because I have nothing to do.*). Students continue the activity in pairs. Then check the answers with the whole class.

> **Answers**
> I am tired because I worked very hard today.
> I am worried because I can't find my keys.
> I am excited because I'm going on holiday tomorrow.
> I am annoyed because I want to go to the picnic but I can't.
> I am interested because we have a good teacher.

Focus attention on the Caution Box. Read the notes with the whole class. Using L1 if possible, explain that adjectives ending in *-ed* often describe a person's feeling or reactions, and that adjectives ending in *-ing* often describe the person or thing that provokes those feelings or reactions.

3   Focus on the pair of sentences in number 1 as an example (*Life in New York is very exciting. The football fans were very excited.*) Students complete the rest.
Check the answers with the whole class.

> **Answers**
> 2   The marathon runners were very **tired**.
>   That game of tennis was very **tiring**.
> 3   The child's behaviour was really **annoying**.
>   The teacher was **annoyed** when nobody did the homework.
> 4   The news is very **worrying**.
>   Everybody was very **worried** when they heard the news.

4   Drill the pronunciation of the pairs of adjectives in exercise 3, making sure students can clearly distinguish the *-ing* and *-ed* forms. Drill the example in the Student's Book chorally and individually.

Continue the activity by asking the following questions and getting students to respond with a suitable adjective in the correct form (sample answers are given in brackets). Elicit a range of answers by asking several students the same question.
Did you enjoy the last book you read? (*Yes, it was interesting.*)
Why don't you run six kilometres every morning? (*Because it's tiring.*)
How do you feel after the lesson? (*A bit tired.*)
How do you feel before an exam? (*Very worried.*)
How do you feel if your friend is late? (*A bit annoyed.*)
Do you like football? (*No, it's very boring.*)
Do you like learning English? (*Yes, it's interesting, but a bit tiring.*)

ADDITIONAL MATERIAL

Workbook Unit 13
Exercises 8 and 9 Adjective suffixes, and *-ed/-ing* adjectives

LISTENING AND READING (SB p102)

The meaning of life

1   Lead in to the theme of the story by asking students *What does a businessman do? And a fisherman? How are their lives different?* Elicit a range of answers from the class.

Focus attention on the picture and ask students to point to the fisherman and the businessman. Elicit any other basic information about the situation.

Read the questions as a class and then give students time to read the first part of the story. Deal with any vocabulary queries. Check the answers.

> **Answers**
> He was on holiday in a fishing village in the south of Mexico.
> He met a young fisherman.
> Yes, he did.
> He said, 'What beautiful tuna!'
> The businessman was American and the fisherman was Mexican.

2   **T 13.4** [CD 2: Track 52] With weaker students, pre-teach/check some of the key vocabulary from the conversation e.g. *fishing village, tuna, siesta, tell jokes, profits, fleet of boats, export* and *advice*. Tell students to close their books. They are going to hear a conversation between the two men. They don't need to understand every word, but should listen for key information about the fisherman's life and the suggestions that the businessman makes.

Play the recording through once. Elicit who the students think has a better life. Encourage them to give reasons for their answers.

> **Tapescript**
> **B = Businessman   F = Mexican fisherman**
> **FC = Fisherman's children**
> **B**   Good morning. What beautiful tuna! How long did it take to catch them?
> **F**   Oh, about two hours.
> **B**   Only two hours! Amazing! Why didn't you fish for longer and catch more?
> **F**   I didn't want to fish for longer. With this I have enough fish for my family.
> **B**   But what do you do with the rest of your day? Don't you get bored?
> **F**   I'm never bored. I get up late, play with my children, watch football, and take a siesta with my wife. Sometimes in the evenings I walk to the village café to see my friends, tell jokes and stories and play cards.

B Really? That's *all* you do? Look, I am a very successful businessman. I went to Harvard University and I studied business. I can help you. Fish for four hours every day and sell the extra fish you catch ...
F But ...
B ... then, with the profits, you can buy a bigger boat, catch more and earn more money.
F But ...
B ... then buy a second boat, a third, and so on, until you have a big fleet of fishing boats.
F But ...
B ... and you can export the fish and leave this village and move to Mexico City, or LA, or New York, and open a fishing business.
F OK, OK, but how long will all this take?
B Er – let me think – er, probably about 15 to 20 years.
F 15 to 20 years! And then what, Señor?
B Why, that's the exciting part. You can sell your business and become very rich, a millionaire.
F A millionaire? Really? But what do I do with all the money?
B Well, let me think. Er – I know, you can stop work and – er, move to a lovely, old fishing village where you can sleep late, play with your grandchildren, watch football, take a siesta with your wife, and walk to the village café in the evenings where you can, tell jokes and stories and play card games with your friends all you want.
F Mmmm – well ...
FC Papa, Papa, did you catch many fish?
F I caught enough for us today and tomorrow and also some for this gentleman. Please, Señor, have some of my beautiful fish. Goodbye, Señor. Come on children, let's go home.

3 Tell students to read the second part of the story. Put students in pairs to do the true/false task.

Answers
1 True.
2 False. He took two hours to catch the tuna.
3 True.
4 False. He is never bored.
5 True.
6 True.

4 **T 13.4** [CD 2: Track 52] Give students time to complete the second part of the story. Monitor and help as necessary.

Allow students to check their answers in pairs. Point out that the recording doesn't have exactly the same wording as the story in the SB, but the dialogue sections are the same and so students should be able to pick out the key words to check their answers.

Play **T 13.4** again. Check the answers with the class. Ask students to spell the Past Simple forms or to write their answers on the board.

Answers
1 two	5 games	9 about
2 didn't	6 went	10 millionaire
3 have	7 studied	
4 late	8 earn	

5 Ask students if they think the businessman will follow the fisherman's advice. Then tell student's to read the last part of the story on page 104.

6 Now tell students to choose the best answer for questions 1–3 and check the answers.

Answers
1 c 2 b 3 b

Vocabulary work

7 Ask students to match each of the seven verbs to a noun a–g. Check the answers.

Answers
1 d 2 e 3 a 4 g 5 c 6 f 7 b

8 This stage gives students the opportunity to retell the story, using their own words where possible. If you have a large class, students can work in groups of about six to give everyone the opportunity to tell a part of the story. Read out the opening of the story: *An American businessman was on holiday in a fishing village in the south of Mexico. One morning ... .* Then get the class to continue the story, each telling a small section before moving on to the next student. Encourage the class to help and prompt each other if they get any of the main events wrong or if they can't remember what happened next. With weaker students, write key words for each section on the board as prompts.

What do you think?

Check comprehension of *moral* (the main lesson of the story) and *what matters* (what is really important). Put students into groups of three or four to discuss their answers. Monitor and help as necessary but don't interrupt or over-correct as this is primarily a fluency task. Allow the discussion to continue for as long as students' interest is held, and exchanges are taking place mainly in English! Elicit a range of opinions from the class and establish the moral of the story ('*Understand what really matters in life.*')

EVERYDAY ENGLISH (SB p105)

Catching a train

> **NOTE**
> You will need to photocopy the information on train times on p131 of the Teacher's Book.

1 Read the introduction as a class. (Bristol is a port in the south-west of England and Bristol Temple Meads is its main station. Oxford is a city in south central England.) If you have a map of Britain in your classroom it would be a nice idea to show your students where Oxford is in relation to Bristol.

Read the Caution Box with the whole class. If necessary, put a few times on the board to help students practise the 24-hour clock:
0645 = oh six forty-five
1219 = twelve nineteen
0835 = oh eight thirty-five
1127 = eleven twenty-seven

T 13.5 [CD 2: Track 53] Students listen and complete the timetable. Check the answers.

> **Answers and tapescript**
> | DEPARTURE TIME | ARRIVAL TIME |
> |---|---|
> | from Oxford | at Bristol Temple Meads |
> | 0816 | **0946** |
> | 0945 | **1114** |
> | 1040 | **1208** |
>
> **T 13.5**
> Trains from Oxford to Bristol Temple Meads. Monday to Friday.
> Here are the departure times from Oxford and arrival times in Bristol.
> 0816 arriving 0946
> 0945 arriving 1114
> 1040 arriving 1208
> 11 . . .

2 **T 13.6** [CD 2: Track 54] Students listen to the conversation and complete it. Play it once through first, then in sections so students have time to write. Check the answers.

> **Answers and tapescript**
> A = Ann B = clerk
> A Good morning. (1) **Can you tell me** the times of trains (2) **from** Bristol (3) **back to** Oxford, please?
> B Afternoon, evening? When (4) **do you want to come back**?
> A About five o'clock this afternoon.
> B About (5) **five o'clock**. Right. Let's have a look. There's a train that (6) **leaves at** 5.28, then there isn't (7) **another one** until 6.50.
> A And (8) **what time do they** get in?
> B The 5.28 gets into Oxford at 6.54 and the 6.50 (9) **gets in at 8.10**.
> A Thanks a lot.

Students practise the conversation in pairs. If students have problems, let them listen to the recording and repeat the conversation, before practising again in pairs.

3 Explain that Ann is now at the ticket office. Students work in pairs to put the conversation in the right order.

T 13.7 [CD 2: Track 55] Students listen and check.

> **Answers and tapescript**
> A = Ann   C = clerk (2)
> A Hello. A return to Bristol, please.
> C Day return or period return?
> A A day return.
> C How do you want to pay?
> A Cash, please.
> C That's eighteen pounds.
> A Here's a twenty-pound note.
> C Here's your change and your ticket.
> A Thank you. Which platform is it?
> C You want platform 1 over there.
> A OK, thanks very much. Goodbye.

Students practise the conversation in pairs. If students have problems, let them listen to the recording and repeat the conversation, before practising again in pairs.

4 Hand out the photocopied information on the train journeys from Oxford. Students work in pairs: A is the passenger and B is the clerk. A decides on a destination, asks for information about times, and then buys a ticket.

Get students to change roles after they have practised one full conversation.

Don't forget!

Workbook Unit 13
Exercise 10 Students read a folk tale. They are then invited to write a story of their own.

Word list
Remind your students of the Word list for this unit on p141. They could write in the translations, learn them at home, and/or write some of the words in their vocabulary notebook.

14

Present Perfect + *ever*, *never*, *yet*, and *just*
At the airport

Have you ever?

Introduction to the unit

This unit introduces one of the most difficult tenses for students of English to learn. The Present Perfect is one of the most commonly used tenses in English, especially spoken English, but its presentation has been deferred until Unit 14. This is because until students have understood the concept that the Past Simple refers to the definite past, they will not be able to grasp the idea that the Present Perfect refers to the indefinite past.

The theme of this unit is 'in my life', and various people's experiences in life are explored. There is a jigsaw reading activity where students read about two people who have never learned to drive, but who have travelled the world. This gives further exposure to and practice in the Present Perfect contrasted with the Past Simple, and also provides a springboard for discussing life and experiences. There is also a *Listening* section with the poem *Why did you leave?*. This links into the *Everyday English* section – *At the airport*.

Language aims

Grammar – Present Perfect In this unit, we introduce one of the main uses of the Present Perfect, that is, to refer to an experience some time in one's life. We also focus on another use (to refer to the present result of a past action) with the adverbs *yet* and *just*. We do not introduce at all the third main use of the Present Perfect, which is to refer to unfinished past (*I have been a teacher for ten years*), nor do we teach the Present Perfect Continuous.

The aim of this unit is to provide an introduction to the Present Perfect, but do not expect your students to master the area quickly! It takes a long time (and a lot of mistakes, correction, and re-teaching) before students feel confident with this tense.

> **POSSIBLE PROBLEMS**
> The Present Perfect tense presents students with problems. In English, the Present Perfect expresses the concept of an action happening at an indefinite time *before now*, and so it cannot be used when a definite time is given. The following sentences are examples of incorrect usage.
> **Common mistakes**
> *I have seen him last week.
> *When have you been to the States?
> *Did you ever try Chinese food?
> *In my life I went to most countries in Europe, but I never went to Greece.
>
> Note that American English can use the Past Simple with *just* and *yet*.
> *Did you do your homework yet? I just did it.*

Vocabulary There is no self-standing vocabulary section in this unit, but a lot of general vocabulary is recycled and extended through the structural input.

Everyday English Language useful in situations at an airport is introduced and practised.

Workbook The Present Perfect is further practised in contrast with Past Simple. The time expressions *ever* and *never*, *ago* and *last week*, *yet* and *just*, and *ever* or *ago* are consolidated with the appropriate tense. The difference between *been* and *gone* is presented.

In the Vocabulary section, phrasal verbs are revised or introduced.

The writing syllabus concludes with a focus on writing a thank-you letter.

Notes on the unit

STARTER (SB p106)

This section is a fun way of getting students into the topic of places people have visited.

1 Focus attention on the first two flags and elicit the names of the corresponding countries. Students continue matching the countries and flags.

Check the answers with the whole class. If students have problems with the pronunciation of the countries, drill them chorally and individually.

Answers
1	Egypt	7	Germany
2	Italy	8	Great Britain
3	Saudi Arabia	9	the USA
4	France	10	United Arab Emirates
5	Brazil	11	Morocco
6	Japan	12	Canada

2 Tell students the countries you have been to. Students then tick off the countries they have visited.

IN MY LIFE (SB p106)

Present Perfect + *ever* and *never*

POSSIBLE PROBLEMS

1 Students find the difference between *He's been to the States* and *He's gone to the States* quite confusing. This is dealt with in exercise 8 of the Workbook. We do not suggest that you attempt to sort this out at this stage of the presentation.

2 Students have already seen a Present Perfect form with the structure *have got*, but we do not suggest that you mention this at all. It would be very confusing for students, as *have got* expresses an essentially present-time concept.

1 **T 14.1** [CD 2: Track 56] Students read and listen to the sentences. Remember that they will probably never have seen the Present Perfect tense before, and *been* will be unfamiliar. Using L1 if possible, explain that *been* is the past participle of the verb *to be*, and sometimes *to go*, and that *have been* is an example of the Present Perfect tense. Don't try to do a full presentation at this stage, but just explain that the sentences refer to the idea of 'some time in your life'.

Ask students to repeat the sentences on the recording (whether they are true for them or not). Do this chorally and individually, and correct mistakes carefully.

Now ask students to make similar sentences, saying which countries they have/haven't been to. Demonstrate this yourself first with true information about the countries you have visited. Then elicit examples from the whole class, so you can check students' accuracy in the use and pronunciation of the structure. Students continue the activity in groups. Monitor and check.

2 **T 14.2** [CD 2: Track 57] This activity introduces the question form. Students read and listen to the conversation. They can practise saying each sentence, either after the recording or with you modelling each one. This exercise highlights the 'experience' use of the Present Perfect, and shows it in contrast to the Past Simple. Draw students' attention to the question form of the Present Perfect, then to *When did you go?* and ask what tense this is (Past Simple). Just name the tenses at this stage and do not try to explain the different uses. (These are given in the *Grammar Spot* on p107.)

Get students to ask you questions about countries you have been to, following the model in exercise 2. Encourage them to ask *When did you go?* and tell them.

Students continue in open pairs asking and answering about countries they have been to, and when. This might sound repetitive and laborious, but remember you are introducing students to a very new concept with the Present Perfect tense and they need practice with forming questions, answers, and negatives.

3 Students write down the names of four cities, and in pairs make similar conversations. Go round and check as they do this. Monitor for accuracy in the use and pronunciation of the two tenses.

4 This practises the third person singular for the first time, so students will need to make the change from *have* to *has*. Focus attention on the examples to highlight this and on the contracted form *'s = has*. Drill the examples chorally and individually. Ask three or four students to talk about their partner.

GRAMMAR SPOT

1 Read the notes with the whole class. Highlight the use of *ever* with the Present Perfect in the question form to mean 'at any time on your life'. Stress that we do not use *ever* in the answer.

2 Read the notes with the whole class. Highlight the use of the Past Simple to say exactly when something happened. Elicit other past time references that can be used with the Past Simple, e.g. *last month*, *a long time ago*, *yesterday*, etc.

3 Read the notes with the whole class and get students to complete the table. Check the answers.

> **Answers**
>
> | | Positive | Negative | |
> |---|---|---|---|
> | I/You/We/They | have | haven't | been to Paris. |
> | He/She/It | has | hasn't | |

4   Students complete the sentences with *ever* or *never*. Check the answers.

> **Answers**
> Has he **ever** been to London?
> He's **never** been to London.

If your students have a similar tense form in their language, and if you can use L1, you might like to make a brief comparison between the way L1 and English use the auxiliary verb *have* + past participle. Be careful, however! Keep it short, and as simple as possible, because it would be very easy to overload students with too much information at this early stage of their exposure to the Present Perfect.

Read Grammar Reference 14.1 on p134 together in class, and/or ask students to read it at home. Encourage them to ask you questions about it.

PRACTICE (SB p107)

Past participles

1   Remind students of the term 'past participle' and give an example: infinitive – *be*, past participle – *been*. Tell students that they will often be able to guess which infinitive a past participle comes from and focus on the example in the Student's Book *eaten – eat*.

Students write in the infinitives for the rest of the verbs. All the verbs are used in exercises that come later in this unit and they are very common verbs when talking about experiences. Get students to check in pairs before checking with the whole class.

> **Answers**
>
> | | | | | | |
> |---|---|---|---|---|---|
> | eaten | **eat** | made | **make** | given | **give** |
> | seen | **see** | taken | **take** | won | **win** |
> | met | **meet** | driven | **drive** | had | **have** |
> | drunk | **drink** | cooked | **cook** | stayed | **stay** |
> | flown | **fly** | bought | **buy** | done | **do** |

2   Ask students to look at the selection of verbs and decide which two are regular. Check the answers.

> **Answers**
> The two regular verbs are *cook* and *stay*.

3   Elicit the Past Simple forms of *eat* (*ate*) and *see* (*saw*) and get students to continue the list in pairs.

4   Refer students to the list of irregular verbs on p142 and get them to check their answers.

The life of Ryan

1   Focus attention on the photo of Ryan and elicit some basic information about him. Pre-teach/check the vocabulary in the list, especially: *foreign, company, jumbo jet, play, tractor, competition*.

Also check the following items from the recording: *first class/business class, politician, farm*.

T 14.3 [CD 2: Track 58] Focus attention on the questionnaire and the column that relates to Ryan. Students listen and tick the things Ryan has done.

Ask students to check in pairs before they give you the answers.

> **Answers and tapescript**
>
> | | |
> |---|---|
> | lived in a foreign country | ✔ |
> | worked for a big company | ✔ |
> | stayed in an expensive hotel | ✘ |
> | flown in a jumbo jet | ✔ |
> | cooked a meal for ten (or more) people | ✘ |
> | met a famous person | ✘ |
> | driven a tractor | ✔ |
> | been to hospital | ✘ |
> | won a competition | ✘ |

> **T 14.3**   Yes, I've lived in a foreign country. In Japan, actually. I lived in Osaka for a year. I enjoyed it very much. I loved the food. And, yes, I have worked for a big company. I worked for Nissan, the car company, that's why I was in Japan. That was two years ago, then I got another job. Have I stayed in an expensive hotel? No, never – only cheap hotels for me, I'm afraid, but I have flown in a jumbo jet – four or five times, actually. Oh, I've never cooked a meal for a lot of people. I love food but I don't like cooking. And I've never met a famous person – oh, just a minute, well not met but I've seen . . . er . . . I saw a famous politician at the airport once – oh, who was it? I can't remember his name. I've driven a tractor though, I had a holiday job on a farm when I was 17. I enjoyed that. Good news – I've never been to hospital. I was born in hospital, of course, but that's different. Bad news – I've never won a competition. I've never, ever won a thing!

2   First ask students to go through the questionnaire to produce some sentences about Ryan. This is to further practise the third person singular. Get some positive sentences first, then some negative ones. Drill them around the class, correcting carefully.

Read the instructions for this exercise. Ask for the positive sentences in the Present Perfect again. This time, where possible, you will ask follow-up questions in the Past Simple, which students will answer in the Past Simple. (You might want to play the recording again

Unit 14 • Have you ever?   115

before you do this to remind students of the information about Ryan.) Although these questions and answers practise the Past Simple, you are also indirectly helping students with the Present Perfect, because you are showing them when the Present Perfect *isn't* applicable.

> **Follow-up questions (and the students' answers)**
> (Note that not all the Present Perfect sentences which students might produce from the questionnaire have a possible follow-up question in the Past Simple.)
> Which city did he live in? (Osaka.)
> Did he enjoy it? (Yes, he did.)
> Did he like the food? (Yes, he did.)
> What sort of company did he work for? (A car company.)
> When did he work there? (Two years ago.)
> Who did he see at the airport? (A famous politician.)
> When did he drive a tractor? (When he worked on a farm.)
> When did he work on a farm? (When he was seventeen.)
> Where was he born? (In hospital.)

3 Students ask a partner the same questions. Monitor and check for correct pronunciation and formation of the questions.

Students tell the class about their partner. Encourage them to give follow-up information in the Past Simple where appropriate, e.g. *Batul has flown in a jumbo jet. She flew from London to New York five years ago.*

ADDITIONAL MATERIAL

Workbook Unit 14
Exercises 1 and 2 Present Perfect and Past Simple
Exercise 3 and 4 Time expressions *ever* and *never*, and *ago* and *last week*

A HONEYMOON IN LONDON (SB p108)

Present Perfect + *yet* and *just*

> **SUGGESTIONS**
> 1 The concepts expressed by *yet* and *just* are very subtle and they are realized by different structures in different languages. We do not ask any questions in the *Grammar Spot* that test concept (only form), because the language required would be more complex than the target item itself. Students should be able to get the meaning through context and use, but you can check comprehension of the two adverbs by translating into L1. Get them to look up the adverbs in dictionaries.
> 2 It might be a good idea to do exercise 8 in the Workbook on *been* versus *gone* before you do the presentation of Present Perfect + *yet* and *just*. This clarifies the difference of meaning between *been* and *gone* as the two past participles of *to go*.

1 Read the introduction and the list as a class. Check that students understand *honeymoon* (a holiday after two people get married). Ask students what they know about places and activities in the list. Refer them to the photos of places and activities in London and use the background information below if necessary.

London
Buckingham Palace – London home of the British king/queen, built in 1703 for the Duke of Buckingham, but bought by George III in 1762. It was reconstructed in 1821–36 and a new front was added in 1913.
the Houses of Parliament – the building where the UK legislative assembly meets which incorporates sections of the medieval Palace of Westminster.
The London Eye – a huge Ferris wheel next to the Thames and near the Houses of Parliament.
Hyde Park – one of the largest open spaces in London which includes a boating lake called the Serpentine.
Harrods – the famous department store in Knightsbridge (London's luxury shopping area) where it is said that you can buy anything!
the Crown Jewels in the Tower of London – the crown, jewels, etc. that the British king/queen wears for ceremonies are housed in the Tower of London and both are popular tourist attractions.
double-decker bus – a bus with two levels. In London, these are red and have become a symbol of the city.
The Ritz – a famous expensive hotel in Piccadilly.

2 **T 14.4** [CD 2: Track 59] Read the instructions as a class. Students listen to the recording and put a tick next to the things Marilyn and Rod have done.

> **Answers and tapescript**
> go to Buckingham Palace ✔
> see the Houses of Parliament ✔
> have a boat ride on the River Thames ✔
> go on the London Eye ✔
> walk in Hyde Park
> go shopping in Harrods
> see the Crown Jewels in the Tower of London
> travel on a double-decker bus ✔
> go to The Ritz
>
> **T 14.4**
> **M = Marilyn   J = Judy**
> **M** We're having a great time!
> **J** Tell me about it! What have you done so far?
> **M** Well, we've been to Buckingham Palace. That was the first thing we did. It's right in the centre of London! We went inside and looked around.
> **J** Have you seen the Houses of Parliament yet?
> **M** Yeah, we have. We've just had a boat ride on the River Thames and we went right past the Houses of Parliament. We saw Big Ben! Then we went on the London Eye. That's the big wheel near Big Ben. That was this morning.

This afternoon we're going to take a taxi to Hyde Park and then go shopping in Harrods. Tomorrow morning we're going to see the Crown Jewels in the Tower of London.
J Wow! You're busy! And what about those big red buses? Have you travelled on a double-decker bus yet?
M Oh, yeah we took one when we went to Buckingham Palace. We sat upstairs. You get a great view of the city.
J Tomorrow's your last night. What are you going to do on your last night?
M Well, we're hoping to go to The Ritz, but we haven't booked it yet.
J Oh, you're so lucky! Give my love to Rod!
M Yeah. Bye, Judy. See you soon!

GRAMMAR SPOT

POSSIBLE PROBLEMS

1 Remember that these questions focus on the form of *yet* and *just*, not the concept, because any questions that tested students' understanding of these items would be more complex than the items themselves. You need to make sure, probably via translation if possible, that students have understood them. Explain that *(not) yet* means *(not) before now* whereas *just* means *a short time before now*, using examples from the text or putting examples on the board.

2 Be prepared to prompt and help with the questions in the *Grammar Spot*, as students may find them hard.

Look at the questions in the *Grammar Spot* as a class.

1 Get students to think about which words they need to complete the gapped sentences. If necessary, refer them back to exercise 1 for the correct information and the past participles. Check the answers.

Answers
1 Have you **seen** the Crown Jewels yet?
2 We **haven't** been shopping in Harrods yet.
3 We've just **had** a boat ride on the Thames.

Focus on the use of *yet* and *just* in the sentences and check comprehension (see *Possible problems* above).

2 Elicit the answers to the questions about the position of *yet* and *just*.

Answers
yet comes at the end of a sentence.
just comes before the past participle.

3 Allow students time to work out the rules for the use of *yet*. Then check the answer.

Answer
We can use *yet* only in questions and negative sentences, not in positive sentences.

Read Grammar Reference 14.2 on p134 together in class, and/or ask students to read it at home. Encourage them to ask you questions about it.

3 Refer students back to the list in exercise 1 on p108. Elicit the past participle of each of the verbs in the list, making sure students give *been* as the participle of *go*. Remind students that the ticks refer to things that Marilyn and Rod *have* done. Drill the examples in the Student's Book and elicit one or two more examples. Students continue working in pairs, saying what Marilyn and Rod have and haven't done. Monitor and check for the correct form of the Present Perfect and the correct position of *yet*.

T 14.4 Play the recording again so that students can check their answers. Then check the answers with the whole class.

Answers
They've been to Buckingham Palace.
They've seen the Houses of Parliament.
They've had a boat ride on the River Thames.
They've been on the London Eye.
They haven't walked in Hyde Park yet.
They haven't been shopping in Harrods yet.
They haven't seen the Crown Jewels yet.
They've travelled on a double-decker bus.
They haven't been to The Ritz yet.

PRACTICE (SB p109)

I've just done it

1 Students haven't practised Present Perfect questions with *yet* or answers with *just*, so now's the time to do it! Drill the question and answer in the Student's Book, making sure students imitate the rising intonation on the question and the falling intonation on the answer. Students give one or two more examples in open pairs. Remind students that they will need to use different pronouns in their answers (*it/him/her/one*) and point out that some questions can have more than one answer.

Students continue working in closed pairs. Then check the answers with the whole class.

> **Answers**
> 2 Have you done the shopping yet?
>   Yes, I've just done it.
> 3 Have you washed your hair yet?
>   Yes, I've just done/washed it.
> 4 Have you cleaned the car yet?
>   Yes, I've just done/cleaned it.
> 5 Have you made the dinner yet?
>   Yes, I've just made it.
> 6 Have you met the new student yet?
>   Yes, I've just met him/her.
> 7 Have you had a coffee yet?
>   Yes, I've just had one.
> 8 Have you given your homework to the teacher yet?
>   Yes, I've just given it to her/him.
> 9 Have you finished the exercise yet?
>   Yes, I've just finished it.

Check it

2 This exercise revises the grammar just covered in the unit. Students work in pairs to choose the correct sentence. Then check the answers with the whole class.

> **Answers**
> 1 I saw John yesterday.
> 2 (Note: both are possible here – 'Did you ever eat . . .' is common in American English.)
> 3 Donna won £10,000 last month.
> 4 I've never drunk Japanese tea.
> 5 Tom has never been to America.
> 6 Have you had the interview yet?
> 7 I haven't finished my homework yet.
> 8 Has he just bought a new car?

ADDITIONAL MATERIAL

Workbook Unit 14
Exercise 5 *yet*
Exercise 6 *yet* and *just*
Exercise 7 Check it
Exercise 8 *been* or *gone*?

READING AND SPEAKING (SB p110)

We've never learned to drive

1 This activity acts as a lead-in to the topic of transport and introduces the two modes of transport described in the texts – hitch-hiking and cycling. Check comprehension of the verbs in the list and give brief examples of your own travel experiences. Divide the class into pairs and get students to ask and answer the questions. Elicit feedback from the class and establish which things most people have done and and which least.

2 This exercise pre-teaches some of the important vocabulary in the texts. If students have access to dictionaries, they can look up the new words. Alternatively, in a monolingual class, get students to work in pairs or small groups to help each other with the translations.

3 Focus attention on the heading and on the photos and elicit possible reasons why Tudor and Josie have never learned to drive. Divide the class into pairs and get the A students to read about Tudor and the B students to read about Josie. They should read their text quickly in order to check their predictions about why Tudor and Josie have never learned to drive (Tudor travels the world by hitch-hiking and Josie fell out of a car when she was young).

4 Get students to read through the questions and check they understand them. Students read the text gain and work in pairs or small groups (A students together and B students together) to answer the questions. If they have access to dictionaries, they can check any unknown vocabulary or they can ask you.

Check the answers with the A and B groups separately before students compare the two travellers.

> **Answers**
> **Tudor Bowen-Jones**
> 1 No, he doesn't. He's retired.
> 2 He likes hitch-hiking.
> 3 He started travelling 60 years ago.
> 4 He went abroad for the first time in 1947.
> 5 He's been to 40 countries.
> 6 Yes, he has.
> 7 Yes, he has.
> 8 Yes, he has. The driver of the car took out a gun, but he cleaned it and put it back again.
> 9 Possible answers: He has hitch-hiked with a horse and cart in Hungary. He has ridden a motorbike across Spain. He sat in the back of a hearse in France. He enjoyed the comfort of a Rolls Royce in Germany.
> 10 He's going to spend his 90th year in Vienna.
>
> **Josie Dew**
> 1 No, she doesn't, but she writes books about her journeys.
> 2 She likes cycling.
> 3 She started travelling in 1985.
> 5 she's been to 40 countries.
> 6 No, she hasn't.
> 7 Yes, she has.
> 8 Yes, she has. A dog attacked her in Bulgaria.
> 9 Possible answers: She has cycled through the Himalayan mountains in Nepal, then down into India. She has cycled through millions of locusts in the Moroccan desert. She has travelled through tornadoes in the USA. She was in Romania when someone killed President Ceauçescu.
> 10 She's going to cycle around New Zealand.

5 Run through the pronunciation of the proper names in the texts that students might have problems with (Tudor /ˈtjuːdə/, Josie /ˈdʒəʊsi:/, Nepal /nɪˈpɔːl/, Romania /ruːˈmeɪnɪə/, Ceauçescu /tʃaʊˈtʃesku:/, Bulgaria /bʌlˈgeərɪə/. Tell students they are going to work with a student from the other group and find out about another traveller. Show them how they can do this in a meaningful way, rather than just read off their answers in order, e.g.

A *Tudor doesn't have a job because he's retired. What about Josie?*

B *She doesn't have a job, but she writes books about her journeys.*

Remind students that they will need to use the Present Perfect, Past Simple and Present Simple tenses in their answers. Students compare the two travellers in pairs. Monitor and check, but don't expect them to get everything right. You can note down and give feedback on common errors, but bear in mind that the main focus is the information exchange through reading and speaking, not grammar accuracy.

What do you think?

Discuss the questions as a class. Encourage students to give reasons for their answers. If you have time, elicit any appropriate anecdotes on a time when students went hitch-hiking or cycling.

VOCABULARY AND PRONUNCIATION (SB p112)

A poem – Why did you leave?

Introduction
Ask students to look at the photo. Ask them a few questions to personalise the topic and prepare for question word practice in exercise 1. Examples: *When did you last travel? Where did you go? How did you travel? Who with? Why?*

1 Ask students to work with a partner to match the question words and answers. If necessary, do the first one(s) with them so that they get the idea. Go round and monitor/help as they do it. Keep this exercise as short as possible as it is just preparation for the main aim of the lesson – reading the poem.

Check the answers with the whole class.

> **Answers**
> What? – a suitcase
> Where? – Spain
> When? – Last September
> Why? – Because I needed a holiday.
> Who? – Nobody.
> How? – By boat.
> Which? – The small brown one.
> Whose? – It's mine.

Ask students what the questions and answers are about. Answer – travel.

2 Ask students to read the poem quite quickly. Tell them not to worry about the words missing at this stage. You just want a general understanding of the poem.

Discuss questions with the whole class. Encourage students to give all kinds of ideas – there are no right or wrong answers.

> **Possible answers**
> **Who do you think is asking the questions?**
> Possibly a parent, a mother or father, or it could be a sister or brother. Even a good friend. It is definitely someone who has been left behind at home (they say 'When are you coming home?'). It someone who is concerned and trying to understand the other person's motives for leaving.
> **Who is answering them?**
> Someone who has left home. A son or daughter who feels they are too old to continue living at home, in the place they grew up in. Perhaps he/she has gone to university, or will look for a job in a new town far away.
> **What is the poem about?**
> It's about the need that some young people feel to get away from the place they've grown up in, where everybody knows them. Sometimes they want to start a new life somewhere else. It can include the search for a new identity, trying to find out who you reallly are, instead of just following other peoples ideas of who you are.

3 Focus students now back onto the poem and away from speculation. Ask them to work with their partner to discuss which words on the right best complete the lines of the poem. Make clear to them that sometimes there is no right or wrong answer but the mood of the poem will suggest what the writer has in mind. Ask a few students to read one or two of their verses aloud to the class. Sometimes ask them why they chose certain words.

4 **T 14.5** [CD 2: Track 60] Play the recording and ask students to compare the words in the poem with the ones they chose. Ask if they think any of their ideas are better than those in the actual poem. See possible reasons for the poet's choice below.

> **Answers and tapescript**
> **Why did you leave?**
> When did you leave?
> I left with the leaves, in **autumn**.
> When did you leave?
> I left when the time was **right**.
>
> Where have you gone?
> To a busy, crowded **city**.
> Where have you gone?
> To a place where I'm not **known**.

What did you take?
Just clothes, and books of **poetry**.
What did you take?
Mostly **memories**, and hope.

How did you travel?
By **plane**, by bus, and taxi.
How did you travel?
On my own. I need to be **alone**.

Why did you leave?
Because I have **grown** up now.
Why did you leave?
Because **birds** must fly the nest.

When are you coming home?
When I have become **someone**.
When are you coming home?
I don't know. Just let me **go**.

The nest is the 'home' that birds build for their eggs. When they are old enough, baby birds have to 'fly the nest', and use their wings to 'leave home'.

5 Point out to your students that the poem is rather simply but cleverly constructed with the repetition of simple questions and answers. They can surely do something similar with other simple questions. Encourage them with their partners to write some more verses for the poem by completing these lines.

> **Sample answers**
> Who did you meet?
> I met *lots of people*.
> Who did you meet?
> I met *nobody interesting*.
>
> How can we help you?
> You *could send me some money*.
> How can we help you?
> You *can't help me at all*.
>
> What have you learned?
> I've learned *how to make friends*.
> What have you learned?
> I've learned *to like myself*.

Invite some students to read their verses to the class. Invite discussion as to whose lines are most interesting.

What do you think?

End the lesson by focusing back on the original poem. The answers to these questions will probably already have been touched upon but they can provide a nice rounding off to the lesson.

> **Sample answers**
> - How old are the people in the poem? *Parents and probably a young person, a teenager or someone in their 20s.*
> - Where has he left? *Probably a small town or village.*
> - Where has he gone? *Probably to a big city a long way away.*

- What is he going to do? *Perhaps he's going to study at university, or look for a job.*
- Do you think he will come back? *Probably yes. He says that he wants to become someone first, i.e. find his own identity, and then he would be ready to come back. But he might change his mind.*

EVERYDAY ENGLISH (SB p113)

At the airport

1 Students read the sentences and then put them in the correct order, working in pairs or small groups.
   Check the answers with the whole class.

> **Answers**
> 5 You wait in the departure lounge.
> 7 You board the plane.
> 2 You get a trolley for your luggage.
> 1 You arrive at the airport.
> 3 You check in your luggage and get a boarding pass.
> 4 You go through passport control.
> 6 You check the departures board for your gate number.

2 **T 14.6** [CD 2: Track 61] Focus attention on the chart and check students understand the headings. Tell students to listen carefully and complete the chart with the missing information. Play the recording and get students to check in pairs. If necessary, play the recording again to let students complete their answers.
   Check the answers with the whole class.

> **Answers**
>
> | Flight Number | Destination | Gate number | Remark |
> |---|---|---|---|
> | BA 516 | Geneva | 4 | LAST CALL |
> | SK 832 | Frankfurt | – | DELAYED **one hour** |
> | AF 472 | Amsterdam | 17 | NOW BOARDING GATE **17** |
> | LH 309 | Miami | 32 | NOW BOARDING GATE **32** |
> | VS 876 | New York | – | WAIT IN LOUNGE |

T 14.6
British Airways flight BA 516 to Geneva boarding at gate 4, last call. Flight BA 516 to Geneva, last call. Scandinavian Airlines flight SK 832 to Frankfurt is delayed one hour. Flight SK 832 to Frankfurt, delayed one hour. Air France flight 472 to Amsterdam is now boarding at gate 17. Flight AF 472 to Amsterdam, now boarding, gate 17.
Lufthansa flight 309 to Miami is now boarding at gate 32. Flight LH 309 to Miami, now boarding, gate 32. Virgin Airlines flight to New York, VS 876 to New York. Please wait in the departure lounge until a further announcement. Thank you. Passengers are reminded to keep their hand luggage with them at all times.

3 Students read the conversations in exercise 4 through quickly and decide who the people are and where they are. Get students to compare in pairs before checking the answers with the whole class.

> **Answers**
> 1 Two passengers in the departure lounge
> 2 Check-in assistant and passenger at the check-in desk
> 3 Rod and Marilyn meeting Marilyn's sister, Judy, in the arrival hall
> 4 Two friends at the departure gate

4 Students complete the conversations with the correct question. Get students to check in pairs.

T 14.7 [CD 2: Track 62] Play the recording and get students to check their answers.

> **Answers and tapescript**
> 1 A Listen! ... BA516 to Geneva. That's our flight.
>   B **Did the announcement say gate 4 or 14?**
>   A I couldn't hear. I think it said 4.
>   B Look! There it is on the departure board. It is gate 4.
>   A OK. Come on! Let's go.
> 2 A Can I have your ticket, please?
>   B Yes, of course.
>   A Thank you. How many suitcases have you got?
>   B Just one.
>   A And **have you got much hand luggage?**
>   B Just this bag.
>   A That's fine.
>   B Oh ... can I have a seat next to the window?
>   A Yes, that's OK. Here's your boarding pass. Have a nice flight!
> 3 A Rod! Marilyn! Over here!
>   B Hi! Judy! Great to see you!
>   A It's great to see you too. You look terrific! **Did you have a good honeymoon?**
>   B Fantastic. Everything was fantastic.
>   A Well, you haven't missed anything here. Nothing much has happened at all!
> 4 A There's my flight. It's time to go.
>   B Oh no! It's been a wonderful two weeks. I can't believe it's over.
>   A I know. **When can we see each other again?**
>   B Soon, I hope. I'll write every day.
>   A I'll phone too. Goodbye.
>   B Goodbye. Give my love to your family.

Students practise the conversations with a partner. If necessary, play the recording again and get students to repeat before practising in pairs.

5 Give students time to decide their roles for each conversation. Encourage them to modify the information in the conversations where possible, e.g.
conversation 1 – different flight numbers, destinations, and gate numbers
conversation 2 – different number of suitcases and lots of hand luggage
conversation 3 – different people, e.g. friends meeting other friends after a holiday, husband meeting wife after a business trip
conversation 4 – different people saying goodbye, e.g. two business colleagues, two teenagers

Be prepared to feed in the language students might need for the characters and contexts they choose. Get students to act out one conversation each for the whole class. If possible, record the conversations and then play them back for students to comment on and correct.

Don't forget!

Workbook Unit 14
Exercise 9 Vocabulary – phrasal verbs
Exercise 10 The writing syllabus concludes with a focus on writing a thank-you letter. The context reintroduces a character from Unit 2 of the Student's Book, Samira, who is writing a thank-you letter to her flatmates. Students are then invited to write a thank-you letter to someone who has looked after them.

Word list
Remind your students of the Word list for this unit on p141. They could write in the translations, learn them at home, and/or write some of the words in their vocabulary notebook.

> **EXTRA IDEAS UNITS 9–14**
> On p132 of the Teacher's Book there is an additional reading activity.
>
> If you have time and feel that your students would benefit from it, you can photocopy it and use it in class. The reading exercise revises all the units so far, particularly Units 9–14. It could also be done for homework. The answers are on p155.

Photocopiable material

UNITS 1–14

Unit 2 Practice 1 (SB p13)
Identity card for Student A

Surname	Binchey
First name	
Country	Ireland
Job	
Address	82, Hill Road, Dublin
Phone number	
Age	47
Married?	

Unit 2 Practice 4 (SB p13)
Identity card for Students A and B

Student A
Name	
Country/town	
Age	
Job	
Phone number	
Married?	

Surname	Binchey
First name	
Country	Ireland
Job	
Address	82, Hill Road, Dublin
Phone number	
Age	47
Married?	

Student B
Name	
Country/town	
Age	
Job	
Phone number	
Married?	

Surname	Binchey
First name	
Country	Ireland
Job	
Address	82, Hill Road, Dublin
Phone number	
Age	47
Married?	

Student A
Name	
Country/town	
Age	
Job	
Phone number	
Married?	

Surname	Binchey
First name	
Country	Ireland
Job	
Address	82, Hill Road, Dublin
Phone number	
Age	47
Married?	

Student B
Name	
Country/town	
Age	
Job	
Phone number	
Married?	

Extra ideas Units 1–4 Revision

Reading

1 A magazine called *Weekend* interviewed a politician, Roberta Tomlinson. Read about her.
2 Complete the questions or answers in the interview with Roberta Tomlinson.

1 **A** What's your name?
   B Roberta Tomlinson.
2 **A** _____ ?
   B T – O – M – L – I – N – S – O – N.
3 **A** Where are you from?
   B _____ .
4 **A** _____ ?
   B I'm forty-three.
5 **A** Are you married?
   B _____ .
6 **A** _____ ?
   B Andrew.
7 **A** What does your husband do?
   B _____ .
8 **A** Do you have any children?
   B _____ .
9 **A** _____ ?
   B Yes. I have two brothers.
10 **A** Do you enjoy your work?
   B _____ .
11 **A** _____ ?
   B Because I meet a lot of people.
12 **A** Where do you live?
   B _____ .
13 **A** Do you have a garden?
   B _____ .
14 **A** _____
       in your free time?
   B Having friends for dinner.

Meet …
Roberta Tomlinson

Me and my family

I'm from Glasgow, in Scotland, and I'm forty-three years old. I'm married, and my husband's name is Andrew. He's a teacher in a school for blind children. We have three children – two boys and a girl. I have two brothers. They still live in Scotland.

Me and my work

I'm a Member of Parliament, so I work in London for part of the week and in Scotland for the rest. I enjoy my work very much. I like it because I meet a lot of people and it is my job to help them. I work about fifty or sixty hours a week.

Me and my home

We have a flat in London, but my home is Glasgow, and we have a large house there. There are about twelve rooms, and the house is like a hotel. So many people come and go! We have a garden where we grow fruit and vegetables.

Me and my free time

Well, I have very little free time, but when I can, I like having friends for dinner. We sit, eat, drink, and talk for hours!

Unit 5 Practice 1 and 2 (SB p37)

Student A

Student B

124 Unit 5 · Photocopiable material © Oxford University Press **Photocopiable**

Unit 7

Suggestion (TB p58)

become	a pilot
win	a medal
break	a record
car	park
orange	juice
news	paper
credit	card
air	port
play	chess
ride	a bike
drive	a car
railway	station

Words that go together

Complete the sentences with verbs and nouns or with compound nouns.

Use the correct form of the verb and check the spelling of the compound nouns (one or two words).

1 **A** Why __*did*__ you __*become a pilot*__ ?
   B I love very fast planes.

2 I'm late for my train. Can you drive me to the _____ ?

3 **A** Can you _____ ?
   B Yes, and I have a new sports car.

4 **A** Would you like an _____ ?
   B No thanks. I'm not thirsty.'

5 I'll pay for the bill on my _____ .

6 **A** Can you _____ ?
   B No, but I'd like to learn.

7 You have to train very hard to _____ at the world championships.

8 **A** What time is the flight?
   B 10.00. I'll see you at the _____ .

9 **A** _____ Carl Lewis _____ in the Olympics?
   B Yes, he won four golds.

10 **A** When did you learn to _____ ?
    B When I was about six – I fell off all the time!

11 We can't leave the bikes in front of the library. We need to find a _____ .

12 I want to read about yesterday's match. Can I borrow your _____ ?

Unit 8 Practice 4 (SB p62)

Student A

Did you know that ...

- ... Buckingham Palace has over 600 rooms?
- ... the Rose Rayhaan Hotel in Dubai has 72 floors?
- ... Shakespeare spelled his name in eleven different ways?
- ... in 1979 it snowed in the Sahara Desert?
- ... the American President George Washington had wooden false teeth?

Student A

Did you know that ...

- ... Buckingham Palace has over 600 rooms?
- ... the Rose Rayhaan Hotel in Dubai has 72 floors?
- ... Shakespeare spelled his name in eleven different ways?
- ... in 1979 it snowed in the Sahara Desert?
- ... the American President George Washington had wooden false teeth?

Student B

Did you know that ...

- ... it took 1,700 years to build the Great Wall of China?
- ... King Henry VIII of England had six wives?
- ... your heart beats over 100,000 times a day?
- ... Shakespeare and the Spanish novelist Cervantes both died on the same day, 23 April 1616?
- ... In Belgium, 172,000 tons of chocolate are made every year?

Student B

Did you know that ...

- ... it took 1,700 years to build the Great Wall of China?
- ... King Henry VIII of England had six wives?
- ... your heart beats over 100,000 times a day?
- ... Shakespeare and the Spanish novelist Cervantes both died on the same day, 23 April 1616?
- ... In Belgium, 172,000 tons of chocolate are made every year?

Extra ideas Units 5–8 Revision

Reading and speaking

1 Work in groups. How good is your memory? Answer the questions.
   1 What did you have to eat last night?
   2 Where were you ten days ago? What did you do that day?
   3 Where were the Olympic Games in 2008?
   4 When was your father born?
   5 How many phone numbers can you remember?

2 Read the newspaper article about Dominic O'Leary, the man with the best memory in the world.

3 Answer the questions.
   1 What are some of the things Dominic can remember?
   2 How did he become world champion?
   3 Was he good at school? Why not?
   4 What did his teachers say about him?
   5 When did he start to improve his memory? What did he see?
   6 What do you think of Dominic's suggestions for a good memory?

   Try his ideas to remember some words in English!

4 Here are the answers to some questions. Write in the questions.
   1 _____ ?
   Wednesday.
   2 _____ ?
   Last October.
   3 _____ ?
   A thousand pounds a day.
   4 _____ ?
   She's a clothes designer.
   5 _____ ?
   He likes number games and crosswords.

5 There are a lot of numbers in the article. What do these numbers refer to?
   Example
   1876   *April 21, 1876 was a Wednesday.*
   1 35   3 4   5 5
   2 34   4 £1,000

WORLD CHAMPION MEMORY MAN

THIS IS DOMINIC O'LEARY, the man with the best memory in the world. He can tell you the day of any date in any year. What day was April 21, 1876? 'Wednesday,' says Dominic. He can remember the teams and the scores of every football match in every World Cup. And he became world champion memory man when he remembered the order of thirty-five packs of playing cards!

At school, Dominic was a pupil who couldn't remember his lessons. 'My maths and English teachers said I was stupid because I could never remember what they taught me.' But four years ago he saw a programme on television which showed people how to improve their memory, and last October he became world champion. 'I remembered the order of thirty-five packs of cards,' said Dominic. 'It was quite easy.'

Dominic, 34, can earn £1,000 a day on European TV programmes. He lives with his wife, Alison, a clothes designer, in a small village near Bath, and he is the manager of an office cleaning company.

In his free time, Dominic loves number games and crosswords. He says children can learn to improve their memory from the age of five. 'Then they can do anything,' says Dominic.

HOW TO IMPROVE YOUR MEMORY

Dominic says anyone can have a good memory. These are his suggestions.

1 When you go to bed, remember everything you did that day.
2 Remember things in pictures, not words. 'Words are difficult to remember, but pictures are easy.' For example, if you want to remember the name Kate, think of a cat. For the number 8814, think of two snowmen, a tree and a bird.
3 If you forget something, remember where you were when you *could* remember it.

Unit 10 Practice 2 (SB p76)

Millionaire A
- 4 houses
- 30 cars – 10 Jaguars, 10 Porsches, and 10 Ferraris
- 100 Arab horses
- 5 boats
- 8 gold watches
- 50 gold and diamond rings
- 10 servants
- 50 million dollars

Millionaire B
- 5 houses – two in France, one in Miami, one in the Caribbean, and a castle in Scotland
- 50 cars – 10 Lamborghinis, 15 Mercedes-Benz, and 25 Rolls-Royces
- 275 Arab horses
- 12 boats
- 18 gold watches
- 80 platinum and diamond rings
- 25 servants
- 150 million dollars

Millionaire A
- 4 houses
- 30 cars – 10 Jaguars, 10 Porsches, and 10 Ferraris
- 100 Arab horses
- 5 boats
- 8 gold watches
- 50 gold and diamond rings
- 10 servants
- 50 million dollars

Millionaire B
- 5 houses – two in France, one in Miami, one in the Caribbean, and a castle in Scotland
- 50 cars – 10 Lamborghinis, 15 Mercedes-Benz, and 25 Rolls-Royces
- 275 Arab horses
- 12 boats
- 18 gold watches
- 80 platinum and diamond rings
- 25 servants
- 150 million dollars

Millionaire A
- 4 houses
- 30 cars – 10 Jaguars, 10 Porsches, and 10 Ferraris
- 100 Arab horses
- 5 boats
- 8 gold watches
- 50 gold and diamond rings
- 10 servants
- 50 million dollars

Millionaire B
- 5 houses – two in France, one in Miami, one in the Caribbean, and a castle in Scotland
- 50 cars – 10 Lamborghinis, 15 Mercedes-Benz, and 25 Rolls-Royces
- 275 Arab horses
- 12 boats
- 18 gold watches
- 80 platinum and diamond rings
- 25 servants
- 150 million dollars

Millionaire A
- 4 houses
- 30 cars – 10 Jaguars, 10 Porsches, and 10 Ferraris
- 100 Arab horses
- 5 boats
- 8 gold watches
- 50 gold and diamond rings
- 10 servants
- 50 million dollars

Millionaire B
- 5 houses – two in France, one in Miami, one in the Caribbean, and a castle in Scotland
- 50 cars – 10 Lamborghinis, 15 Mercedes-Benz, and 25 Rolls-Royces
- 275 Arab horses
- 12 boats
- 18 gold watches
- 80 platinum and diamond rings
- 25 servants
- 150 million dollars

Unit 11 **Practice 5** (SB p84)

A

B

Unit 12 **The weather 3** (SB p96)

WORLD WEATHER: NOON YESTERDAY

		°C
Athens	S	18
Berlin	___	___
Bombay	R	31
Edinburgh	___	___
Geneva	C	12
Hong Kong	___	___
Lisbon	C	19
London	___	___
Los Angeles	Fg	21
Jeddah	___	___
Milan	Fg	19
Moscow	___	___
Oslo	Sn	2

S = sunny
Fg = foggy
Sn = snowy
C = cloudy
R = rainy

WORLD WEATHER: NOON YESTERDAY

		°C
Athens	S	18
Berlin	___	___
Bombay	R	31
Edinburgh	___	___
Geneva	C	12
Hong Kong	___	___
Lisbon	C	19
London	___	___
Los Angeles	Fg	21
Jeddah	___	___
Milan	Fg	19
Moscow	___	___
Oslo	Sn	2

S = sunny
Fg = foggy
Sn = snowy
C = cloudy
R = rainy

WORLD WEATHER: NOON YESTERDAY

		°C
Athens	S	18
Berlin	___	___
Bombay	R	31
Edinburgh	___	___
Geneva	C	12
Hong Kong	___	___
Lisbon	C	19
London	___	___
Los Angeles	Fg	21
Jeddah	___	___
Milan	Fg	19
Moscow	___	___
Oslo	Sn	2

S = sunny
Fg = foggy
Sn = snowy
C = cloudy
R = rainy

WORLD WEATHER: NOON YESTERDAY

		°C
Athens	S	18
Berlin	___	___
Bombay	R	31
Edinburgh	___	___
Geneva	C	12
Hong Kong	___	___
Lisbon	C	19
London	___	___
Los Angeles	Fg	21
Jeddah	___	___
Milan	Fg	19
Moscow	___	___
Oslo	Sn	2

S = sunny
Fg = foggy
Sn = snowy
C = cloudy
R = rainy

Unit 13 Catching a train 4 (SB p105)

DEPARTURE TIME from Oxford	ARRIVAL TIME at London Paddington
0858	0951
0915	1010
0921	1031
1745	1844
1815	1915
1825	1932
Day return	£15.50
Period return	£22.50

DEPARTURE TIME from Oxford	ARRIVAL TIME at London Paddington
0858	0951
0915	1010
0921	1031
1745	1844
1815	1915
1825	1932
Day return	£15.50
Period return	£22.50

DEPARTURE TIME from Oxford	ARRIVAL TIME at Stratford-upon-Avon
0912	1018
1023	1127
1218	1325
1746	1904
1857	2031
1945	2110
Day return	£17.50
Period return	£25.50

DEPARTURE TIME from Oxford	ARRIVAL TIME at Stratford-upon-Avon
0912	1018
1023	1127
1218	1325
1746	1904
1857	2031
1945	2110
Day return	£17.50
Period return	£25.50

DEPARTURE TIME from Oxford	ARRIVAL TIME at Reading
0739	0808
0815	0838
0920	0943
1630	1715
1645	1709
1720	1754
Day return	£8.50
Period return	£15.50

DEPARTURE TIME from Oxford	ARRIVAL TIME at Reading
0739	0808
0815	0838
0920	0943
1630	1715
1645	1709
1720	1754
Day return	£8.50
Period return	£15.50

Extra ideas Units 9–14 Revision

Vocabulary

The following words are either flowers or colours. Put them into the correct column. If you have a dictionary, use it to check new words.

tulip   pink   orange   daffodil   grey
rose   red   gold   white   snowdrop
yellow   primrose   brown

Flowers	Colours

The Garden that Moved House!

Artist Verena Devoy loves gardening. It is her passion. Until three days ago she lived in a lovely little thatched cottage in a village near Cambridge. She spent ten years and thousands of pounds to make her garden there beautiful. She had flowers and plants for every season of the year.

In autumn, big orange chrysanthemums grew next to the gold of the trees and bushes. In winter, little white snowdrops grew in the grass and under the trees. In spring there were bright yellow daffodils all over her front lawn and tulips and primroses next to the path. And summer! Summer was the prettiest season of all! She bought hundreds of roses to fill every part of the garden: she bought climbing roses to put round the windows and doors, pink roses for the front garden, and red and white roses for the back. A lot of people came to the village especially to see Verena's garden. It was more beautiful than the park.

Then last summer she decided that she would like to move to a bigger house. It was easy to sell her beautiful cottage. Mr and Mrs Grey from London came to see it. **'We fell in love with it immediately,'** especially the garden – we couldn't believe the colours of the roses. We wanted to move from London because we didn't have a garden there.'

Of course Mr and Mrs Grey bought the cottage and at the end of the summer they moved from London. They arrived at the cottage.

'There was no garden! There was a brown field with some stones and rocks. There weren't any flowers or trees and there wasn't any grass! It looked terrible! We couldn't believe our eyes!'

But it was true! Verena Devoy loved her garden so much that she took it with her when she left. Five large lorries carried all the flowers, trees, and plants to her new house five miles away. It cost £1,000! She says:

'I've got a much bigger garden now' and I'm going to make it even more beautiful than my first garden. I'm going to plant all the flowers and trees again and this time I'm going to have a pond with some goldfish.'

And Mr and Mrs Grey? What do they say? 'She can't do this! We bought the garden with the house! We're going to see our solicitor!'

Reading

Read the text and answer the questions. If you have a dictionary, use it to help with new words.

1. What is Verena's hobby?
2. Why did she spend thousands of pounds?
3. Which was the most colourful season in her garden?
4. Why did Verena want to move?
5. Did Mr and Mrs Grey like the cottage when they first saw it?
6. Why were they shocked when they arrived at the cottage?
7. How much did Verena pay to move her garden?
8. What are her plans for her new garden?
9. What are Mr and Mrs Grey going to do?

Language work

1 Here are some answers. Complete the questions.

1. How much **did she spend to make her garden beautiful?**
   Thousands of pounds.
2. Which was _____?
   Summer. Because of all the roses.
3. Why _____?
   To see Verena's garden.
4. Was _____?
   Yes, it was. Very easy.
5. Why _____?
   Because they wanted to have a garden.
6. When _____?
   At the end of the summer.
7. What _____ like?
   It looked terrible. There weren't any flowers, just stones and rocks.
8. Has Verena _____ now?
   Yes, she has. It's much bigger.
9. What _____?
   She's going to make it even more beautiful and she's going to have a pond.
10. Who _____?
    Their solicitor.

2 Find examples of the following in the text. <u>Underline</u> them.

1. The present and past of *have got*
2. a comparative sentence
3. a superlative sentence
4. three irregular past tenses
5. three sentences about the future
6. an infinitive of purpose
7. a sentence with *some*
8. a sentence with *any*

NOTES

NOTES

NOTES

NOTES

Test material

Stop and check 1

UNITS 1–4

Correct the mistakes

Each sentence has a mistake. Find it and correct it.

Example
Antonia is ~~Italiana~~. **Antonia is Italian.**

1. London is a city very big.
2. My mother works in a hotel is a receptionist.
3. My father watch TV in the evening.
4. He's like watching football.
5. On Sundays we go in a restaurant.
6. Hans is businessman.
7. You family is very nice.
8. I like listen to the radio.
9. Our school have a lot of students.
10. The childrens go to school near here.
11. We have the dinner at 7.00.
12. Buses in London are reds.
13. My brother no have a job.
14. Do you want a ice-cream?
15. Is near here, my flat.

[15]

Word order

Put the words in the correct order.

Example
Cairo Yasmina from comes. **Yasmina comes from Cairo.**

1. policeman from is John a New York
   _____
2. married brother is your?
   _____
3. mountains sister skiing goes the in my
   _____
4. isn't coffee nice English very
   _____
5. your what name teacher's is?
   _____
6. surname how spell do your you?
   _____
7. often weekends go I at swimming
   _____

[7]

Choose the correct sentence

One sentence is correct. Which one?

Example
Where she from? ✗
Where does she from? ✗
Where is she from? ✓

1. a Sally is a nice girl, and I like.
   b Sally is a nice girl, and I like her.
   c Sally is a nice girl, and I like him.
2. a He has 27 years old.
   b He's 27 years.
   c He's 27.
3. a Peter works with his father.
   b Peter works with he's father.
   c Peter works with him father.
4. a Sally and Tim live in Madrid. They're flat is lovely.
   b Sally and Tim live in Madrid. Their flat is lovely.
   c Sally and Tim live in Madrid. There flat is lovely.
5. a She lives in a house or a flat?
   b Does she lives in a house or a flat?
   c Does she live in a house or a flat?
6. a I don't like going to meetings.
   b I don't like go to meetings.
   c I no like going to meetings.
7. a How many languages you speak?
   b How many languages do you speak?
   c How many languages does you speak?
8. a My brother work in a bank.
   b My brother he works in a bank.
   c My brother works in a bank.

[8]

Questions

1 Match a line in A with a line in B to make questions.

A	B
What	do you go to bed?
Where	languages do you speak?
What time	is a cup of coffee and a sandwich?
Who	do you usually sit next to?
How much	do you do at weekends?
How many	do you go on holiday?

[5]

2 Here are the answers to some questions. Write the questions. Use the words in brackets.

Example
What do you do? (you/do) I'm a hairdresser.

a _____ ?
  (Peter / start work) At 8.00.
b _____ ?
  (Sylvie and Jacques / come)   From France.
c _____ ?
  (your wife's)   Jackie.
d _____ ?
  (you / have)   Three. Two girls and a boy.
e _____ ?
  (you / like / gardening)
  Yes, I do. I grow a lot of vegetables.

[5]

Prepositions

Complete the text with the prepositions in the box.

| at   in   about   after   for   with   by   to   on   after |

Example
James lives ____in____ a small flat.

James lives (1)_____ Cambridge. He lives (2)_____ two other boys who are students (3)_____ Cambridge University. They work hard during the week, but (4)_____ weekends they invite a lot of friends to their house. They cook a meal (5)_____ their friends, and then they go out (6)_____ a café (7)_____ a coffee, or they stay (8)_____ home and listen (9)_____ the radio.
James has two jobs. (10)_____ Mondays, Tuesdays, and Wednesdays he works (11)_____ a hospital, where he helps to look (12)_____ children who are ill. He goes to the hospital (13)_____ bus. He starts (14)_____ ten o'clock and works until quarter (15)_____ five. On Thursdays and Fridays he works (16)_____ home. He has a computer (17)_____ his bedroom and he writes stories. (18)_____ the evening, one of the boys cooks a meal. (19)_____ dinner they look in the newspaper to see what's on TV or they talk (20)_____ their day. They usually go to bed at about midnight.

[20]

Vocabulary

Put the words in the correct column. There are five words for each column.

| egg   menu   scientist   favourite   tuna   accountant |
| collect   hotel   cake   island   want   deliver   letter |
| easy   expensive   chicken   journalist   dictionary |
| sell   friendly   interpreter   magazine   orange   café |
| beach   nurse   office   newspaper   busy   listen |

Things to read	Professions	Things to eat	Places	Verbs	Adjectives
		egg			

[30]

am/is/do/does (not)

Complete the sentences with the verbs in the box.

| am/'m not   is/isn't   are/aren't   does/doesn't   do/don't |

Example
I _'m not_____ English.

1 Fez _____ in Morocco.
2 Where _____ you from?
3 I _____ on holiday. I'm at work.
4 My teacher _____ very funny.
5 What time _____ the bank open?
6 My sister _____ eat meat because she _____ like it.
7 I _____ hungry. How much _____ a tuna sandwich?
8 Where _____ you usually go on holiday?
9 Daddy, we _____ want to go to bed. We _____ tired.
10 Learning English_____ boring! It's interesting!

[10]

TOTAL [100]

TRANSLATE

Translate the sentences into your language. Translate the *ideas*, not word by word.

1 I am a student.
   _____
2 My brother is a teacher.
   _____
3 She isn't at home. She's at work.
   _____
4 I live in a flat.
   _____
5 My mother works in a bank.
   _____
6 I don't drink coffee.
   _____
7 My father doesn't like football.
   _____
8 What do you do at weekends?
   _____
9 John's flat is in the centre of town.
   _____
10 Can I have a cup of tea, please?
   _____

Stop and check 2

UNITS 5–8

Correct the mistakes

Each sentence has a mistake. Find it and correct it.
Example
~~Where you live?~~ Where do you live?

1. There no is a supermarket.
2. Look at this pictures.
3. Is a bank near here?
4. I arrive at Heathrow airport at ten o'clock last night.
5. She could to speak three languages when she was ten.
6. Where did you went last night?
7. The plant is in front the window.
8. I don't can go out because I have a lot of homework.
9. In the kitchen is a table.
10. I was to the museum last weekend.
11. Who are these people over there?
12. I buyed a new DVD.
13. Did you watch the football on TV last evening?
14. Italian people is very friendly.
15. I like cities because I can to go to the shopping mall.

[15]

Past Simple

Complete the text with the Past Simple form of the verbs in brackets. There are regular and irregular verbs.
Example
Isaac Newton ____lived____ in England in the seventeenth and eighteenth century.

He was a student in Cambridge, where he (1)_____ (study) philosophy and astronomy. He (2)_____ (begin) to work on a new mathematical theory as a student, and later this (3)_____ (become) the system of calculus.
Newton (4)_____ (not be) just a mathematician. He (5)_____ (work) on a theory of colour, and he also (6)_____ (invent) a telescope with mirrors.
Newton is most famous for his work on gravity and the movement of planets. In 1684, he (7)_____ (write) the *Principia*, which (8)_____ (explain) the movement of the planets around the sun.
Newton was also a Member of Parliament, but he only (9)_____ (say) something once in parliament – asking for the window to be closed! Throughout his life, Newton didn't find it easy to make friends, and in fact he (10)_____ (make) a lot of enemies.

[20]

Irregular verbs

Write the Past Simple form of these irregular verbs.

1. give _____
2. leave _____
3. sell _____
4. speak _____
5. lose _____
6. make _____
7. break _____
8. meet _____
9. win _____
10. take _____

[10]

can/could/was/were (not)

Complete the sentences with the verbs in the box.

| can can't was wasn't were weren't could couldn't |

Example
I ___can't___ drive. I'm only 14 years old.

1. Our teacher _____ at school last week because she _____ ill.
2. He _____ a student in Florence. He _____ draw and design buildings.
3. We _____ see football match last night.
4. 'Where _____ you last night? You _____ at home. I phoned you, but there _____ no answer.'
5. 'I _____ get into my flat because I lost my keys. I _____ at a friend's house.'

[10]

Questions and negatives

Write the statements as questions and negatives.
Example
He can swim. **Can he swim?**
              He can't swim.

1. There's a good restaurant _____
   in this town.   _____
2. There are some eggs in _____
   the fridge.   _____

3 You can speak French. _____

4 He was born in 1985. _____

5 She could play chess when she was three. _____

6 They were in class last week. _____

7 Your parents studied German at school. _____

8 The students went to the library last night. _____

[16]

some/any/a/an

Complete the sentences with *some*, *any*, *a*, or *an*.
Example
Heathrow is ___an___ international airport.

1 Did Charles Dickens have _____ children?
2 I bought _____ newspaper and _____ magazines.
3 Jane lives in _____ old house in France.
4 There are _____ trees in my garden, but there aren't _____ flowers.
5 Do you have _____ books by Gabriel García Márquez?
6 There are _____ letters for you on the table.

[8]

Vocabulary – connections

Match a line in A with a line in B.

A	B
ski	kitchen
sofa	second
computer	operator
2nd	plane
telephone	living room
fridge	wedding
son	snow
season	Internet
Congratulations!	war
ticket	sun
pharmacy	month
soldier	aspirin

[11]

Vocabulary – opposites

Match a word in A with its opposite in B.

A	B
hot	rich
clean	far
win	under
old	left
near	cold
before	lose
happy	finish
poor	after
on	sad
begin	dirty
right	modern

[10]

TOTAL [100]

TRANSLATE

Translate the sentences into your language. Translate the *ideas*, not word by word.

1 Is there a pharmacy near here?
_____
2 There are two books on the table.
_____
3 There are some flowers in the living room.
_____
4 Are there any glasses?
_____
5 I can ski, but I can't swim.
_____
6 I couldn't go to the meeting last night.
_____
7 I was ill.
_____
8 Where were you born?
_____
9 I was born in Iran.
_____
10 She started work when she was twelve.
_____
11 He didn't like his first job.
_____
12 Where did you go on holiday last year?
_____

Stop and check 3

UNITS 9–12

Correct the mistakes

There is a mistake in each sentence. Find it and correct it.

Example
~~Where you live?~~ Where do you live?

1. It's very hot today – do you like something to drink?
2. Peter's got a lot of books because he'd like reading.
3. How many children do you got?
4. How many money has he got?
5. Who's is that new car?
6. I'm go home now because it's late.
7. Last night I went to a café for to meet my friends.
8. We're going have a test next week.
9. I'm wear my old clothes because I'm going to clean the car.
10. Pierre is French, he's coming from Paris.
11. What you doing this evening?
12. My sister is more old than me.
13. I think is going to rain.
14. Your house is bigger than my.
15. Who is the most rich person in the world?

[15]

Questions and answers

Match a question in A with an answer in B.

A	B
Where does your sister work?	Yes, of course. What can I do for you?
Whose is this coat?	Yes. I think he's very nice.
How many sons have you got?	To buy some toothpaste.
How much did your bike cost?	To Turkey.
Could you help me, please?	In a bank.
Would you like some more to eat?	I stayed at home.
Do you like Henry?	Three.
Where are you going on holiday?	It's Jane's.
Why are you going to the pharmacy?	£195.
What did you do last night?	Her name's Mrs Taylor.
Who's the new teacher?	No, thanks. I'm full.

[10]

Comparatives and superlatives

Complete the chart.

Adjective	Comparative	Superlative
big	_____	_____
_____	more beautiful	_____
_____	_____	worst
exciting	_____	_____
noisy	_____	_____

[10]

Comparing hotels

1. Look at the information about the two hotels. Write five sentences about the hotels using the comparative forms of the adjectives in the box.

   Example
   The Ritz is a better hotel than The Strand.

good	big	expensive	near	far	modern

	The Strand	The Ritz
Number of stars	★★★	★★★★
Number of rooms	102	55
Price	£80–£100	£120–£140
How many minutes to the sea?	10 minutes	15 minutes
How many minutes to the town centre?	20 minutes	8 minutes
Old or new?	New–1990	Old–1870

   a _____
   b _____
   c _____
   d _____
   e _____

   [10]

2. Look at the information about The Star Hotel. Write five more sentences, comparing the three hotels. Use the superlative form of the adjectives.

   Example
   The Star is the best hotel.

	The Star
Number of stars	★★★★★
Number of rooms	45
Price	£150–£175
How many minutes to the sea?	1 minute
How many minutes to the town centre?	15 minutes
Old or new?	Old–1920

a _____
b _____
c _____
d _____
e _____

[10]

some/any/a

Complete the sentences with *some*, *any*, or *a*.

Example
I don't have ___any___ brothers or sisters.

1 Would you like _____ cup of tea?
2 You have _____ lovely pictures on the walls!
3 Is there _____ water in the fridge?
4 Can I have _____ grapes, please?
5 I'd like _____ burger and _____ chips, please.
6 Do you want _____ sandwich?
7 The shop doesn't have _____ potatoes, peas, or bread.
8 There are _____ eggs in the cupboard, but there isn't _____ sugar.

[10]

Present Simple and Continuous

Complete the sentences with the correct form of the verbs in brackets.

Example
I often ___watch___ (watch) TV in the evenings, but tonight ___I'm going___ (go) to a restaurant.

1 Pierre _____ (drink) five cups of coffee, but he _____ (not drink) now because he's in class.
2 Alice and Peter _____ (look) for a new house. They _____ (not like) living in London.
3 I always _____ (wear) nice clothes for work. Today I _____ (wear) a blue jacket and skirt.
4 'Why _____ you _____ (go) to bed? It's only 10.00.' 'I always _____ (go) to bed early.'
5 Jane _____ (work) in a bank, but today she's at home. She _____ (write) letters.

[10]

going to

Complete the sentences with *going to*. Use a verb and a place or person from the boxes.

Example
I'm going to do my homework in the living room.

buy	write	see	borrow	have

my friend	Malta	library	museum	baker's

1 Peter _____ some bread at _____ .
2 I _____ some books from _____ .
3 We _____ an exhibition at _____ .
4 They _____ a holiday in _____ .
5 I _____ a letter to _____ .

[10]

Vocabulary

Put the words in the correct column.

| tea fruit a dress a suit mushrooms milk a shirt cheese coffee rice a sweater water juice shorts meat |

Clothes shop	Food	Drinks
a dress		

[15]

TOTAL 100

TRANSLATE

Translate the sentences into your language. Translate the *ideas*, not word by word.

1 I like orange juice. I'd like an orange juice.
_____
2 There is some bread on the table. There isn't any coffee.
_____
3 You're older than me, but Tim is the oldest in the class.
_____
4 My sister has got three children.
_____
5 I usually wear jeans, but today I'm wearing a suit.
_____
6 'Whose is this book?' 'It's mine.'
_____
7 We're going to have a picnic.
_____
8 I went into London to buy some books.
_____

Stop and check 4

UNITS 13–14

Correct the mistakes

There is a mistake in each sentence. Find it and correct it.
Example
We ~~was~~ in Paris last year.   **We were in Paris last year.**

1 Why you want to learn Portuguese?
2 She hasn't never been to Madrid.
3 I've wrote to her three times and she hasn't answered yet.
4 I didn't enjoy the book. It was very bored.
5 How many times you been to Greece?
6 I'm very exciting about my holiday.
7 The students worked very hardly.
8 Say me when you want to stop for lunch.
9 What sort magazines do you like reading?
10 Did you ever been to Ireland?

[10]

Questions and tenses

Ask questions about the statements.
Example
John went to New York.   When _did he go_ ?

1 Anna's tired.
   Why _____ ?
2 I don't go to work by car.
   How _____ you _____ ?
3 This pen isn't mine.
   Whose _____ ?
4 I met a famous tennis player.
   Who _____ you _____ ?
5 Simon's bought a new car.
   What sort _____ ?
6 We saw Bill yesterday.
   Where _____ you _____ ?
7 Sue's watching television.
   What _____ ?
8 They're going on holiday.
   Where _____ ?
9 Peter's left the picnic.
   Why _____ ?
10 She drank a lot of juice.
   How much _____ ?

[20]

Past Simple and Present Perfect

1 Underline the correct tense.
   Example
   I _saw_/have seen Jill yesterday.

   1 I _met_/have met Anna ten years ago.
   2 My sister _did never go_/_has never been_ to France.
   3 I'm sorry. I _didn't finish_/_haven't finished_ my work yet.
   4 I _ate_/_have eaten_ a lot of ice-cream when I was a child.
   5 They _climbed_/_have climbed_ Everest in 1953.

[5]

2 Put the verb in brackets in the correct form, the Present Simple or the Present Perfect.
   Example
   I travelled (travel) by plane for the first time last year.

   1 We _____ (go) to Paris two years ago.
   2 _____ you ever _____ (eat) Japanese food?
   3 I _____ never _____ (be) to hospital.
   4 Where _____ you _____ (live) when you were a student?
   5 I can't give you your book back, because I _____ (not read) it yet.

[10]

Adverb or adjective?

Underline the correct form.
Example
I'm driving careful/_carefully_ because it is raining.

1 Our village is always very _quiet/quietly_. Nothing happens.
2 Please speak more _slow/slowly_. I can't understand you.
3 He's a very _good/well_ driver.
4 My brother doesn't drive very _good/well_.
5 My grandparents are very strong and _healthy/healthily_ for their age.

[5]

Word order

Put the words in the correct order.

Example
letter you yet have written?
Have you written the letter yet?

1 many got you how cousins have?
   _____
2 Rome they just have in arrived
   _____
3 well speak you very English
   _____
4 quickly road along man the walked the
   _____
5 by book a have Shakespeare read ever you?
   _____
6 exam students the yesterday a had difficult
   _____
7 carefully work you did your check?
   _____
8 exercise this do please quickly
   _____
9 people going many invite picnic how are to to your you?
   _____
10 up is because she tired she got early
   _____

[10]

Auxiliaries

Complete the sentences with an auxiliary verb from the box.

am/is/are	do/does	did	have/has

Example
I ___am___ listening to the radio.

1 Look at those children – they _____ swimming in the river!
2 _____ your daughter speak French well?
3 _____ you learn German when you were at school?
4 _____ Ben ever been to India?
5 We _____ never played volleyball.
6 I _____ going to have driving lessons soon.
7 _____ Mark and Jane live near you?
8 _____ John going to phone you tomorrow?
9 When _____ you start work? A long time ago?
10 _____ you written to thank Sue and Bill yet?

[10]

Vocabulary – word groups

Put the words in the correct column. Each column has a different number of words.

| quiet day return annoying jumbo jet departure lounge |
| worried niece station husband arrival hall platform |
| tiring aunt flight grandson badly-behaved boarding pass |
| gate widow lovely |

Travel by train	Travel by plane	Adjectives	Family

[20]

Prepositions

Complete the sentences with the prepositions in the box.

| about | in | out of | by | on | for | to | from |

Example
Pamela lives ___on___ the second floor.

1 I'm reading a book _____ the history of France.
2 *Oliver Twist* is a book _____ Charles Dickens.
3 Is it far _____ your house to the station?
4 Is Mexico City the biggest city _____ the world?
5 Jane's worried _____ her exam.
6 What's _____ television tonight?
7 Are you interested _____ photography?
8 She works _____ a big company.
9 Can I speak _____ you for a moment?
10 He drove _____ the garage and down the street.

[10]

TOTAL 100

TRANSLATE

Translate the sentences into your language. Translate the *ideas*, not word by word.

1 Tim drives carefully. Tim's a careful driver.
   _____
2 Have you ever been to China? I went to China last year.
   _____
3 He hasn't finished his homework yet.
   _____
4 I've just finished my homework.
   _____
5 I want to go home.
   _____
6 I'm interested in history.
   _____

Progress test 1

UNITS 1–5

Exercise 1 Asking about people

Surname	Smith
First name	John
Country	Britain
Age	30
Address	94 East St, Oxford OX1 9HJ
Job	Teacher
Place of work	School in Oxford
Married	No
Free time	Football

Read the information about John Smith. Write the questions.

Example
What's his first name?
His first name's John.

1 _____
   His surname is Smith.
2 _____
   He's from Britain.
3 _____
   He's 30.
4 _____
   94 East St, Oxford OX1 9HJ.
5 _____
   He's a teacher.
6 _____
   In a school in Oxford.
7 _____
   No, he isn't. He's single.
8 _____
   He plays football.

[8]

Exercise 2 Word order

Put the words in the correct order.
Example
you from are Where?
Where are you from?

1 do at What weekends you do?
   _____
2 work she does Where?
   _____
3 a television There photo is the on
   _____
4 near there pharmacy a Is here?
   _____
5 coffee please I a Can have?
   _____
6 children How they do have many?
   _____
7 skiing in Hans Switzerland teaches
   _____
8 any Is milk the there fridge in?
   _____
9 not work Rosy go by does to car
   _____
10 Sue going Dave and restaurants like to
   _____

[10]

Exercise 3 Questions

Match a line in A with a line in B to make a question. Then find an answer in C.

A	B	C
Who	do you do on Sundays?	At seven o'clock.
How much	do you meet on Saturday evenings?	To the gym.
What	do you go on Friday evenings?	My friends, Dave and Paul.
Where	do you get up?	I play tennis.
How	is a chicken sandwich?	By bus.
What time	do you travel to work?	£2.50.

[5]

Exercise 4 some, any, a, and an

Complete the sentences with some, any, a, or an.
Example
There are __some__ flowers in the garden.

1 There are _____ pictures on the wall.
2 Can I have _____ apple, please?
3 Are there _____ books in the living room?
4 There aren't _____ good restaurants in our city.
5 There's _____ newsagent's opposite the post office.
6 John has _____ trees in his garden.
7 Are there _____ Japanese students in your class?
8 There's _____ orange on the table.
9 There aren't _____ photographs on the wall.
10 There are _____ plates next to the sink.

[10]

Exercise 5 Present Simple

Complete the text with the correct form of the verb in brackets.

I (1)_____ (have) two brothers, Simon and Chris. They (2)_____ (live) in London. Simon (3)_____ (be) a pilot and Chris (3)_____ (work) in a garage. Simon (5)_____ (like) flying, but Chris (6)_____ _____ (not like) mending cars. At weekends I (7)_____ (go) to London and I (8)_____ (stay) with them. We (9)_____ (go) to a football match on Saturday, and on Sunday we (10)_____ (walk) in Hyde Park.

[10]

Exercise 6 be and do

Complete the sentences with a verb from the box.
Example
Peter __is__ a teacher.

| am / am not | does / does not | is / is not |
| do / do not | are / are not | |

1 I _____ hungry. Can I have an apple?
2 How _____ you travel to work?
3 Rome _____ in Spain. It _____ in Italy.
4 Mary and Sarah _____ like milk.
5 _____ James have two jobs?
6 Ben _____ like travelling by bus.
7 We aren't from Spain – we _____ from Portugal.
8 '_____ you like ice-cream?' 'No, I _____ .'

[9]

Exercise 7 Plural forms

Write these sentences in the plural.
Example
She's a doctor.   They_'re doctors_.

1 I go swimming on Saturdays.
   _____

2 He watches TV every day.
   _____

3 The dictionary is over there.
   _____

4 This watch is expensive.
   _____

5 Look at that lovely flower.
   _____

6 Do you have a stamp?
   _____

7 She's our child.
   _____

8 He's an interesting person.
   _____

9 That man is American.
   _____

10 The school doesn't have a computer.
   _____

[10]

Exercise 8 Prepositions

Complete the sentences with the correct preposition.
Write one word on each line.

1 There are two chairs _____ the living room.
2 The sofa is _____ _____ the table.
3 There's a lamp _____ the sofa.
4 There's a picture _____ the wall.
5 The chairs are _____ the television.
6 There's a cat _____ _____ _____ the fire.
7 The telephone is _____ the table.

[7]

Exercise 9 Choose the correct sentence

Tick (✓) the correct sentence.
Example
Let's go to home.
Let's go home. ✓

1 a Kate and Ann are students in Cambridge University.
   b Kate and Ann are students at Cambridge University.
2 a Let's go out to the park!
   b Let's go out at the park!
3 a On Thursdays I get home at six o'clock.
   b In Thursdays I get home at six o'clock.
4 a Richard lives at London.
   b Richard lives in London.
5 a To weekends I go swimming.
   b At weekends I go swimming.

[5]

Exercise 10 Which one is different?

Underline the different word.
Example
Cambridge London Oxford Rome

1 magazine	pen	newspaper	book
2 milk	apple	ice-cream	bread
3 house	palace	street	flat
4 architect	dentist	policeman	teach
5 boring	interesting	like	funny
6 father	sister	mother	man
7 house	bathroom	kitchen	living room
8 often	near	next to	opposite
9 France	England	American	Hungary
10 my	we	his	your

[10]

Exercise 11 Adjectives

Match the opposites.

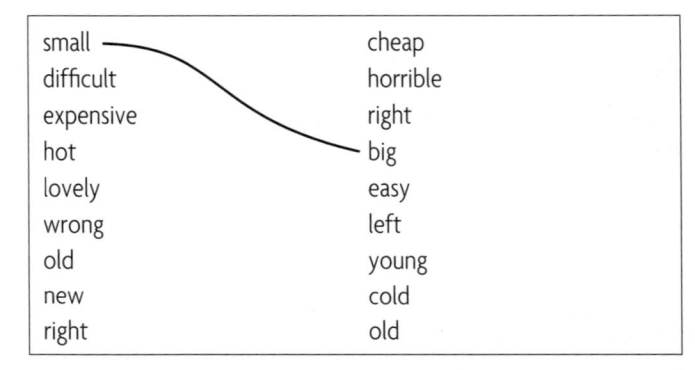

small	cheap
difficult	horrible
expensive	right
hot	big
lovely	easy
wrong	left
old	young
new	cold
right	old

[8]

Exercise 12 Words that go together

Match a verb in A with a line in B.

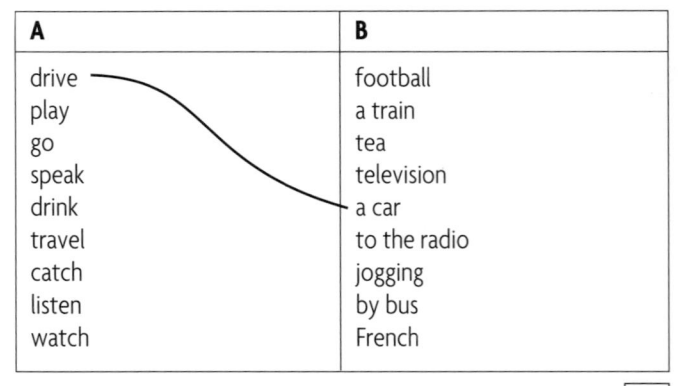

A	B
drive	football
play	a train
go	tea
speak	television
drink	a car
travel	to the radio
catch	jogging
listen	by bus
watch	French

[8]

TOTAL 100

Progress test 2

UNITS 6–10

Exercise 1 The past tense of the verb *to be*

What are the past tense forms of the verb *to be*?

		Positive	Negative
Example	I	was	wasn't
1	You	_____	_____
2	He/She/It	_____	_____
3	We	_____	_____
4	They	_____	_____

[8]

Exercise 2 *can* and *can't*

Read the information, then complete the sentences with *can* or *can't* and a verb.

	swim	play tennis	speak German	speak Italian
Sylvia	✓	✗	✓	✓
Linda	✓	✓	✗	✓
Marianne	✗	✗	✓	✓

Example
Linda **can swim** and she **can play** tennis.

1 Sylvia can swim, but she _____.
2 Marianne _____ and she _____.
3 Linda _____, but Sylvia and Marianne can.
4 Everybody _____.
5 Only Linda _____.
6 Sylvia and Linda _____, but Marianne can't.

[7]

Exercise 3 Past Simple

Write the Past Simple of these verbs.

Regular	Irregular
1 work ____	6 have ____
2 live ____	7 come ____
3 earn ____	8 give ____
4 move ____	9 go ____
5 stay ____	10 buy ____

[10]

Exercise 4 Past Simple and Present Simple

Complete the text with the correct form of the verb in brackets: the Past Simple or the Present Simple.

My friend Jack is 40. He (1)_____ (leave) Britain when he was 20 and (2)_____ (go) to Italy. He (3)_____ (work) in Naples for ten years, then he (4)_____ (move) to Rome. There he (5)_____ (meet) Antonella. They (6)_____ (get) married in 1982 and now they (7)_____ (live) in Florence. Jack (8)_____ (teach) English in a language school. And what (9)_____ (do) Antonella do? She (10)_____ (sell) computer software.

[10]

Exercise 5 Past Simple: negative

Make these positive sentences negative.
Example
He bought a new shirt. *He didn't buy a new shirt.*

1 We enjoyed the football match.
   _____
2 I took a photograph of my sister.
   _____
3 Angela wrote a letter to her friend.
   _____
4 Charles Dickens became a journalist when he was 18.
   _____
5 Germany won the World Cup in 1986.
   _____
6 Her father died when she was 14.
   _____
7 I lost £10 last night.
   _____
8 People flew by plane 100 years ago.
   _____
9 That book was very interesting.
   _____
10 We arrived at school at eight o'clock.
   _____

[10]

Exercise 6 would like

Tick (✓) the correct sentence.
Example
A Would you like | a drink? ✓
   Do you like | ✗
B No thanks, I'm not thirsty.

1 A Would you like | some fruit?
      Do you like |
   B Yes. An apple, please.
2 A Would you like | windsurfing?
      Do you like |
   B Yes, but I prefer swimming.
3 A What | do you like | for dinner this evening?
           | would you like |
   B Steak and chips.
4 A Would you like | Mr Brown?
      Do you like |
   B No. He's not very nice.
5 A Can I help you?
   B Yes. | I like | a bottle of mineral water, please.
           | I'd like |

[5]

Exercise 7 Countable and uncountable

Write C next to the count nouns and U next to the uncount nouns.
Example
book **C**   rice **U**

1 pencil ___   5 apple   ___
2 water   ___   6 money   ___
3 rain   ___   7 bread   ___
4 flower ___

[7]

Exercise 8 some, any, or a

Write some, any, or a in the gaps.
Example
Do you have ___**any**___ rice?

1 I've got _____ pens in the office.
2 Can I have _____ bottle of water, please?
3 There isn't _____ sugar in the dining room.
4 Have you got _____ photographs of Jim?
5 I'd like _____ fruit, please.
6 Peter put _____ water and _____ glasses on the table.
7 There wasn't _____ petrol or oil in the car.

[8]

Exercise 9 How much and How many

Complete the questions with How much or How many.

1 _____ milk is there in the fridge?
2 _____ stamps do you need?
3 _____ oranges and apples are there on the table?
4 _____ juice is there in the kitchen?
5 _____ money did you take to France?

[5]

Exercise 10 Comparatives and superlatives 1

Read about the castles.

Abergoran Castle
Price: £200,000
Built: 1072
Rooms: 0

Footleby Castle
Price: £10 million
Built: 1835
Rooms: 160

Haywood Castle
Price: £2 million
Built: 1450
Rooms: 20

These sentences are false. Correct them.
Example
Abergoran Castle is more modern than Haywood Castle.
No, it isn't. It's older.

1 Footleby Castle is cheaper than Haywood Castle.
　_____
2 Abergoran Castle is bigger than Footleby Castle.
　_____
3 Abergoran Castle is the biggest.
　_____
4 Abergoran Castle is more expensive than Footleby Castle.
　_____
5 Footleby Castle is the cheapest.
　_____
6 Footleby Castle is older than Haywood Castle.
　_____
7 Abergoran Castle is the most modern.
　_____

7

Exercise 11 Comparatives and superlatives 2

Complete the chart.

Adjective	Comparative	Superlative
_____	more dangerous	_____
_____	_____	best
bad	_____	_____
interesting	_____	_____

8

Exercise 12 Ordinal numbers

Write the ordinal numbers in words.
Example
6th **sixth**

1 1st _____
2 2nd _____
3 3rd _____
4 12th _____
5 20th _____

5

Exercise 13 Opposites

Choose a word from the box and write it next to its opposite.
Example
big **small**

| interesting | old | buy | before | start |
| quiet | east | day | new | same |

1 boring _____
2 stop _____
3 night _____
4 sell _____
5 different _____
6 noisy _____
7 old _____
8 modern _____
9 west _____
10 after _____

10

TOTAL 100

Progress test 3

UNITS 11–14

Exercise 1 Present Continuous: -ing form

Write the correct -ing form.
Example
walk   walking
leave   leaving

1 drive _____
2 stop _____
3 work _____
4 use _____
5 look _____
6 get _____
7 buy _____
8 think _____
9 swim _____
10 cry _____

[10]

Exercise 2 Present Continuous

Complete the sentences with the Present Continuous form of the verb in brackets.
Example
Julie _is wearing_ earrings. (wear)

1 I _____ on holiday tomorrow. (not go)
2 A Why _____ you _____? (smile)
  B Because Mr Black didn't give us any homework.
3 A Where's Richard?
  B He _____ next to Jane. (stand)
4 Tom _____ at his desk. (not sit)
5 A What _____ Sue _____? (eat)
  B A tuna sandwich.
6 A What _____ you _____? (do)
  B I _____ my shoes. (clean)
7 I can't phone my wife. The telephone _____. (not work)

[8]

Exercise 3 Present Simple and Continuous

Complete the sentences with the Present Simple or the Present Continuous form of the verbs in brackets.
Example
'Be quiet! I_'m watching_ (watch) this programme!'

1 We usually _____ (take) the bus to town, but today we _____ (go) by car.
2 A Where _____ you usually _____ (go) on Wednesday evenings?
  B To a restaurant.
3 A It's 11.30. Why _____ you _____ (work) so late?
  B Because I _____ (have) a lot of homework.
4 A Where _____ your parents _____? (live)
  B In a small village near Oxford.
  A _____ they _____ (like) living in the country?
  B Yes, they do.
5 A What _____ you usually _____ (have) for breakfast?
  B Toast. But today I _____ (have) some fruit because there isn't any bread.
6 A The telephone _____ (ring). Can you answer it?
  B OK.

[10]

Exercise 4 Possessive pronouns

Write the sentences using a possessive pronoun.
Example
It's my pen. **It's mine.**
They're her socks. **They're hers.**

1 It's your newspaper.
   _____
2 They're his books.
   _____
3 It's her T-shirt.
   _____
4 They're our DVDs.
   _____
5 This is their house.
   _____

[5]

Exercise 5 going to

Make positive sentences, negative sentences, and questions using *going to*.
Examples
she / pilot **She's going to be a pilot.**
he / not / bus driver **He isn't going to be a bus driver.**
you / hairdresser? **Are you going to be a hairdresser?**

1 they / architects
   _____
2 he / not / writer
   _____
3 you / pilot?
   _____
4 I / not / policeman
   _____
5 we / shop assistants
   _____
6 she / not / chef
   _____
7 he / vet?
   _____
8 I / accountant
   _____
9 he / not / travel agent
   _____
10 you / English teacher?
   _____

[10]

Exercise 6 Infinitive of purpose

Rewrite these sentences using the infinitive of purpose.
Example
I went to Holland because I wanted to see the tulips.
I went to Holland to see the tulips.

1 I'm going to Moscow because I want to see the Kremlin.
   _____
2 Paul is going to London because he wants to buy some clothes.
   _____
3 Roger went to Dubai because he wanted to visit the Jumeirah beach.
   _____
4 Tracey often goes to the library because she wants to read.
   _____
5 Tim is going to America because he wants to see the Niagara Falls.
   _____
6 Frank is learning French because he wants to get a better job.
   _____
7 Peter is saving money because he wants to buy a car.
   _____
8 Henry went to Japan because he wanted to visit Kyoto.
   _____
9 Chris went to the newsagent's because he wanted to buy a newspaper.
   _____
10 Brian and Jane are going to Paris because they want to climb the Eiffel Tower.
   _____

[10]

Exercise 7 Adverbs

Write the adverbs next to the adjectives.
Example
quick **quickly**

1 slow   _____   5 hard   _____
2 early   _____   6 sudden _____
3 careful _____   7 fast   _____
4 good   _____   8 bad   _____

[8]

Exercise 8 Question words

Complete the questions with a word from the box.

Example
A __How__ tall is your brother?
B 1m 52.

| Where | Which | Why | How | Who | What | When |

1. A _____ often do you go to the library?
   B About once a month.
2. A _____ time does the programme start?
   B At nine o'clock.
3. A _____ did you close the window?
   B Because I'm cold.
4. A _____ colour is Andrew's new car?
   B Red.
5. A _____ did you go to town with?
   B Jim and Lucy.
6. A _____ newspaper do you want – the Italian one or the English one?
   B The English one.
7. A _____ is Edinburgh?
   B It's in Scotland.
8. A _____ are you going to clean your room?
   B When this programme has finished.
9. A _____ is your favourite season?
   B I like summer best.

[9]

Exercise 9 Past Simple and Present Perfect

Write the Past Simple and the Past Participle of these verbs.

Example
stay   stayed   stayed
sing   sang   sung

1. eat   _____   _____
2. win   _____   _____
3. live   _____   _____
4. have   _____   _____
5. do   _____   _____
6. cook   _____   _____
7. go   _____   _____
8. drive _____   _____

[8]

Exercise 10 Present Perfect and Past Simple

Tick (✓) the correct sentence.

1. a I went to London last week.
   b I have been to London last week.
2. a Have you ever been to France?
   b Did you ever go to France?
3. a Kate has finished her homework two hours ago.
   b Kate finished her homework two hours ago.
4. a Did he go to the dentist last week or the week before?
   b Has he been to the dentist last week or the week before?
5. a I haven't seen that exhibition yet.
   b I didn't see that exhibition yet.
6. a I've just bought my plane ticket to Paris – here it is!
   b I just bought my plane ticket to Paris – here it is!
7. a Jim and Cathy won £1,000 last month.
   b Jim and Cathy have won £1,000 last month.

[7]

Exercise 11 Word groups

Put the words in the correct column.

blue	T-shirt	foggy	green	sweater
tie	sunny	brown	cloudy	snowing
pink	suit	skirt	yellow	windy

Colours	Clothes	Weather

[15]

TOTAL [100]

Answer keys

Extra ideas Units 1–4

Answers
2 **A** How do you spell it?
3 **B** Glasgow, in Scotland.
4 **A** How old are you?
5 **B** Yes, I am.
6 **A** What's your husband's name?
7 **B** He's a teacher. (He teaches blind children.)
8 **B** Yes, I do. I have two sons and a daughter.
9 **A** Do you have any brothers or sisters?
10 **B** Yes, I do.
11 **A** Why do you enjoy your job?
12 **B** In London and Glasgow.
13 **B** Yes, I/we do.
14 **A** What do you like doing in your free time?

Extra ideas Units 5–8

Answers
1 3 Beijing
3 1 the day of any date in any year; the teams and the scores of every football match in every World Cup.
   2 He remembered the order of 35 packs of playing cards.
   3 No, he wasn't. He couldn't remember his lessons.
   4 They said he was stupid.
   5 Four years ago. He saw a programme on TV which showed people how to improve their memory.
4 1 What day was April 21, 1876?
   2 When did he become world champion?
   3 How much can he earn a day on European TV programmes?
   4 What does his wife do?
   5 What does he like doing in his free time?
5 1 He remembered the order of 35 packs of cards.
   2 Dominic is 34 years old.
   3 He started to improve his memory 4 years ago.
   4 He earns £1,000 a day.
   5 Children can learn to improve their memory from the age of five.

Extra ideas Units 9–14

Answers
Vocabulary

Flowers	Colours	
tulip	pink	red
rose	yellow	gold
daffodil	orange	white
snowdrop	brown	
primrose	grey	

(Note that *pink* is also a flower, a type of carnation, but it is not necessary to mention this.)

Reading
1 Her hobby is gardening.
2 To make her garden beautiful. / Because she wanted to make her garden beautiful.
3 Summer, because there were hundreds of red, white, and pink roses.
4 Because she wanted a bigger house.
5 Yes, they did. (They fell in love with it immediately.)
6 Because there was no garden, just a brown field with some stones and rocks. Also there weren't any flowers or trees.
7 £1,000.
8 She's going to plant all the flowers and trees again and she's going to have a pond with some goldfish.
9 They're going to see their solicitor.

Language work
1 2 Which was the prettiest season?
   3 Why did a lot of people come to the village?
   4 Was the cottage easy to sell?
   5 Why did Mr and Mrs Grey want to move from London?
   6 When did they move?
   7 What was the garden like?
   8 Has Verena got a bigger house (now)?
   9 What is she going to do (with it)?
   10 Who are Mr and Mrs Grey going to see?
2 1 **Present**
      I've got a much bigger garden
      Past
      She had flowers and plants for every season
      … *we didn't have* a garden there.
   2 It was *more beautiful than* the park.
      … she would like to move to a *bigger* house.
      …I'm going to make it even *more beautiful than* my first garden.
   3 Summer was *the prettiest season of all.*
   4 *spent, had, grew, bought, came, fell, left, (was/were).*
   5 *I'm going to make* it even more beautiful than my first garden
      I'm going to plant all the flowers and trees again.
      I'm going to have a pond.
      We're going to see a solicitor.
   6 She spent ten years and thousands of pounds *to make* her garden there beautiful.
      A lot of people came to the village especially *to see* Verena's garden.
      Mr and Mrs Grey came *to see* it.
   7 There was a brown field with *some stones and rocks.*
      I'm going to have a pond with *some goldfish.*
   8 There weren't *any flowers or trees* and there wasn't *any grass*!

Stop and check 1

Correct the mistakes
1 London is a very big city.
2 My mother works in a hotel. She's a receptionist. *or* My mother is a receptionist in a hotel.
3 My father watches TV in the evening.
4 He likes watching football.
5 On Sundays we go to a restaurant.
6 Hans is a businessman.
7 Your family is very nice.
8 I like listening to the radio.
9 Our school has a lot of students.
10 The children go to school near here.
11 We have dinner at 7.00.
12 Buses in London are red.
13 My brother doesn't have a job.
14 Do you want an ice-cream?
15 My flat is near here.

Word order
1. John is a policeman from New York.
2. Is your brother married?
3. My sister goes skiing in the mountains.
4. English coffee isn't very nice.
5. What is your teacher's name?
6. How do you spell your surname?
7. I often go swimming at weekends./I go swimming often at weekends.

Choose the correct sentence
1b 2c 3a 4b 5c 6a 7b 8c

Questions
1. Where do you go on holiday?
   What time do you go to bed?
   Who do you usually sit next to?
   How much is a cup of coffee and a sandwich?
   How many languages do you speak?
2. a What time does Peter start work?
   b Where do Sylvie and Jacques come from?
   c What's your wife's name?
   d How many children do you have?
   e Do you like gardening?

Prepositions
1 in	8 at	15 to
2 with	9 to	16 at
3 at	10 On	17 in
4 at	11 in	18 In
5 for	12 after	19 After
6 to	13 by	20 about
7 for	14 at	

Vocabulary

Things to read	Professions	Things to eat
menu	scientist	egg
letter	accountant	tuna
dictionary	journalist	cake
magazine	interpreter	chicken
newspaper	nurse	orange

Places	Verbs	Adjectives
hotel	collect	favourite
island	want	easy
café	deliver	expensive
beach	sell	friendly
office	listen	busy

am/is/do/does (not)
1. is
2. are
3. 'm not
4. is/isn't
5. does/is
6. doesn't doesn't
7. 'm is
8. do
9. don't aren't
10. isn't

Translate
The idea behind this is that students begin to be aware of similarities and differences between English and L1. Emphasize that they must not translate word by word. Obviously it will only be possible to check their answers in a monolingual class but even in a multi-lingual class students can discuss their answers together in nationality groups.

Stop and check 2

Correct the mistakes
1. There isn't a supermarket.
2. Look at this picture/these pictures.
3. Is there a bank near here?
4. I arrived at Heathrow airport at ten o'clock last night.
5. She could speak three languages when she was ten.
6. Where did you go last night?
7. The plant is in front of the window.
8. I can't go out because I have a lot of homework.
9. There is a table in the kitchen.
10. I went to the museum last weekend.
11. Who are those people over there?
12. I bought a new DVD.
13. Did you watch the football on TV last night/yesterday evening?
14. Italian people are very friendly.
15. I like cities because I can go to the shopping mall.

Past Simple
1. studied   6. invented
2. began   7. wrote
3. became   8. explained
4. wasn't   9. said
5. worked   10. made

Irregular verbs
1. gave   5. lost   9. won
2. left   6. made   10. took
3. sold   7. broke
4. spoke   8. met

can/could/was/were (not)
1. wasn't was
2. was could
3. can
4. were weren't was
5. couldn't was

Questions and negatives
1. Is there a good restaurant in this town?
   There isn't a good restaurant in this town.
2. Are there any eggs in the fridge?
   There aren't any eggs in the fridge.
3. Can you speak French?
   You can't speak French.
4. Was he born in 1985?
   He wasn't born in 1985.
5. Could she play chess when she was three?
   She couldn't play chess when she was three.
6. Were they in class last week?
   They weren't in class last week.
7. Did your parents study German at school?
   Your parents didn't study German at school.
8. Did the students go to the library last night?
   The students didn't go to the library last night.

some/any/a/an
1. any
2. a some
3. an
4. some any
5. any
6. some

Vocabulary – connections
(Suggested answers but do award points for any sensible alternatives!)

sofa – living room
computer – Internet
2nd – second
telephone – operator
fridge – kitchen
son – sun
season – month
Congratulations! – wedding
ticket – plane
pharmacy – aspirin
soldier – war

Vocabulary – opposites
clean – dirty   happy – sad
win – lose   poor – rich
old – modern   on – under
near – far   begin – finish
before – after   right – left

Translate

See note about translation on p156.

Stop and check 3

Correct the mistakes

1 It's very hot today – would you like something to drink?
2 Peter's got a lot of books because he likes reading.
3 How many children have you got/do you have?
4 How much money has he got?
5 Whose is that new car?
6 I'm going home now because it's late.
7 Last night I went to a café to meet my friends.
8 We're going to have a test next week.
9 I'm wearing old clothes because I'm going to clean the car.
10 Pierre is French, he comes from Paris.
11 What are you doing this evening?
12 My sister is older than me.
13 I think it is going to rain.
14 Your house is bigger than mine.
15 Who is the richest person in the world?

Questions and answers

Whose is this coat? – It's Jane's.
How many sons have you got? – Three.
How much did your bike cost? – £195.
Could you help me, please? –
　Yes, of course. What can I do for you?
Would you like some more to eat? –
　No, thanks. I'm full.
Do you like Henry? –
　Yes. I think he's very nice.
Where are you going on holiday? –
　To Turkey.
Why are you going to the pharmacy? –
　To buy some toothpaste.
What did you do last night? –
　I stayed at home.
Who's the new teacher? –
　Her name's Mrs Taylor.

Comparatives and superlatives

Adjective	Comparative	Superlative
big	bigger	biggest
beautiful	more beautiful	most beautiful
bad	worse	worst
exciting	more exciting	most exciting
noisy	noisier	noisiest

Comparing hotels

1 a The Strand is bigger than the Ritz.
　b The Ritz is more expensive than the Strand.
　c The Strand is nearer the sea than the Ritz.
　d The Strand is farther from the town centre than the Ritz.
　e The Strand is more modern than the Ritz.
2 a The Strand is the biggest.
　b The Star is the most expensive.
　c The Star is the nearest to the sea.
　d The Strand is the farthest from the town centre.
　e The Strand is the most modern.

some/any/a

1 a　　　　　5 a　some
2 some　　　6 a
3 any　　　　7 any
4 some　　　8 some　any

Present Simple and Present Continuous

1 drinks　isn't drinking
2 are looking　don't like
3 wear　'm wearing
4 are you going　go
5 works　's writing

going to

1 Peter **is going to buy** some bread at **the baker's**.
2 I **am going to borrow** some books from **the library**.
3 We **are going to see** an exhibition at **the museum**.
4 They **are going to have** a holiday in **Malta**.
5 I **am going to write** a letter to **my friend**.

Vocabulary

Clothes shop	Food	Drinks
a dress	fruit	tea
a suit	mushrooms	milk
a shirt	cheese	coffee
a sweater	rice	water
shorts	meat	juice

Translate

See note about translation on p156.

Stop and check 4

Correct the mistakes

1 Why do you want to learn Portuguese?
2 She hasn't ever been to Madrid./She has never been to Madrid.
3 I've written to her three times and she hasn't answered yet.
4 I didn't enjoy the book. It was very boring.
5 How many times have you been to Greece?
6 I'm very excited about my holiday.
7 The students worked very hard.
8 Tell me when you want to stop for lunch.
9 What sort of magazines do you like reading?
10 Have you ever been to Ireland?

Questions and tenses

1 Why **is she tired**?
2 How **do** you **go to work**?
3 Whose **is this pen**?
4 Who **did** you **meet**?
5 What sort **of car did he buy**?
6 Where **did** you see **him**?
7 What **is she watching**?
8 Where **are they going**?
9 Why **did he leave**?
10 How much **juice did she drink**?

Past Simple and Present Perfect

1　1 met　　　　　　4 ate
　2 has never been　5 climbed
　3 haven't finished

2　1 went　　　　　4 did ... live
　2 Have ... eaten　5 haven't read
　3 have ... been

Adverb or adjective?

1 quiet　　4 well
2 slowly　5 healthy
3 good

Word order

1 How many cousins have you got?
2 They have just arrived in Rome.
3 You speak English very well.
4 The man walked quickly along the road.
5 Have you ever read a book by Shakespeare?
6 The students had a difficult exam yesterday.

7 Did you check your work carefully?
8 Please do this exercise quickly.
9 How many people are you going to invite to your picnic?
10 She is tired because she got up early.

Auxiliaries

1 are   6 am
2 Does   7 Do
3 Did   8 Is
4 Has   9 did
5 have   10 Have

Vocabulary – word groups

Travel by train	Travel by plane
day return	jumbo jet
station	departure lounge
platform	arrival hall
	flight
	boarding pass
	gate

Adjectives	Family
quiet	niece
annoying	husband
worried	aunt
tiring	grandson
badly-behaved	widow
lovely	

Prepositions

1 about   5 about   9 to
2 by   6 on   10 out of
3 from   7 in
4 in   8 for

Translate

See note about translation on p156.

Progress test 1

Exercise 1
1 What's his surname?
2 Where's he from?
3 How old is he?
4 Where does he live? / What's his address?
5 What does he do? / What's his job?
6 Where does he work / teach?
7 Is he married?
8 What does he do in his free time?

Exercise 2
1 What do you do at weekends?
2 Where does she work?
3 There is a photo on the television.
4 Is there a pharmacy near here?
5 Can I have a coffee, please?
6 How many children do they have?
7 Hans teaches skiing in Switzerland.
8 Is there any milk in the fridge?
9 Rosy does not go to work by car.
10 Sue and Dave like going to the restaurant.

Exercise 3
How much is a chicken sandwich? £2.50.
What do you do on Sundays? I play tennis.
Where do you go on Friday evenings? To the gym.
How do you travel to work? By bus.
What time do you get up? At seven o'clock.

Exercise 4
1 some   6 some
2 an   7 any
3 any   8 an
4 any   9 any
5 a   10 some

Exercise 5
1 have   6 doesn't like
2 live   7 go
3 is   8 stay
4 works   9 go
5 likes   10 walk

Exercise 6
1 am   5 Does
2 do   6 does not
3 is not, is   7 are
4 do not   8 Do, don't

Exercise 7
1 We go swimming on Saturdays.
2 They watch TV every day.
3 The dictionaries are over there.
4 These watches are expensive.
5 Look at those lovely flowers.
6 Do you have any stamps?
7 They're our children.
8 They're interesting people.
9 Those men are American.
10 The schools don't have any computers.

Exercise 8
1 in   5 near
2 next to   6 in front of
3 behind   7 on
4 on

Exercise 9
1b   2a   3a   4b   5b

Exercise 10
1 pen (You can read the others.)
2 milk (You can drink milk.)
3 street (The others are buildings.)
4 teach (The others are professions.)
5 like (The others are adjectives.)
6 man (The others are names of family members.)
7 house (The others are rooms.)
8 often (The others describe position.)
9 American (American is an adjective.)
10 we (The others are possessive adjectives.)

Exercise 11
difficult – easy
expensive – cheap
hot – cold
lovely – horrible
wrong – right
old – young
new – old
right – left

Exercise 12
play football
go jogging
speak French
drink tea
travel by bus
catch a train
listen to the radio
watch television

Progress test 2

Exercise 1
1 were   weren't
2 was   wasn't
3 were   weren't
4 were   weren't

Exercise 2
1. can't play tennis
2. can speak German / can speak Italian
3. can't speak German
4. can speak Italian
5. can play tennis
6. can swim

Exercise 3
1. worked
2. lived
3. earned
4. moved
5. stayed
6. had
7. came
8. gave
9. went
10. bought

Exercise 4
1. left
2. went
3. worked
4. moved
5. met
6. got
7. live
8. teaches
9. does
10. sells

Exercise 5
1. We didn't enjoy the football match.
2. I didn't take a photograph of my sister.
3. Angela didn't write a letter to her friend.
4. Charles Dickens didn't become a journalist when he was 18.
5. Germany didn't win the World Cup in 1986.
6. Her father didn't die when she was 14.
7. I didn't lose £10 last night.
8. People didn't fly by plane 100 years ago.
9. That book wasn't very interesting.
10. We didn't arrive at school at eight o'clock.

Exercise 6
1. Would you like …
2. Do you like …
3. What would you like …
4. Do you like …
5. Yes. I'd like a bottle …

Exercise 7
1C 2U 3U 4C 5C 6U 7U

Exercise 8
1. some
2. a
3. any
4. any
5. some
6. some some
7. any

Exercise 9
1. How much
2. How many
3. How many
4. How much
5. How much

Exercise 10
1. No, it isn't. It's more expensive.
2. No, it isn't. It's smaller.
3. No, it isn't. It's the smallest.
4. No, it isn't. It's cheaper.
5. No, it isn't. It's the most expensive.
6. No, it isn't. It's more modern.
7. No, it isn't. It's the oldest.

Exercise 11

Adjective	Comparative	Superlative
dangerous	more dangerous	most dangerous
good	better	best
bad	worse	worst
interesting	more interesting	most interesting

Exercise 12
1. first
2. second
3. third
4. twelfth
5. twentieth

Exercise 13
1. interesting
2. start
3. day
4. buy
5. same
6. quiet
7. new
8. old
9. east
10. before

Progress test 3

Exercise 1
1. driving
2. stopping
3. working
4. using
5. looking
6. getting
7. buying
8. thinking
9. swimming
10. crying

Exercise 2
1. am not going
2. are … smiling
3. is standing
4. isn't sitting
5. is … eating
6. are … doing am cleaning
7. isn't working

Exercise 3
1. take are going
2. do … go
3. are … working have
4. do … live Do … like
5. do … have am having
6. is ringing

Exercise 4
1. It's yours.
2. They're his.
3. It's hers.
4. They're ours.
5. It's theirs.

Exercise 5
1. They're going to be architects.
2. He isn't going to be a writer.
3. Are you going to be a pilot?
4. I'm not going to be a policeman.
5. We're going to be shop assistants.
6. She isn't going to be a chef.
7. Is he going to be a vet?
8. I'm going to be an accountant.
9. He isn't going to be a travel agent.
10. Are you going to be an English teacher?

Exercise 6
1. I'm going to Moscow to see the Kremlin.
2. Paul is going to London to buy some clothes.
3. Roger went to Dubai to visit the Jumeirah beach.
4. Tracey often goes to the library to read.
5. Tim is going to America to see the Niagara Falls.
6. Frank is learning French to get a better job.
7. Peter is saving money to buy a car.
8. Henry went to Japan to visit Kyoto.
9. Chris went to the newsagent's to buy a newspaper.
10. Brian and Jane are going to Paris to climb the Eiffel Tower.

Exercise 7
1. slowly
2. early
3. carefully
4. well
5. hard
6. suddenly
7. fast
8. badly

Exercise 8
1. How
2. What
3. Why
4. What
5. Who
6. Which
7. Where
8. When
9. Which

Exercise 9

1 ate   eaten
2 won   won
3 lived   lived
4 had   had
5 did   done
6 cooked   cooked
7 went   gone
8 drove   driven

Exercise 10

1a 2a 3b 4a 5a 6a 7a

Exercise 11

Colours	Clothes	Weather
blue	sweater	cloudy
yellow	skirt	snowing
pink	T-shirt	foggy
green	tie	sunny
brown	suit	windy

Workbook key

UNIT 1

1 **A** Hello. What's your name?
  B Scott. What's *your* name?
  A My name *is* John. Where *are* you *from*, Scott?
  B *I'm* from London. *Where are* you from?
  A *I'm* from New York.

2 3 I'm from Germany. 4 I'm from Japan.
  5 I'm from Jordan. 6 I'm from Italy.
  7 We're from England.

3 1 She's Jana Al-Majali. 2 She's from Jordan. 3 She's a student. 4 She's 19.
  5 They're Ilona and László Novak.
  6 They're from Hungary. 7 They are teachers. 8 Ilona is 26. 9 László is 28.

4 2 What is your name? 3 She is from Italy. 4 I am twenty years old. 5 They are from the USA. 6 You are English.
  7 We are students.

5 2 My name's Maria. 3 He's married.
  4 They're from Brazil. 5 I'm from Mexico. I'm not from Spain. 6 We're from the USA. 7 He's a teacher. He's not a doctor.

6 1 My 2 your 3 your 4 my

7 1 her 2 His 3 His 4 Her

8
Country	Nationality
England	English
Germany	German
Italy	Italian
France	French
Spain	Spanish
Portugal	Portuguese
Egypt	Egyptian
Japan	Japanese
the United States	American
Russia	Russian
Hungary	Hungarian
Brazil	Brazilian
Mexico	Mexican

9 1
A ••	B •○
Russia Ireland	Brazil
Spanish German	
Egypt	

2
C ••○	D •••○
Portugal Italy	Japanese
Mexico Mexican	

10 4 a teacher 5 an apple 6 a car
  7 newspapers 8 a house 9 magazines
  10 a camera 11 a telephone 12 stamps

11 2 Pierre is *a French name*.
  3 Oxford is *an English university*.
  4 English is *an international language*.
  5 Milan is *an Italian city*.
  6 A Mercedes is *a German car*.
  7 A Pentax is *a Japanese camera*.

12 3 Where's she from? 4 What's her name? 5 I'm a student. 6 I have two sisters. 7 They're from Japan. 8 It's a Spanish orange. 9 His name's Jamal.
  10 Her name is Fatima.

13 1 one 2 two 3 three 4 four 5 five
  6 six 7 seven 8 eight 9 nine 10 ten
  11 eleven 12 twelve 13 thirteen
  14 fourteen 15 fifteen 16 sixteen
  17 seventeen 18 eighteen 19 nineteen
  20 twenty

14 b nine oranges c fifteen students
  d five cars e six tickets f three letters
  g twelve keys h four postcards
  i twenty stamps j two dictionaries

UNIT 2

1 1 d 2 e 3 f 4 a 5 c 6 b

2 2 How *old is he*? 3 Where *is he* now?
  4 What's *his address*? 5 Where *is she* now? 6 What's *her job*? 7 What's *her phone number at work*? 8 How old are the children? 9 Where are they now?

3 Students' own answers

4 2 Cairo isn't in Turkey. It's in Egypt.
  3 Snow isn't hot. It's cold.
  4 Five and six isn't twelve. It's eleven.
  5 You aren't English. You're Saudi Arabian.
  6 We aren't in a Russian class. We're in an Arabic class.
  7 Rolls-Royce cars aren't cheap. They're expensive.

5 3 Yes, it is. / No, it isn't.
  4 Yes, it is. / No, it isn't.
  5 Yes, I am. / No, I'm not.
  6 Yes, I am. / No, I'm not.
  7 Yes, they are. / No, they aren't.

6 2 It isn't hot today. 3 I'm not married.
  4 Where's the newspaper? 5 They aren't from Oxford. 6 We're at work.
  7 You're a student.

7 2 You are not old. 3 My flat is small.
  4 Her son is not an accountant. 5 His wife is a journalist. 6 They are at work.
  7 We are not rich.

8 3 is 4 is 5 P 6 is 7 P 8 P 9 is 10 P

9 2 Cathy *is Louise's* sister. 3 Stephen *is David's son*. 4 Ann *is Stephen's* aunt.
  5 George *is Mary's* husband. 6 Mary *is Cathy's grandmother*. 7 David *is Cathy's uncle*. 8 David *is Ann's brother*.

10 Students' own answers

11 2 a hot day 3 a young girl 4 an old man
  5 an easy exercise 6 a difficult language
  7 a fast car 8 an expensive camera

12 1 cars 2 classes 3 cities 4 women
  5 families 6 addresses 7 people
  8 boys 9 sandwiches 10 universities

13 2
one 1	two 2
ten 10	twelve 12
one hundred 100	twenty 20
3 three	fourteen 14
13 thirteen	forty-five 45
30 thirty	fifty-four 54
5 five	sixteen 16
15 fifteen	twenty-six 26
50 fifty	sixty-one 61
7 seven	eighteen 18
17 seventeen	eighty-seven 87
78 seventy-eight	ninety-eight 98
19 nineteen	40 forty
90 ninety	65 sixty-five
99 ninety-nine	82 eighty-two

14 2 90p Ninety p.
  3 £1.30 One pound thirty p.
  4 £7.15 Seven pounds fifteen p.
  5 £13.75 Thirteen pounds seventy-five p.
  6 £81.00 Eighty-one pounds.
  7 £125.50 One hundred and twenty-five pounds fifty p.

UNIT 3

1 **She's a flight attendant.** She wears a uniform. She travels a lot. She speaks three languages. She serves drinks.
  She's a doctor. She works in a hospital. She helps sick people. She works with nurses. She wears a white coat.
  He's a receptionist. He works in a hotel. He answers the phone. He speaks four languages. He works with a computer.
  He's a postman. He works outside. He walks a lot. He delivers letters. He starts work at 5.00 a.m.

2 2 lives 3 flies 4 has 5 goes, plays
  6 studies 7 starts

3 1 Students' own answers

2 2 He *has a shower*.
   3 Then he *gets dressed*.
   4 He *has* tea and toast for breakfast.
   5 He *leaves* his flat at half past eight.
   6 He *goes* to work by bus.
   7 He works in a bookshop. He *starts* work at nine o'clock.
   8 At one o'clock he *has* lunch in a small café.
   9 He leaves work at half past five and *goes* home.
   10 First he *has* dinner.
   11 Then he *watches* television.
   12 He *goes* to bed at eleven o'clock and *reads* a book.

4 1 c 2 g 3 d 4 h 5 e 6 f 7 a 8 b

5 1 2 What does he have for breakfast?
      3 How does he go to work?
      4 Where does he have lunch?
      5 What does he do in the evenings?
      6 When does he go to bed?
   2 1 When/What time does he start work?
      2 Where does he work?
      3 When/What time does he have lunch?
      4 When/What time does he go home?
      5 What does he do in the evenings?

6 A My sister *is* very clever.
   B What *does* she do?
   A She *is* an interpreter.
   B Where *does* she live?
   A She *has* a lovely flat in London.
   B *Is* she married?
   A Yes. Her husband's name *is* Rob.
   B *Does* she have any children?
   A Yes. She *has* one son. He *is* eight years old.

7 1 2 Does she like reading?
      3 Does she speak a foreign language?
      4 Does she have a car?
      5 Does she like her job?
   2 2 Yes, he does. 3 No, he doesn't.
      4 No, he doesn't. 5 Yes, he does. He's an accountant.

8 1 2 doesn't have 3 doesn't like
      4 doesn't speak 5 doesn't have
   2 2 The Queen of England doesn't live in New York. She lives in London.
      3 Our teacher doesn't arrive late every day. She arrives on time.
      4 An architect doesn't translate things. He designs buildings.
      5 School doesn't start at six o'clock in the morning. It starts at nine o'clock.
      6 *Headway* doesn't teach German. It teaches English.

9 1 f 2 d 3 g 4 i 5 c 6 a 7 h 8 e 9 b

10

1 Jobs	2 Transport
scientist	boat
interpreter	taxi
nurse	bus
shopkeeper	car
policeman	plane

3 Places	4 Adjectives
house	exciting
hospital	busy
country	cheap
city	new
office	horrible

11 2 It's ten past eight. 3 It's twenty to six.
    4 It's quarter past one. 5 It's ten to eleven. 6 It's twelve o'clock. 7 It's five past two. 8 It's twenty-five to one. 9 It's quarter to seven. 10 It's half past five.
    11 It's nine o'clock. 12 It's five to eight.

12 1

Subject pronouns	Object pronouns	Possessive adjectives
I	me	my
you	you	*your*
he	him	his
she	her	*her*
it	it	its
we	us	*our*
they	them	their

   2 2 He, them 3 it 4 She, him 5 We, us 6 us 7 her 8 She, it 9 me 10 She, them

13 2 Mona Halalsheh is Jordanian, but *she* lives in New York because *she* works as an interpreter for the UN. *She* is an interpreter. She likes New York because *it* is interesting, but *her* husband, Hussain, doesn't like *it*. He wants to leave and go back to Jordan. *They* have two children. Hussain takes *them* out of the city in *his* free time. *They* go walking in summer and skiing in winter. Mona doesn't go with *them* because *she* doesn't have any free time.

UNIT 4

1 1 2 has 3 come 4 speak 5 don't speak 6 speaks 7 like 8 have 9 go 10 work 11 works 12 love
   2 2 starts 3 don't start 4 gets up 5 stay 6 don't get up 7 meet 8 finishes 9 go 10 have 11 go
   3 2 does, do 3 do, work 4 do, speak 5 Do, speak 6 Does, speak 7 do, start 8 do, love

2 Correct order: c 1 f 2 a 3 i 4 b 5 h 6 e 7 g 8 d 9

3 1 2 do 3 don't 4 do 5 doesn't 6 does
   2 2 Yes, I do. / No, I don't.
      3 Yes, I am. / No, I'm not.
      4 Yes, I do. / No, I don't.
      5 Yes, I am. / No, I'm not.
      6 Yes, I do. / No, I don't.

4 1 am 2 Does 3 do 4 Is 5 do 6 are 7 does

5 (Sample answers)
   2 I like coffee, but I *don't like* tea.
   3 We like playing tennis, but we *don't like swimming*.
   4 Sue likes fruit, but she *doesn't like vegetables*.
   5 I speak French, but I *don't speak Japanese*.
   6 Tom speaks Arabic, but he *doesn't speak German*.
   7 Mr and Mrs Green have a son, but they *don't have a daughter*.

6 1 We always go to France in spring.
   2 We usually stay in a hotel. / Usually we stay in a hotel.
   3 We sometimes go by plane. / Sometimes we go by plane.
   4 We sometimes go by train. / Sometimes we go by train.
   5 Our children never come with us.
   6 We often go to a restaurant on Thursday evenings.

7 1 (Sample answers)
     2 I usually have a shower. 3 I always have coffee. 4 I sometimes watch a DVD. 5 I sometimes go for a walk. 6 I often go to Egypt. 7 No, never. 8 We usually have dinner together at my parents' house.
   2 (Sample answers)
     2 Never. 3 Every morning/evening. 4 Every Friday. 5 Every day. 6 Three or four times a year.

8 1 In, on 2 at 3 at 4 in 5 on 6 in

9 1 1 c 2 e 3 d 4 a 5 f 6 h 7 b 8 g
   2 2 closes 3 finishes 4 go to bed 5 goes 6 early 7 arrives 8 relax

UNIT 5

1 1 ✓ 2 ✓ 3 ✗ 4 ✗ 5 ✗ 6 ✗ 7 ✓ 8 ✓ 9 ✗ 10 ✗

2 1 2 A *Are* there any cups?
        B Yes, *there are*. They're *on* the coffee table.
      3 A Is *there a book*?
        B Yes, it's in the bag.
      4 A *Is there an* umbrella?
        B No, *there isn't*.
      5 A *Are there any* flowers?
        B No, *there aren't*.
      6 A *Are there any* letters?
        B Yes, *there are*. They're *next to* the fax machine.
   2 2 A Is there a fax machine?
        B Yes, *there is*.
        A Where *is it*?
        B It's *on a table*.
      3 A Are there *any* pictures?
        B Yes, *there are*.
        A Where *are they*?
        B They're *on the wall* behind the sofa.
      4 A Are there any people?
        B Yes, *there are*.
        A Where *are they*?
        B They're *sitting on the sofa*.
      5 A *Is there a* coffee table?
        B *Yes, there is*.
        A Where *is it*?
        B It's *in front of* the sofa.

3 1 2 are there 3 There are 4 Is there 5 there is 6 some 7 there is 8 in 9 near 10 Are, any 11 there is 12 Is there

2 2 some 3 a, a 4 any 5 a 6 any 7 an 8 a 9 some 10 an

4 2 Yes, there is. / No, there isn't.
3 Yes, there is. / No, there isn't.
4 Yes, there are / No, there aren't.
5 Yes, there are. / No, there aren't.
6 Yes, there is. / No, there isn't.
7 Yes, there are. / No, there aren't.

5 1 d 2 b 3 a 4 c

6 1 b 2 d 3 a 4 c

7 2 Take *these* bags into the kitchen.
3 I don't like *this* game.
4 A Is *this* book John's?
  B Yes, *it* is.
5 A Are *these* books Mary's?
  B Yes, *they* are.
6 A How much are *these* glasses?
  B *They're* very cheap.
7 A *This* exercise is very easy.
  B No, *it* isn't. *It's* difficult.

8 1 Is *that* your brother over there?
2 Look at *those* beautiful flowers!
3 What's *that* in your bag?
4 A Is *that* house Ann's?
  B Yes, *it* is.
5 A Are *those* boys your brothers?
  B Yes, *they* are.
6 A How much is *that*?
  B *It's* £350.
7 A Do you like *those* shoes?
  B No, I don't. *They're* horrible.

9 1 2 bedroom 3 wardrobe 4 toilet 5 bathroom 6 shower 7 bath 8 window 9 armchair 10 coffee table 11 fireplace 12 bookshelves 13 sofa 14 living room 15 washing machine 16 cooker 17 dishwasher 18 kitchen 19 door 20 garden

2 1 c 2 h 3 a 4 e 5 g 6 b 7 d 8 f

3 2 I cook dinner in the kitchen.
3 I wash my hair in the bathroom.
4 I clean my teeth in the bathroom.
5 I go to bed in the/my bedroom.
6 I have a shower in the bathroom.
7 I get dressed in the/my bedroom.
8 I do my homework in the living room.

10 2 so 3 but 4 because 5 but 6 so 7 so 8 but 9 because

UNIT 6

1 2 can ride, can drive 3 can use, can't program 4 can drive, can't ride 5 can play chess 6 can program a computer 7 can't ride a motorbike 8 can play golf 9 can drive a car

2 1 f *Can* you *play* football?
2 a *Can* you *speak* any other languages?
3 e *Can* you *play* golf?
4 c *Can* you *ride* a motorbike?
5 b *Can* you *use* a computer?
6 d *Can* you *cook* Italian food?
7 g *Can* you *drive* a car?

3 2 am, am 3 were, was 4 was, was 5 is, was 6 are, were 7 was 8 were, was, was

4 1 1 bag 2 camera 3 trainers 4 television 5 briefcase 6 pens

2 2 A How much is the camera?
   B It's only £150.
   A How much was it before?
   B It was £200.
   A Well … what a bargain!

3 A How much are the trainers?
   B They're only £50.
   A How much were they before?
   B They were £80.
   A Well … what a bargain!

4 A How much is the television?
   B It's only £250.
   A How much was it before?
   B It was £500.
   A Well … what a bargain!

5 A How much is the briefcase?
   B It's only £45.
   A How much was it before?
   B It was £90.
   A Well … what a bargain!

6 A How much are the pens?
   B They're only £15.
   A How much were they before?
   B They were £45.
   A Well … what a bargain!

5 2 Yes, she does. 3 They were in bed. 4 Yes, he was. 5 Yes, he was. 6 No, she wasn't. 7 She was on the bus. 8 Yes, he can. 9 She was at work. 10 They were at home watching TV.

6 Students' own answers

7 1 stay in a hotel
ask a question
know the answer
start work
go home
get up early
live alone
speak English fluently
make a phone call
play football

2 1 know 2 play (football) 3 get up early 4 start work 5 speaks English fluently 6 live alone 7 go home

8 1 at, on 2 at, with 3 in, with 4 to, by, at 5 at, with, on 6 in, in 7 with, Of, to 8 at, of

9 1 1 Road 2 Street 3 receptionist 4 am twenty-eight 5 live 6 am a (tourist) 7 was 8 like 9 can 10 (foreign) languages 11 use 12 was

UNIT 7

1 1 I usually *work* eight hours a day, but yesterday I *started* work at 9.00 a.m. and *finished* at 9.00 p.m.
2 Max usually *drives* to work, but yesterday he *walked*.
3 Ann usually *watches* TV in the evenings, but yesterday evening she *listened* to the radio.
4 Ann and Max usually *go* sailing at weekends, but last weekend they *played* tennis.
5 It usually *rains* a lot in winter, but last year it *snowed* for three months.
6 Max and I usually *go* camping in August, but last summer we *stayed* in a hotel.

2 2 A Does Max usually drive to work?
   B Yes, *he does*.
   A Did he *drive to work* yesterday?
   B No, *he didn't. He walked*.

3 A Does Ann usually watch TV in the evenings?
   B Yes, *she does*.
   A Did she *watch* TV yesterday evening?
   B No, *she didn't. She listened to the radio*.

4 A Do Ann and Max usually go sailing at weekends?
   B *Yes, they do*.
   A *Did they go sailing last weekend*?
   B *No, they didn't. They played tennis*.

5 A Does it usually rain a lot in winter?
   B *Yes, it does*.
   A *Did it rain a lot last year*?
   B *No, it didn't. It snowed for three months*.

6 A Do you and Max usually go camping in August?
   B Yes, we *do*.
   A *Did you go camping last August*?
   B *No, we didn't. We stayed in a hotel*.

3 A Hi Talal! How are you?
B Hi Bob! I'm really well. I *had* a really great weekend.
A Really? What *did* you do?
B Well, I *had* an exam on Wednesday, but it *was* my last one. So I went out for a big meal on Wednesday night.
A *Did* you go to that new Malaysian restaurant?
B Yes!
A Ah, I want to go there next weekend. *Was* it good?
B Yes! The food *was* excellent, and the people *were* really friendly. And yesterday me and some friends *had* a picnic in the desert.
A Fantastic! Oh well, Saturday again, and some of us have got a job to go to. Bye!
B Bye. See you later!

4 Regular verbs

Infinitive	Past Simple
visit	visited
enjoy	enjoyed
paint	painted
travel	travelled
stay	stayed

Irregular verbs

Infinitive	Past Simple
write	wrote
leave	left
lose	lost
buy	bought
do	did
see	saw
go	went
take	took
have	had
drive	drove
speak	spoke
come	came
meet	met

5 2 met 3 left 4 saw 5 bought 6 knew
7 lost 8 had 9 wrote 10 began

6 2 What time did you get up this morning?
3 What did you have for dinner last night?
4 When did you last travel by train?
5 What did you do last weekend?
6 Where did you go on holiday last summer?
7 When did you last visit a museum?
8 How did you come to school today?
Students' own answers

7 1 3 found 4 broke 5 talks 6 owns
7 helps 8 gives 9 happened
10 gave 11 took 12 loved
13 started 14 became 15 enjoys
16 use 17 delivers 18 lost
19 learnt 20 made

2 3 Yes, he is. 4 No, he doesn't.
5 Yes, he does. 6 No, he didn't.
7 Yes, he does. 8 Yes, it did.

3 2 Where does he live now?
3 Why did he have a difficult time at school?
4 What is his company called?
5 When did his father give him a computer?
6 How much money did he lose?

8 1 (adj) nice (v) enjoy (n) holiday
(adj) new (n) airport (prep) in
(v) see (adj) warm (adj) famous
(prep) near (v) earn (v) win
(n) postman (prep) at (v) relax

2 2 Did you *see* Frank's *new* car this morning? It's red.
3 I play tennis with her *at* weekends and she always *wins*.
4 I *relaxed* and watched television yesterday evening. It was so *warm* in front of the fire.
5 I saw a *famous* sports star at the *airport*.

6 He worked as a *postman* until he died, and he only *earned* £10,000 a year.
7 They had a *holiday in* Dubai and they *enjoyed* it very much.

9 1 to 2 over 3 to, about 4 about
5 with, at 6 about 7 after 8 at, in, at
9 with, for 10 to, for

10 2 2 When did he go? Last June.
3 How long did he go for? Three weeks.
4 How did he travel? By plane.
5 Where did he stay? In a tent.
6 What did he do? He took photographs of wild animals.
7 What did he see? Elephants, lions, giraffes; not any crocodiles.
8 Did he enjoy the holiday? Yes, he did.

3 1 went 2 travelled 3 stayed 4 took
5 saw 6 didn't see 7 enjoyed

4 Last October Alison went to Scotland for a week. She travelled by train and she stayed in a hotel. She went walking in the mountains. She saw some beautiful lakes, but she didn't see the Loch Ness Monster. She enjoyed the holiday very much.

5 Students' own answers

UNIT 8

1 2 became 3 had 4 won 5 went
6 could 7 learnt 8 couldn't
9 invented 10 used 11 could
12 visited 13 understood 14 began
15 started 16 died 15 knew

2 2 His father wasn't a teacher. He was a leather worker.
3 He didn't become blind when he was six. He became blind when he was three.
4 He didn't go to school in London. He went to a school in Paris.
5 The books for blind people weren't cheap. The books were very expensive.
6 He didn't invent 'night writing'. Charles Barbier invented it.
7 He didn't begin to develop 'Braille' when he was ten. He began when he was fifteen.
8 He didn't die when he was fifty-three. He died when he was forty-three.

3 2 I didn't go to school on Monday.
3 Our teacher didn't come to school today.
4 Anna wasn't in Paris last month.
5 They weren't at home.
6 Paul couldn't read until he was eight.

4 3 My aunt didn't give me a new watch.
4 It rained a lot during our holiday.
5 I drank the coffee, but I didn't eat the sandwich.
6 She brought her homework.
7 She was tired, so she went to bed.
8 He didn't forget his passport and he didn't lose his plane ticket.

9 It cost a lot of money.
10 I had a lot of time, so I did the shopping.

5 1 1 this morning 2 yesterday evening
3 the day before yesterday 4 last winter 5 ten years ago 6 in 1980

2 Students' own answers

6 (Sample answers: adjust according to current date/time)
2 I had breakfast two hours ago.
3 They got married twenty years ago.
4 We saw John two days ago.
5 We met thirty-five years ago.
6 My daughter started school nine months ago.
7 My uncle died three years ago.
8 Alice came back from America a month ago.
9 Their son was born eight hours ago.

7 2 1 on 24 February 1304
2 nearly half his life
3 at the age of twenty-one
4 eighteen months
5 for just three weeks
6 In November 1327
7 during the day
8 for a second time
9 in the winter of 1332
10 in 1344

3 1 Where was Ibn Battuta born?
2 He studied religion and law.
3 When did he first go to Mecca?
4 How did he travel?
5 He studied and visited religious places.
6 Why did he travel at night?
7 He wanted to see the different lengths of night and day.
8 How old was he when he went to China? He was forty.
9 Did he like people using paper money?
10 Both cities were nearly empty because of the Black Death.

8 2 drink drinks 3 cooked cook
4 watched watch 5 walked walk
6 fish fish 7 visit visited
8 name name

9 1 bicycle 2 train 3 television
4 camera 5 plane 6 computers
7 fridge 8 telephone 9 washing
10 jeans

All these things are inventions.

11 945 nine hundred and forty-five
590 five hundred and ninety
471 four hundred and seventy-one
999 nine hundred and ninety-nine
115 one hundred and fifteen
603 six hundred and three
425 four hundred and twenty-five
144 one hundred and forty-four
508 five hundred and eight
862 eight hundred and sixty-two
238 two hundred and thirty-eight

734 seven hundred and thirty-four
616 six hundred and sixteen
310 three hundred and ten
800 eight hundred

12 1 2 one hundred and forty-five
3 six hundred and ten
4 eight hundred and ninety
5 three hundred and eighty-seven
6 one hundred and fifty
7 five hundred and thirty-two
2 1 three hundred and sixty-five
2 one hundred and twenty
3 eighty-eight
4 students' own answers
5 two hundred and eight
6 four hundred and seventy-three

13 1 I left the meeting early because I didn't feel well.
2 Peter couldn't speak until he was nearly four.
3 Tim didn't see the Colosseum when he was in Rome.
4 Eva didn't start learning English until she was thirty.
5 I didn't enjoy maths lessons when I was at school.
6 Sally didn't buy the red shoes because she couldn't afford them.
7 They didn't go to bed until after midnight.
8 We met Ken's wife last Saturday when they came for dinner.

14 1 1 when   2 and   3 because   4 and
5 until   6 but   7 when   8 and
9 because   10 so   11 but   12 so
13 and   14 so
2 Students' own answers

UNIT 9

1 1 rice U   2 money U   3 bread U
4 stamp C   5 milk U   6 apple C
7 banana C   8 strawberry C
9 biscuit C   10 fruit U   11 sandwich C
12 cheese U   13 cup C   14 egg C

2 2 some   3 some   4 a, some   5 a
6 an, some   7 some   8 some   9 a, a
10 some   11 an

3 2 Because I love listening to the radio.
3 Because he likes doing crosswords.
4 Because I like watching DVDs in bed.
5 Because she loves taking photographs.
6 Because I love learning about the past.
7 Because they like swimming and windsurfing.
8 Because he likes playing computer games.

4 1 2 What sort of food does she like? Italian and Mexican.
3 What does she like doing? Going to restaurants and meeting friends.
4 What sort of books does she like? Science fiction.

5 Does she like Chinese food? No, she doesn't.
6 Does she like playing football? No, she likes tennis and volleyball.
7 Does she like going to restaurants? Yes, she does.
8 Does she like going shopping? No, she doesn't.
2 2 Do you like cooking?
3 Do you like shopping?
4 Do you like playing computer games?
5 Do you like doing homework?
6 Do you like learning English?
Students' own answers

5 1 f   2 g   3 a   4 b   5 d   6 e   7 c

6 (Sample answers)
3 He likes cooking.   4 I'd like a new one.
5 She'd like a bigger one.   6 He likes fruit.   7 I'd like to watch it.   8 He likes reading.   9 I'd like to stay at home and watch TV.   10 They like skiing.

7 1 2 any   3 any   4 some   5 some
6 any   7 any   8 any   9 some, any
10 Some   11 some
2 2 any chairs   3 any photos   4 any food   5 some petrol   6 any stamps
7 some, people   8 some books

8 2 How many English books do you have?
3 How much does a cup of coffee cost?
4 How many languages do you speak?
5 How many people are there in your class?
6 How many weeks' holiday do you have in summer?
7 How much coffee do you drink a day?
Students' own answers

9 2 1 Would you like some coffee?
2 Would you like to order something to drink?
3 Fizzy or still mineral water?
4 We'd like a table for two.
5 Can we have the bill?
6 Could we have the menu?
7 Is service included?
8 First I'd like the pâté.
9 I'd like the chicken for the main course.
10 What vegetables would you like?
3 1 We'd like a table for two … 2 Could we have the menu … 3 First I'd like the pâté.   4 I'd like the chicken for the main course.   5 What vegetables would you like?   6 Would you like to order something to drink?   7 Fizzy or still mineral water?   8 Would you like some coffee?   9 Can we have the bill?
10 Is service included?

UNIT 10

1 1 3 fast   4 safe   5 friendly   6 big
7 noisy   8 hot   9 exciting   10 modern
2 3 smaller   4 more expensive
5 dirtier   6 more interesting
7 easier   8 hotter   9 nearer   10 worse

2 2 is newer than   3 is more modern than
4 is … bigger than   5 is … hotter than
6 is better than   7 is dirtier than   8 is … more difficult than

3 3 'Has he got a computer?' 'No, he hasn't.'
4 He's got a motorbike. He hasn't got a car.
5 They've got a flat. They haven't got a house.
6 'Have you got any brothers?' 'Yes, I have.'
7 'Has she got a new job?' 'Yes, she has.'
8 'Has he got a new camera?' 'No, he hasn't.'
9 We haven't got much money. They've got a lot.

4 1 Have   2 Does   3 have   4 Do   5 Has
6 Do; do   7 Does; does

5 2 They've got a big classroom.
3 He's got a bike, but he hasn't got a car.
4 We don't have much money. We're poor.
5 She's got a big house. She's rich.
6 He doesn't have an English dictionary.

6 1 1 Ismail is younger than Matt.
2 Ismail is taller than Matt.
3 'How many brothers has Ismail got?' 'Two.'
4 Ismail hasn't got any sisters.
5 Matt hasn't got any brothers or sisters.
6 Matt and Ismail have both got a flat.
7 Matt has got a car, but Ismail hasn't got one.
8 They have both got a camera.
9 'Has Matt got a computer?' 'No, she hasn't.'
2 Students' own answers

7 3 younger; the youngest   4 happier; the happiest   5 more beautiful; the most beautiful   6 bigger; the biggest
7 busier; the busiest   8 more intelligent; the most intelligent   9 worse; the worst
10 further; the furthest   11 newer; the newest   12 more dangerous; the most dangerous

8 2 My sister is younger than me.
3 Who is the oldest in the class?
4 Concorde was the fastest passenger plane in the world.
5 Your book is more interesting than my book.
6 Peter bought the most expensive watch in the shop.
7 Did you buy the cheapest watch in the shop?
8 English is much more difficult than German.
9 The weather today is much better than yesterday.

9 2 What is the highest mountain in the world? (Everest)
3 What is the biggest city in your country?
4 What is the most popular sport in your country?
5 Where is the oldest university in Europe? (Bologna)

6 Who is the youngest person in your family?
7 Who is the most intelligent student in your class?

10 2 1 c 2 e 3 i 4 g 5 h 6 a 7 b 8 d 9 j 10 f

3 1 railway station 2 river bank 3 car park 4 bookshop 5 bus stop 6 post office 7 town centre 8 travel agent 9 phone box 10 airport

4 1 phone box 2 railway station 3 bookshop 4 airports 5 bus stop 6 travel agent

11 1 Jack wrote the letter which arrived this morning.
2 There's the park where we play football.
3 This is the hotel where I always stay.
4 Robert's got a car which is faster than yours.

12 1 1 d 2 c 3 a 4 f 5 e 6 b

UNIT 11

1 1 d 2 c 3 f 4 a 5 g 6 b 7 e

2 2 having 3 reading 4 stopping 5 using 6 listening 7 running 8 saying 9 swimming 10 coming 11 doing 12 putting 13 riding 14 driving 15 thinking

3 Students' own answers

4 1 He's wearing a jumper and jeans. He's cooking.
2 He's wearing a shirt, a watch and a hat. He's writing a letter.
3 He's wearing a T-shirt, trousers, and trainers. He's sitting on a sofa playing computer games.

5 2 What are you cooking?
3 Are you going out this evening?
4 What time are we playing tennis?
5 Why is your daughter crying?
6 When are Ken and Ellen coming for dinner?

6 3 He's having dinner. 4 She's an architect. 5 No, she isn't. 6 She's skiing. 7 He's a postman. 8 Yes, he is. 9 She's a shop assistant. 10 No, she isn't. 11 She's swimming.

7 1 1 have 2 It's raining 3 are you doing; Are you going 4 are we having 5 do you usually go 6 are you doing 7 I'm trying

2 2 'm reading; read 3 're walking; walk 4 works; 's working 5 'm not eating; don't eat 6 is speaking; does … speak 7 do … do; are … doing

8 1 doesn't 2 are; am 3 does 4 am; do 5 is; is 6 don't; don't 7 do; don't; is

9 2 Whose is the bike? It's his.
3 Whose is the hat? It's hers.
4 Whose is the car? It's theirs.
5 Whose are the sunglasses? They're hers.
6 Whose are the trainers? They're his.
7 Whose is the suncream? It's hers.
8 Whose is the sports bag? It's his.
9 Whose is the ball? It's his.
10 Whose are the children? They're theirs.

10 2 It's mine. 3 It's yours. 4 They're theirs. 5 They're hers. 6 It's mine. 7 It's yours. 8 They're yours.

11 2 I'm *going* to a restaurant this evening.
3 *Whose* is this jacket on your chair?
4 We *don't* wear a uniform at my school.
5 That's my husband over there. He *is standing* near the window.
6 What *are* you doing after school today?
7 Sorry. You can't speak to Jenny. She *is having* a bath.
8 *Who's* that girl over there? She looks sad.
9 Peter's a businessman. *He works* all over the world.
10 At the moment Peter *is working* in Russia.

12 2 face 3 hair 4 feet 5 eyes 6 arm 7 hand 8 leg

13 1 too 2 both 3 because 4 but 5 Although 6 For example

14 1 both 2 too 3 For example 4 but 5 because 6 Although 7 For example 8 but 9 because 10 but 11 Although

UNIT 12

1 2 He's going to be a teacher.
3 She's going to be an interpreter.
4 She's going to be a journalist.
5 They're going to be doctors.
6 She's going to be an architect.
7 He's going to be an accountant.
8 She's going to be an athlete.

2 2 What are you going to buy?
3 What are you going to cook?
4 What is she going to study?
5 When are they going to get married?
6 Is she going to fly?
7 Are you going to study for it?
8 Is it going to rain?

3 2 2 They are going to travel by plane.
3 They are going to stay in the Atlantis Hotel.
4 They are going to stay for ten days.
5 They are going to visit Jumeirah beach.

3 1 Where are you going on holiday next summer?
2 Are you going to fly there?
3 Where are you going to stay?
4 How long are you going to stay?
5 And what are you going to do?
6 I'm going to visit the old town centre.

4 Students' own answers

4 2 She isn't going to have one this year.
3 We're not going there this year.
4 I'm not going to wear it today.
5 They aren't going to do it today.
6 He isn't going to get married this year.
7 He isn't going to pass it this year.

5 2 'm going to be sick 3 's going to snow 4 're going to leave 5 's going to have a job interview 6 're going to be late 7 'm going to drive

6 2 To buy/get some aspirin. 3 To buy/get a dictionary. 4 To get a holiday brochure. 5 To buy/get some stamps. 6 To buy/get a ticket. 7 To buy/get some milk.

7 She went to the dry cleaner's to collect her dress. Then she went to the pharmacy to buy some suncream and a new pair of sunglasses. After that she went to the bank to get some Euros, and to the travel agent's to collect some tickets. Then she went home to pack her suitcase. An hour later a taxi arrived to take her to the airport to catch a plane to Madrid.

8 1 Did 2 Is 3 do 4 Did 5 am 6 are 7 Do 8 are 9 did 10 does

9 Students' own answers

10

••	••
mountain	perhaps
suitcase	police
homework	hotel
cousin	dessert
airport	afraid

•●•	●••
tomorrow	yesterday
important	hospital
expensive	dangerous
delicious	video
umbrella	beautiful

11 2 weather 6 listen 3 forget 7 evening 4 frightened 8 relax 5 special

12 1 at 2 for 3 from 4 in 5 than 6 for 7 of 8 like 9 at 10 at 11 On 12 in

13 1 Dear Julie and Pete,
We're having *a wonderful* time here in Majorca. The weather *is lovely* so we *go to the beach* most of the time and *swim*. Yesterday it was very *hot and sunny* and we *got very red*. Tomorrow we're not going to *sit in the sun*, we're going to buy some souvenirs.
See you both soon,
Love János and Irén

Dear Julie and Pete,
We're having *quite a good* time here in Majorca. The weather *isn't very nice* so we *stay in the hotel* most of the time and *play table tennis*. Yesterday it was very *cold and foggy* and we *couldn't see the sea*. Tomorrow we're not going to

stay in the hotel, we're going to buy some souvenirs.
See you both soon,
Love János and Irén

UNIT 13

1 1 1 g (When) 2 h (What's) 3 b (How)
      4 i (Who) 5 a (What) 6 c (How)
      7 f (Where) 8 e (Which) 9 d (Who)

   2 2 What 3 how 4 where
      5 Which 6 why 7 How 8 Who
      9 When 10 How

2 2 What time does the football match start?
   3 What colour is your car?
   4 What day is it today?
   5 What sports do you like best?
   6 What size shoes do you take?

3 2 How many English lessons do you have a week?
   3 How often do you watch TV?
   4 How fast can your car go?
   5 How tall are you?
   6 How big is Peter's house?

4 2 Which one does she go to?
   3 Which one did you buy?
   4 Which one did you go to?
   6 Which one would you like?

5 1 1 1859 2 Edinburgh 3 medicine
      4 thirty-two 5 romances, adventure stories, and historical novels 6 1887
      7 fifty 8 Baker Street, London
      9 Doctor Watson 10 1930

   2 2 Which university did he go to?
      3 What did he study?
      4 How old was he when he became a full-time writer?
      5 What sort of books did he write?
      6 When did he write his first (detective) story?
      7 How many (detective) stories did he write?
      8 Where did Sherlock Holmes live?
      9 Who did he work with?
      10 When did Sir Arthur Conan Doyle die?

6 1 happily 2 happy 3 well 4 good
   5 well 6 quick 7 quickly 8 quietly
   9 slow

7 2 Listen *carefully*. I want you to come home *immediately*.
   3 I work *hard* and at night I sleep *well*.
   4 I know Peter *well* because we play tennis *together*.
   5 I like swimming *very much*. Jack likes swimming, *too*.
   6 Please speak *slowly* and explain *clearly*.

8 colourful beautiful sunny
   peaceful dangerous healthy
   romantic careful noisy
   angry

9 1 interested 2 bored 3 boring
   4 worried 5 interesting 6 exciting

10 2 unhappy 3 terrible 4 dirty
   5 slowly 6 Suddenly 7 quickly
   8 angrily 9 afraid 10 sadly
   11 fantastic 12 happily 13 quietly
   14 happy

UNIT 14

1 | Infinitive | Past Simple | Past participle |
   |---|---|---|
   | leave | left | left |
   | write | wrote | written |
   | speak | spoke | spoken |
   | see | saw | seen |
   | have | had | had |
   | do | did | done |
   | meet | met | met |
   | take | took | taken |
   | ride | rode | ridden |
   | give | gave | given |
   | finish | finished | finished |
   | fly | flew | flown |
   | buy | bought | bought |

2 1 1 has already won 2 started 3 went
      4 have travelled 5 went 6 played
      7 didn't win 8 hasn't played

   2 3 Yes, she did. 4 Yes, they have.
      5 Yes, they have. 6 Yes, they did.
      7 No, she didn't. 8 No, she hasn't.

   3 1 met 2 Have … been 3 went
      4 didn't like 5 have … been 6 Have … seen 7 went 8 saw 9 didn't enjoy 10 have … returned 11 Have … visited 12 went 13 climbed

3 1 3 Have you ever been to Rome?
      4 Have you ever ridden a motorbike?
      5 Have you ever been to London?
      6 Have you ever ridden on a double-decker bus?
      7 Have you ever worked in Berlin?

   2 3 He's been to Rome twice.
      4 He's never ridden a motorbike.
      5 He's been to London four times.
      6 He's never ridden on a double-decker bus.
      7 He's worked in Berlin once.

4 2 It arrived five minutes ago.
   3 We saw the Eiffel Tower in 1997.
   4 She wrote the letter yesterday.
   5 I did my homework after supper.
   6 They had lunch at twelve o'clock.

5 2 She hasn't washed it yet.
   3 They haven't seen it yet.
   4 He hasn't had one yet.
   5 We haven't moved (house) yet.
   6 She hasn't given it to me yet.

6 2 A Ann, have you spoken to the bank manager yet?
      B Yes, I've just spoken to him.
   3 A Mark, have you made a cup of tea yet?
      B Yes, I've just made one.
   4 A Have you done your homework yet?
      B Yes, I've just done it.
   5 A Mr Jones, have you read the report yet?
      B Yes, I've just read it.
   6 A Have you called a taxi yet?
      B Yes, I've just called one.

7 2 Have you *ever* tried Japanese food?
   3 Have you finished writing your book *yet*?
   4 I've *never* seen anyone who eats more than you.
   5 Are there any letters for me? I've *just* seen the postman.
   6 We went out to a restaurant *yesterday*.

8 2 1 gone 2 gone 3 been 4 been
      5 gone 6 been 7 gone

9 1 grow up 2 Take off 3 gets up
   4 looking after 5 put … on / turn … on 6 give up 7 try on 8 turn on
   9 Put … on 10 go out

10 1 just/now 2 but 3 had 4 much
   5 going 6 has 7 lot 8 couldn't/ didn't
   9 quickly 10 going 11 like 12 visit

REVISION

Verb *to be*

1 2 j 3 b 4 f 5 g 6 h 7 i 8 d 9 c 10 a

2 2 Bananas aren't blue. They're yellow.
   3 Tokyo isn't the capital of China. It's the capital of Japan.
   4 I'm not from Britain. I'm from (Italy).
   5 The day after Thursday isn't Wednesday. It's Friday.
   6 London and Paris aren't small cities. They're big cities.

3 2 How old are your children?
   3 What is her phone number?
   4 Is your flat in the centre of London?
   5 Is your brother at home?
   6 How much are the chicken sandwiches?
   7 What is your first name?

4 2 My brother isn't married. 3 I'm not a student. 4 Where's the university?
   5 You're twenty-nine. 6 We're at school. 7 She's cold and I'm hot.

Present Simple

1 2 speaks 3 flies/travels/goes 4 stay
   5 goes 6 watches 7 come

2 2 They don't live in Scotland.
   3 He doesn't write letters every day.
   4 We don't have a car.
   5 Eric and Lina don't like getting up.
   6 Richard doesn't drive.
   7 It doesn't cost $50.

3 2 What time do they get up?
   3 What languages does she speak?
   4 Where do you live?
   5 What time do you finish school?
   6 Where do you work?
   7 What does she have for breakfast?

Workbook key 167

4 1 (Answers will vary.)

2 2 Tom has tea and orange juice for breakfast. I have (answers will vary).
   3 Tom goes to work by car.
   4 Tom has lunch in a restaurant.
   5 Tom finishes work at 5.30.
   6 Tom has dinner at 7.15.
   7 Tom watches TV in the evening.
   8 Tom goes to bed at 11.30.

5 1 lives 2 studies 3 gets up 4 has
   5 doesn't eat 6 starts 7 works 8 goes
   9 finishes 10 doesn't finish 11 eats
   12 doesn't like 13 fly 14 visit 15 stay
   16 want 17 love

6 2 doesn't; isn't 3 Does 4 Do; is
   5 don't; are; aren't 6 don't; do
   7 don't; is 8 Does; is 9 are; aren't

there is/are

1 (Answers will vary.)

2 1 There are 2 Are there 3 there aren't
   4 there's 5 are there 6 there are
   7 Is there 8 there isn't 9 is there
   10 there is 11 there's 12 is there
   13 There are

can/can't

1 2 can't; can 3 swim; can't 4 cook
   5 can; can't

2 2 Can; play (Answers will vary.)
   3 Can; speak 4 Can; drive 5 Can; use
   6 Can; play 7 Can; ride

Past Simple

1 2 worked; met; went 3 sold; bought
   4 played; rained; studied 5 drove; visited
   6 lost; left; stole 7 retired; moved

2 2 They didn't win a holiday in the Caribbean.
   3 We weren't at home yesterday.
   4 Dickens didn't write sixteen novels.
   5 Columbus wasn't born in Genoa.
   6 She didn't spend a week in the Alps.
   7 I didn't bring you a present.

3 2 Where were you born? (Answers will vary.)
   3 Where were you at 10.00 yesterday morning?
   4 What time did you go to bed last night?
   5 When did you last wash the car?
   6 How many books did you read last month?
   7 Did you eat in a restaurant last week?

4 1 went 2 did … spend 3 came back
   4 did … travel 5 flew 6 drove
   7 did … stay 8 didn't have 9 stayed
   10 did … do 11 went 12 drank
   13 ate 14 took 15 went 16 didn't have 17 Did … enjoy 18 was
   19 did … bring 20 brought

like

1 (Answers will vary.)

2 2 I'm hungry. I'd like a sandwich. ✓
   3 **B** Yes, I do. ✓
   4 Would you like a coffee? ✓
   5 I like red cars. ✓
   6 **B** I'd like two tickets, please. ✓
   7 **B** No, thanks. ✓
   8 She likes going to the library. ✓
   9 **B** Yes, I do. ✓

do, does, have, or has?

2 haven't; have 3 Do; do 4 Have; have
5 doesn't; do 6 Do; don't; haven't
7 Has; hasn't

Present Continuous

1 2 are … looking 3 isn't working
   4 is … feeling 5 aren't swimming
   6 are … laughing 7 'm getting up
   8 'm not cooking 9 is taking

2 2 Are they going shopping tomorrow?
   3 Is she driving or going by bus?
   4 How many potatoes are you buying?
   5 Why aren't you wearing your sunglasses?
   6 What are you making for dinner tonight?
   7 Why is he studying Russian?

3 2 Sally's having breakfast at the moment.
   3 They're not coming to the class today.
   4 I don't understand what you mean.
   5 What are you doing this weekend?
   6 He drives to work every day.
   7 John doesn't like studying.

4 1 teaches 2 starts 3 finishes 4 likes
   5 meets 6 isn't working 7 's travelling
   8 're spending 9 're camping 10 has
   11 loves 12 doesn't like 13 wants
   14 're flying

going to

1 1 2 g 3 f 4 a 5 b 6 d 7 e

2 2 I'm going to buy new ski boots.
   3 Lynn and Pat are going to buy a Spanish phrase book.
   4 Jeff's going to buy ten water bottles.
   5 Anne's going to buy insect repellent.
   6 We're going to buy new swimsuits.
   7 I'm going to buy an umbrella.

2 2 She isn't going to swim two miles today.
   3 They aren't going to catch the bus this week.
   4 It isn't going to rain this week.
   5 The other team aren't going to win this match.
   6 I'm not going to have a big breakfast today.
   7 Liam and Elton aren't going to make lots of money this month.

3 2 Are they going to share a flat?
   3 What's Mark going to study?
   4 Is Sara going to get a part-time job?
   5 Where are they going to buy books?
   6 Is Mark going to have enough money?
   7 Are they going to visit their parents?

Question forms

1 2 Did he go to Bahrain?
   3 Have you got much money?
   4 Was she here yesterday?
   5 Do they like skiing?
   6 Does he play golf?
   7 Did they go swimming yesterday?

2 2 What are you going to do this evening?
   3 Were you at the conference last week?
   4 Where did you go on holiday last year?
   5 How many languages do you speak?
   6 What is Martha studying at university?
   7 Does he like playing sports?

Present Perfect

1 3 Frank has ridden a motorbike but Angela hasn't.
   4 Frank has spoken in public but Angela hasn't.
   5 Angela and Frank have both seen the Queen.
   6 Frank has broken an arm but Angela hasn't.
   7 Angela has read *War and Peace* but Frank hasn't.
   8 Angela and Frank have both studied French.

2 2 Have you ever driven a sports car? (Answers will vary.)
   3 Have you ever seen anyone famous?
   4 Have you ever lost your keys?
   5 Have you ever made a cake?
   6 Have you ever drunk Turkish coffee?
   7 Have you ever played basketball?

3 He flew to Australia three times last year.
   She's written ten letters this year.
   They spent £600 on clothes last year.
   I bought a new car last year.
   I've broken my leg twice this year.
   We've given £65 to charity this year.

4 1 1 was 2 studied 3 got
   4 has worked 5 has just decided
   6 hasn't thought 7 have opened
   8 has always been 9 cooked
   10 came 11 told 12 was

2 2 When did he start cooking?
   3 How long did he study at cookery school?
   4 Where did he get his first job?
   5 Where has he worked?
   6 Where has he just decided to open a restaurant?
   7 How many top restaurants have opened there this year?
   8 When did he cook for the Italian President?

168   Workbook key